Bourdieu, Language and Linguistics

Books also available from Continuum

Pierre Bourdieu: Agent Provocateur, Michael James Grenfell
Pierre Bourdieu: Education and Training, Michael James Grenfell

Bourdieu, Language and Linguistics

By
Michael Grenfell
with contributions from
Adrian Blackledge, Cheryl Hardy,
Stephen May, and Robert Vann

continuum

Continuum International Publishing Group

The Tower Building   80 Maiden Lane
11 York Road   Suite 704
London SE1 7NX   New York, NY 10038

www.continuumbooks.com

British Library Cataloguing-in-Publication Data
A catalogue record for this book is available from the British Library.

ISBN: 978-1-8470-6569-8 (hardcover)

Library of Congress Cataloging-in-Publication Data
Bourdieu, language and linguistics / [editor] Michael James Grenfell.
   p. cm.
ISBN: 978-1-8470-6569-8 (hardcover)
1. Language and culture. 2. Bourdieu, Pierre, 1930–2002. 3. Sociolinguistics. I. Grenfell, Michael, 1953– II. Title.

P35.B625 2010
306.44–dc22   2010008974

Typeset by Newgen Imaging Systems Pvt Ltd, Chennai, India
Printed and bound in Great Britain by the MPG Books Group

Contents

Part III: Towards a Science of Language and Linguistic Study

List of Illustrations

Tables

Graph

Figures

Acknowledgements

The idea for this book grew out of a symposium organized by the Linguistic Ethnography Forum, a special interest group of the British Association of Applied Linguistics. I would like to acknowledge the input of the members of this Forum and their encouragement to undertake this project. In particular, I thank Brian Street of Kings College, London, and Adrian Blackledge from University of Birmingham for their discussion and support. The book began life as a joint project between Adrian and I. Although he later had to drop out from steering the project through to completion, I appreciate the work he did, especially at the initial, planning stages of the book.

Some 8 years after his death, I still feel a need to acknowledge Pierre Bourdieu for the time and support he afforded me over a number of years. We discussed issues of language and linguistics at length together during our meetings, and he also gave me invaluable feedback on my corpus study work from Orléans. I remember him as a friend and mentor who offered an example to us all, and as one who still guides my own endeavours to actualize a reflexive science.

I acknowledge with gratitude and respect the individual contributors, who worked on the practical chapters of the book: Adrian Blackledge, Cheryl Hardy, Stephen May, Robert Vann.

Special thanks to Cheryl Hardy for input and feedback way beyond her own individual contribution.

Finally, I acknowledge the patience and interest extended to me by my colleagues at Trinity College, Dublin, while I was preoccupied with work on the book, especially, Andrew Loxley, Paula McDonagh, Carmel O'Sullivan, Adrian Seery and Michael Shevlin.

Chapter 1

Introduction

Michael Grenfell

Since the death of the French sociologist Pierre Bourdieu in 2002, it seems that his influence has continued to grow unabated. Born of 'peasant stock' in 1930, Bourdieu's academic trajectory took him from local boarding school to the highest echelons of the Parisian intellectual world. Perhaps last of the old-style *philosophes*, his work is now studied and his name cited alongside those other twentieth-century giants of the French thought: De Beauvoir, Sartre, Derrida and Foucault. His output was both enormous and extensive, including many hundreds of books, articles and talks on a wide range of subjects, from philosophy to the French fashion industry. It is now commonplace to see Bourdieu's ideas adopted in such academic fields as education, economics, the media, philosophy, culture, art and music, management, gender studies, literature, sport, photography, religion and politics – among others.

Although I have described Bourdieu as a 'sociologist', his was a special kind of sociology, one that was founded on a central European philosophical tradition; and Bourdieu was heavily influenced by such philosophers as Heidegger, Wittgenstein, Husserl and Nietzsche, albeit that this influence was often as much thinking against them as with them. His mentors also included French philosophers, for example, the phenomenologist Merleau-Ponty, and philosophers of the history of science such as Bachelard, Canguilhem and Koyré. Besides these philosophical roots, Bourdieu's brand of sociology was constructed through a synthesis of the founding fathers of the discipline: Comte, Marx, Weber and Durkheim. He also embraced anthropology at an early stage in his career, mostly noticeably through the work of Claude Lévi-Srauss. Bourdieu's sociology was therefore very much a 'social philosophy', and one that continually confronted issues of fact and value in exploring the limits of science and truth. Of course, 'language' was a central concern for many of the writers cited above. However, up until now, and somewhat curiously, Bourdieu has been generally overlooked by language specialists and linguists. This book sets out to redress this imbalance, and to raise issues of theory and practice with respect to the study of language from a Bourdieusian perspective.

Twentieth-century philosophy was dominated by questions of language. This is seen in the 'language games' of Wittgenstein and the 'force of the word' of Nietzsche, and also in the developing terminology of Husserl and the phenomenologists, as well as in the etymology of words which is at the core of Heidegger's work. Of course, modern-day linguistics also has its roots in the last century with the seminal work of Ferdinand de Saussure. From the meeting point of these writers, post-modernism emerged as the dominant philosophical source of the latter part of the twentieth century. Through the work of Lyotard, Derrida and Foucault, among others, language as a conveyor of sense and meaning was challenged, as was the very form of writing and speech. Here, 'discourse' became a guiding metaphor, and was used to explain human practice as a space of meaning-based signs and symbols – each mutually referential and defining. In a way, the philosophy of man became the philosophy of language. It is therefore unsurprising that Bourdieu should share this preoccupation. We can discern at least four ways in which language features in his work. First, it appears in the study of language use itself, and we shall see this in Bourdieu's early work of observations about linguistic usage in Algeria and the Béarn, and the meaning he attributed to such use. Second, it is seen in his critique of academic fields – including sociology, philosophy and psychology – which undertake linguistic analyses. Here, he is particularly critical of the Saussurian tradition. Third, it is raised in the issue of Bourdieu's own theoretical language. Throughout his academic studies, Bourdieu developed a highly sophisticated set of concepts which he referred to as his 'thinking tools', for example, *habitus, field, capital*, etc. He used these not simply as metaphors for narrative heuristics, but as philosophically charged instruments of analysis in a range of social contexts. In the course of this book, we shall see what each of these concepts signifies, as well as the use they have or that could be made of them with respect to language and linguistics, in particular. Fourth, it is portrayed in the 'power of words' themselves. For Bourdieu, words are never 'value-neutral', never used in isolation, but arise in contexts which need to be seen as dynamic social spaces where issues of power are always at stake. This is true for Bourdieu's own theoretical concepts, and is one of the reasons for the development of his own specific language – in order 'to break' from the everyday use of language. Whether in specific, specialist fields, or in everyday use, Bourdieu encourages us to think of language as representing and carrying a whole social dynamic, as well as occulting the processes that constitute it.

I pointed out that Bourdieu's work has been relatively underused by language specialists. Why might this be the case? In a sense, a rather fuller answer to this question will emerge in the course of the book. However, we can note immediately that the study of language is itself a highly specialized and compartmentalized academic field where, besides the philosophy of language and linguistics, we can count sociolinguistics, social psycholinguistics, psycholinguistics, the sociology of language and ethnomethodological approaches, together with applied linguistics itself. Each of these sub-fields constructs language in a certain way for its study; consequently, each has an interest in seeing language through its own particular lens. In the course of this book, we shall see how Bourdieu's perspective to language is distinct from each of these, and consider in what way his approach offers a way of understanding aspects of language which others do not. At one point, Bourdieu mounted an explicit attack on the paradigm which has dominated modern linguistics – Chomsky's – and we shall ask whether linguists' reluctance to engage with him is really because they feel that the best way of countering this attack is to ignore it, or whether the divide between the two is irreconcilable because language is here simply being conceptualized as two quite distinct objects of research?

Part II of this book offers a selection of practical chapters which show others exploring Bourdieu's ideas on language and developing understandings in a range of linguistic contexts. We look at phonetics and phonology, ideology, multilingualism, language policy and language and education from a Bourdieusian perspective. However, we precede this exemplification of Bourdieu's method in practice by setting out his main ideas and guiding principles. Part I begins with an account of 'Bourdieu the man': where he came from and what shaped his main theoretical approaches. The intention here is more than biographical. Bourdieu often argued for a 'socio-genetic' reading of his work; in other words, the need to set the ideas he expressed in the context of the time, both in terms of intellectual and actual socio-historical events of the day. Chapter 1 does this by showing the range of issues that shaped Bourdieu's thinking at various parts of his career, and the intellectual currents of which he was a part. Chapter 2 then gives an account specifically of Bourdieu's work on language and linguistics. All his major publications are included as well as his critiques of others writing on language and linguistics. His approach is contrasted with these, as well as the important academic disciplines which have dominated the study of language. Key analytical concepts are addressed in Part I as a way of exploring both Bourdieu's particular approach to language and the theory of practice which underpins it. Part I is a contextual and theoretical preparation for the practical studies in Part II.

Part III finally offers a synthesis of the first two parts – of theory and practice – as a way of distilling out the essential features of Bourdieu's view of language as an object of study. Here, further methodological principles and their implications for research practice are discussed in terms of what might be termed Bourdieu's 'science of language'. In this respect, the book offers a unique account of Bourdieu on language and linguistics. It is intended as a way of opening up the possibilities and routes for other researchers to follow.

Part I

Theory

Part I is concerned with questions of theory. Chapter 2 sets out a background to Bourdieu's theory of practice in terms of his own biography, both in terms of personal trajectory and his formative intellectual influences. By raising philosophical issues and methodological implications, the chapter highlights the main features of Bourdieu's approach and discusses how they are justified. Bourdieu's key concepts –*habitus*, *field*, *capital*, etc. – are presented and exemplified. Finally, their methodological significance and application are addressed.

Chapter 3 then extends this theory of practice to language and linguistics per se. It begins by addressing the way that language featured in the range of Bourdieu's work: from the early studies in Algeria and the Béarn, to education and culture, economics and politics. It then gives an account of Bourdieu's major critique of the sciences of language – most notably modern-day linguistics. The main features of this critique are presented along with the key concepts for language for which he developed an alternative approach. Bourdieu's approach is contrasted with that of others. The notion of the *linguistic market* is also addressed. Finally, the chapter considers Bourdieu's analysis of language as it operated in specific *field* contexts: religion, philosophy, education and politics. Once again, methodological issues conclude the chapter.

The aim of Part I is to provide a theoretical background to the practical chapters that follow in Part II.

Chapter 2

Bourdieu: A Theory of Practice

Michael Grenfell

Introduction

This chapter offers an account of Pierre Bourdieu and his work. As noted in the Introduction, Bourdieu always argued for a 'socio-genetic' reading of his work, meaning that individual statements should be read in the context in which they were written. But how to define that context? Clearly, there are various biographical aspects which are important in understanding what Bourdieu wrote and why; experience, both from a personal and intellectual perspective, is bound to shape individual responses and actions. Moreover, that experience is set within the social and historical events of the day which, themselves, have antecedents. A 'socio-genetic' reading must therefore take account of biographical details and intellectual currents, as well as social, historical and political factors. This approach is all the more important when the writer concerned originally published most of his work in his native French, some of which did not appear in English until 25 years later. In the present context, it is also important to keep in mind the fact that Bourdieu's writings covered a very wide range of topics and themes. Our present concern is language and linguistics. However, it is only really possible to understand Bourdieu's position with respect to these topics by appreciating the way they situate themselves in the body of his work as a whole, and the significance a wide range of themes has for language and linguistics and vice versa.

This chapter therefore begins with a straight biographical account of Bourdieu and his major works. This section gives the bare bones of Bourdieu's life and his output. That life is then set within a socio-historical framework. The world that Bourdieu grew up in and the main events of the day are described. Here, the discussion will necessitate some account of the history of contemporary France. These biographical and socio-historical details will then provide a basis for addressing Bourdieu's principal 'thematic concerns' – what preoccupied him and why? Here, both the social and political issues are reviewed, and the salient questions raised which Bourdieu posed over the course of his career. Bourdieu's own pre-occupations will then be set against a range of intellectual currents – both from the past and contemporary with Bourdieu – in order to understand the range of academic perspectives that might be taken on these issues, and how Bourdieu's position distinguishes itself from these. The chapter will develop the main themes of Bourdieu's 'theory of practice', and set out exactly how we might understand it. Furthermore, the range of conceptual terms that Bourdieu developed – for example, *habitus, field, capital*, etc. – will also be presented and explored. Finally, the chapter concludes by addressing further issues of methodology and practice by considering the key features of undertaking research from a Bourdieusian perspective. The chapter is intended to provide a background context against which the rest of the book can be read.

Bourdieu: A Life and Work

Bourdieu was born on 1 August 1930 in a small village within the French Pyrénées-Atlantiques. We know very little about his childhood experiences. The family were apparently of modest means; both parents left school relatively early, as was the norm at that time. For all intents and purposes, they seem to have lived the life of an average 'peasant' family. His father was an itinerant crop-picker cum temporary post office worker. His mother was a housewife who raised the family. This background was scarcely unusual for that time and place. The 1930s were a period of international economic hardship and political unrest, but we can imagine that life in this relative rural backwater, with its attachment to local traditions and customs, remained very much as it had done for centuries. Gascon, a now moribund dialect of French, was spoken at home, and Bourdieu seems to have been reared in the same way as most of the neighbours' children.

However, we do know that Bourdieu's father was politically astute and his mother was educationally ambitious (for further details of Bourdieu's biography, see Bourdieu 2007/2004 and Grenfell 2004a). Both influences were to have a formative effect on Bourdieu. After local elementary school, Bourdieu went to the *lycée* in Pau, a local medium-sized town of the South-West Region. The distance from his home village necessitated Bourdieu staying on site as a boarder during the week, only returning to his home at weekends and for holidays. This experience created an early separation for Bourdieu, one which would have echoes for the rest of his life. In the school in Pau, the division between town and country was even more evident. In addition to his distinct rural accent, Bourdieu, as a boarder, was forced to wear a smock while the local day-pupils from the town were able to dress in the latest styles. Apparently, fights were common and Bourdieu was punished on several occasions for a range of misdemeanours. He also seemed to develop an enthusiasm for rugby and, with it, a disposition for the 'games play' of life and a fierce sense of competitiveness. Despite somewhat kicking against the system, Bourdieu clearly achieved academic recognition as he eventually passed the entrance to the *Lycée Louis Le Grand* in Paris, one of the highly reputed preparatory schools for those looking to gain a seat in the prestigious *Grandes Écoles*. Entrance to one of these is by competitive examination – the *concours* – and Bourdieu was subsequently successful in gaining entry to the *École Normale Supérieur* (ENS), which represented (and still does) the main academic university for any aspirant to the French intellectual elite in France. Sartre and de Beauvoir were both former pupils of this school, and Bourdieu spent his time there with one student who would later become a leading figure in post-modernist thinking – Jacques Derrida.

Passing as an *agrégé* in Philosophy, Bourdieu would have normally been destined for a university career as a lecturer. Indeed, he did teach for one year at the *Lycée de Moulins*. However, at the time, all young Frenchmen were obliged to undertake military service, and so Bourdieu went to Algeria as a young conscript. The experience proved to be an epiphany for him. The country itself was in a state of almost complete meltdown. It had become a French colony in 1830, more as a diversionary tactic on the part of the restored monarchy who sought to galvanize national support. However, once there, France proved itself to be an enthusiastic colonialist, pursuing a strict policy of assimilation. Algeria literally became a French territory. It returned a member to the French parliament, and local languages were suppressed in favour of French. The ruling class became a mixture of Algerians, fully assimilated to the French way of thinking and doing things, and Frenchmen and women themselves who took up positions in this French outpost. Later still, and in times of economic depression, thousands of unemployed Frenchmen were encouraged to settle there and create a life for themselves. Arriving poor and with no shoes, these men and women were christened *pieds noirs*, a name which is still used. By the 1950s, however, times had changed. The indigenous populace were in open revolt against their French rulers. Algeria was in the throes of a cruel war of independence and society was split into a number of divisions. On the one side were the traditional peasants who had been uprooted from their traditional lands and placed in compounds.

On the other side, an emerging politically sensitive class took inspiration from both the Second World War and other wars of independence to organize opposition to the French Regime. However, the situation was complex. Many Frenchmen and women considered Algeria their home, and still others believed it a matter of national pride, wounded by German defeat in the Second World War, that it should remain the jewel in the crown of the French Empire. Bourdieu was catapulted into such a context; one that was both dangerous and yet socio-politically intriguing. At first, he worked 'in the field', as it were, where he took literally thousands of photos (see Bourdieu 2003a). Soon, however, he moved to the capital city of Algiers where he undertook administrative duties in the General Government. This placement also allowed him close proximity to one of the most impressive libraries of Algeria, which gave him the opportunity to continue his studies. In fact, he eventually also taught at the *faculté de lettres* at the university in Algiers (see Grenfell 2006 for further details).

The effect on Bourdieu could not have been more significant. Coming as he did from a rarefied, intellectual training – a philosophical one at that – the immediate experience could hardly have been more demanding. Besides the challenges and dangers of living in such an environment, there was the evident need to make sense of what was happening there. At one point, Bourdieu explained how he set to work to understand what this 'thing' Algeria was – a phenomenon that was poorly understood, in his opinion, by the majority of Frenchmen and women (see Bourdieu and Grenfell 1995). Besides taking photographs, he also conducted many interviews with a range of the Algerian populace, and undertook field studies of indigenous people. The results of this work eventually appeared in his first publication, *Sociologie de l'Algérie* (1958), where he sets out to give a topography of the country, its various tribes and the dynamics at play within a society at war. Besides this first book, the outcome of his experiences appeared in several other publications, specifically *Travail et travailleurs en Algérie* (1963) and *Le déracinement, la crise de l'agriculture tradionelle en Algérie* (1964a), although the content of his work here also informed many of his subsequent other works.

Bourdieu returned to France in 1960, when he was appointed to assist the leading French intellectual of the time, Raymond Aron. From 1961 to 1964, he divided his time between Paris and teaching at the University of Lille, and was nominated as Director of Studies at the *École Pratique des Hautes Études* (later to be named *École des Hautes Études en Sciences Sociales* – EHESS) and as Director of the *Centre de Sociologie Européenne* (CES) (founded by Aron). The CES gave Bourdieu an institutional powerbase – positioned outside of the main University system but within the French academic space – on which to build his career. His initial research topics included education and culture: *Les héritiers* (1979a/1964), *La reproduction* (1977a/1970) on education; *Un art moyen* (1990a/1965) and *L'amour de l'art* (1990b/1966) on photography and museums. These studies also allowed Bourdieu to develop a particular methodological perspective – what he subsequently referred to as a 'theory of practice'. A seminal methodological statement appeared with *Le métier de sociologue* (1991a/1968), which offered illustrative extracts from key thinkers as a background to the approach described, for example, Marx, Weber, Durkheim, Mauss, Saussure, Bachelard and Canguilhem. This book was followed up by a major exposition of method: *Esquisse d'une théorie de la pratique* (1977b/1972) (which includes further studies from his Algerian work).

Bourdieu married Marie-Claire Brizzard in 1962, and they had three sons – Jérôme, Emmanuel and Laurent. In 1964, he also took over the editorship of *Le Sens Commun*, a series from the leading French publishing house, *Les Éditions de Minuit*. This series published translations of texts from international academics, for example, Erving Goffman and Erwin Panofsky, as well as much of Bourdieu's own subsequent work. Bourdieu's work as editor expanded when, in 1975, he founded the *Actes de la recherche en sciences sociales*, a journal aimed at an international, academic audience, which offered a vehicle for work from Bourdieu and the network of collaborators he had by then established at home in France and abroad.

The 1980s were marked by the publication of the three principal texts which now form the core of his oeuvre: *La distinction* (actually published in 1979 (1984a/1979)) on the sociology of 'taste'; *Homo academicus* (1988a/1984) on the academic field itself; and *La noblesse d'état* (1996a/1989), an examination of the French system of *Grandes Écoles*. A reconsideration of his Algerian studies, including extended discussion of methodology as begun in *Esquisse* and *Métier*, was also published as *Le sens pratique* (1990c/1980). During this particularly fecund period, a collection of previously published articles and talks also appeared: *Questions de sociologie* (1993a/1980) indicated the extent of Bourdieu's thinking on such diverse topics as fashion, language, art, sport, politics, philosophy, literature and education; *Choses Dites* (1990d/1987) further developed many of the methodological issues and themes in a series of interviews and lectures; while *L'ontologie de politique de Martin Heidegger* (1991b/1988) offered a socio-historical reading of a key twentieth-century philosopher. And, a major book-length statement on language also appeared: *Ce que parler veut dire* (1982a). Some of the key themes across these publications will be developed below.

The 1980s marked a turning point in Bourdieu's public profile. Until this point, Bourdieu seemed content to occupy a rather private academic milieu; indeed, he positively eschewed opportunities to appear before the general public and criticized intellectuals with ambitions to 'change the world'. However, all this was about to change. In 1981, the French electorate voted for a socialist president – François Mitterand – and then a socialist government, the first of the Fifth Republic. This change of political colour acted as a mobilizing force for French intellectuals and Bourdieu was caught up in the general call to arms. In 1981, Bourdieu was elected as Chair in Sociology at the *Collège de France*, an august institution of just 52 members which groups together the leading thinkers in France in their respective fields. This position gave Bourdieu an unchallenged base on which to construct his subsequent career. The period was marked by two key features. First, his increasing involvement in public life: in both 1984 and 1988, Bourdieu took part in committees set up by the Mitterand government with a review to reforming school curricula (see Bourdieu and Salgas, 1985a and Bourdieu 1992/1989). Second, the appearance of further major works in such areas as the art field – *Les règles de l'art* (1996b/1992); gender politics – *La domination masculine* (2001a/1998); philosophy/methodology–*Réponses* (1992b), *Raisons pratiques* (1998a/1994), *Méditations pascaliennes* (2000a/1997), *Science de la science et réflexivité* (2001c); and economics – *Les structures sociales de l'économie* (2000b/2005).

Bourdieu's affair with politics was brief. The Mitterand government itself was forced to perform a *volte-face* in the face of economic instability after its early phase of social reform. This change led to an abandonment of key features of its social welfare programme, and the embracing of neo-liberal economics, as espoused by international leaders such as Margaret Thatcher and Ronald Reagan, which were so fashionable at the time. Bourdieu's response was to take an increasingly combative line with respect to the emerging policies and their harmful results for significant sections of the populace. If *Actes* offered Bourdieu a vehicle for addressing an academic audience, he now needed an outlet for a more general public. Consequently, he founded *Liber-Raisons d'Agir* in 1998, a series aimed at the production of small publications accessible to a more general reader. His own contributions to the series – *Contre-feux* (1998b) and *Contre-feu 2* (2001b) – included a collection of shorter political and polemical texts. The series also included his critique of the machinations of modern media in *La télévision* (1998c).

The most significant publishing event at the time for Bourdieu was the appearance of *La misère du monde* (The Weight of the World) in 1993

(1999a/1993). This book documents a range of human suffering in contemporary France – suffering that had arisen as a direct result of government policy. The book was a sensation: time was made available on TV to consider its findings; the book became a best-seller; and some sections of the text were used in drama productions as a form of *theatre de realité*. Bourdieu's public profile increased still further: he now became a frequent attendee at activist meetings, strikes and political discussions. This activity led to his support – through petitions etc. – for various pressure groups. He was also active at an international level, networking with other academics, writers and artists in what increasingly came to be seen as practical 'acts of resistance' (see Bourdieu, 2008a/2002).

Bourdieu retired from the *Collège de France* and died from cancer on 23 January 2002. The next section now places Bourdieu's life and work in their socio-historic context.

Historical Context

In a sense, Bourdieu could not have been born at a more significant point in the twentieth century. His age set him apart from pre-war intellectuals and key figures such as Simone de Beauvoir and Jean-Paul Sartre, although in disposition he was still a member of this generation, the end of which was marked by his death. In this section, I want to reflect a little on the historical heritage that surrounded Bourdieu. This is important in understanding the events to which he was responding, both personally and intellectually. Clearly, the Second World War marked a watershed for France, but I wish to begin this account some years prior to that to show its antecedents and traditions.

It is arguable that France gave the world the first humanist revolution. The Great Revolution of 1789 was against the *ancien régime*. Before this revolt, political power rested with the monarch, and was legitimized by appeals to 'birthright' and the will of God. Thus, when France executed their King, it was as if God had died with him. However, from the mid eighteenth century, contributors to the *Encyclopédie* – Diderot, Voltaire, Helvetius and D'Alembert – were publishing articles on the sciences, arts and trade which distinguished themselves from traditional religious accounts of the universe. In a sense, this was an intellectual revolution which predated the social and political one, and which certainly contributed to it. The Great Revolution was a bourgeois revolt, in that it represented the overthrow of traditional social structures by an emerging middle class.

However, this middle class was entrepreneurial rather than industrial, and France did not yet undergo the full-blown industrial revolution that was taking place in England. It is almost as if France shocked itself. The Revolution of 1789 did indeed separate the State from the King and Church, but was followed by decades of reaction, further revolution and counter-revolution. There would be two more Republics, two Empires, two Revolutions and further flirtations with monarchy before France finally extinguished the active forces of the *ancien régime*.

When Bourdieu was born, in 1930, the Third Republic was barely 60 years old. What was the French world that surrounded him like? The Franco-Prussian war of 1870–1871, which resulted in France losing it north-east frontier to its Prussian neighbours as confiscated lands, marked the end of the Second Empire, which in turn precipitated popular insurrection in Paris where the Commune held out against France's own military forces. It was not until 1905 that the Church finally separated from the State, and secular education was not fully introduced until the 1880s. The First World War – fought mainly on French territory – had been a trauma for France. Emerging on the side of the victors, it felt justified in reclaiming Alsace–Lorraine as its own and adding its weight to claims for heavy financial retribution from the Germans as punishment for their military aggression. The inter-war period was then marked by a sense of deepening crisis. Faced with economic depression, with all that it entailed in terms of rising unemployment and poverty, the French political class came under increasing pressure to find a solution to the troubles which afflicted France. When war with Germany eventually broke out, Marc Bloc called the resultant capitulation on the part of the French as '*une étrange défaite*' (1990/1946) in order to indicate that what had occurred was more than a simple military defeat. Rather, it seemed to involve the very moral fabric of the country. Once again, the result was that the forces of reaction and revolution came to the surface. For many, collaboration with the German invaders was unthinkable, and resistance became an immediate necessity. However, among the political elite, there was enough consensus, and apparent empathy with the fascist cause, that a successful armistice was signed which placed the war veteran Pétain at the head of a collaborationist government. France was divided in two, compulsory transfer of certain groups of workers to German factories was introduced and the rallying principles of the Republic – *Liberté, Fraternité, Égalité* – were replaced with the more traditional *famille, travail, patrie*. Such was the popular appeal to the French that literally thousands of photos of Pétain were sold.

We do not know how much these events impacted on the young Bourdieu, growing up in the South-West region of France – he would have been nine when the war broke out and an adolescent (already set on his academic career) when it ended. What is significant is that he would have been aware of the trauma of war at a young age, and that he was coming to intellectual maturity in its aftermath and through further experience of war in Algeria. As noted in the previous section, his personal experience in Algeria needs to be seen as an extension of the internal and external problems that France was experiencing as a nation state. It may seem that the forces of conservatism had been banished forever as a result of the defeat of the collaborationists. But this was only partly true. Charles de Gaulle, the army officer who almost single-handedly initiated French resistance, and who headed new governments when the Fourth Republic was formed, was also fiercely nationalist. This issue can only really be understood as one which challenged the way the French viewed their position and standing in the world. As we shall see in the next section, these experiences of war and colonialism also led to the emergence of various themes which were to preoccupy Bourdieu: education and culture, of which language played a significant part.

1968 was the next watershed year for the French. The initial post-war years had been marked by the need to rebuild a country in defeat. Such a task required centralized planning and strong political leadership, the latter provided by the resistance war veteran, Charles de Gaulle. Economic planning was equally strong, centralized and active. The result was often referred to as an 'economic miracle', and certainly an extensive programme of social housing had been undertaken and key industries located in a series of what were known as *métropoles d'équilibre*. Education too had expanded at a dramatic rate. However, there was a cost. Planning had been effective, but it had also seemed to be heavy-handed and authoritarian. Moreover, what had worked in the immediate post-war years increasingly seemed rigid and inflexible. And, of course, the cultural revolution of the 1960s was also taking place, establishing a young emergent generation who had not experienced the trauma of war. By 1968, there was a feeling that Frenchmen had had enough. A minor incident over access to female dormitories sparked a student demonstration, which soon engulfed the whole country. Strikes were widespread; fighting between students, workers and the 'forces of order' was often hand-to-hand in the streets of Paris and the major cities of France. For Bourdieu, these were 'critical moments', and he took the opportunity to collect data from students and academics to inform the core of his major publications of the 1980s, in particular,

Homo academicus. Nonetheless, France did not fully abandon its habit of veering between reaction and revolution. Once again, shocked by the 'events of May', the French populace ousted De Gaulle and restored conservative presidents when they first elected George Pompidou and then his successor Valery Giscard D'Estaing. These times can be seen as perhaps a period of liberalization and reform. Concessions were certainly made to both students and striking workers in the name of *autonomie, participation* and *autogestion.* However, it is widely acknowledged that as the establishment regrouped, many of the newly introduced reforms were watered down and, soon, what was left of them was little more than a slightly more flexible system than the one which had been so severely shaken in 1968.

It is worth connecting these times and events with Bourdieu's biography. As noted earlier, the 1970s saw Bourdieu publish key methodological texts, as well as further work on his principal empirical research studies: education, language and culture. He was also preparing the major texts of *La distinction, La noblesse d'état* and *Homo academicus.* The 1980s were to see a change of political complexion in French government and, with it, the priorities embedded in policy.

That Bourdieu was engaged in a political way, both with a small and a large 'p', is evident from the range of his activities on a number of fronts. But what were his major concerns? The next section considers this question.

Thematic Concerns

As noted previously, Bourdieu took many thousands of photographs in the course of his academic career. In another publication (Grenfell 2004a), I have evoked the image of Bourdieu the photographer as a way of understanding just how his perspective on the social world emerged. Two images are paramount. One is of a village celebration in his home town of the Béarn, a simple Christmas feast. There is a ball going on where the men and women of the village gather to dance. However, around the perimeter of the dance floor are gathered a group of men. They seem to have something in common – they are about the same age and have a similar demeanour. But they do not dance. Why not (see Bourdieu 2008b/ 2002)? The second image is taken from one of his Algerian photos of a young Algerian market seller. However, instead of having a fixed position on a market stall, these sellers carry their wares on their bikes (see 2003a: 164). In both cases, it is as if Bourdieu is asking: Who are these men? What are they doing here? What social forces produced them? With what are they struggling? What structures determine their future course of actions? Of course, these questions are easily posed, but complex to respond to. In fact, Bourdieu's response to the photographic images entailed detailed empirical investigations, analyses and theoretical developments over a number of years. He seemed to constantly come back to this issue, to unpick the range of factors involved in answering these questions. In both Algeria and the Béarn, Bourdieu uses statistics, ethnography and theoretical elaboration in an integrated way to uncover the social forces 'creating' these individuals. In the case of the Béarnais peasant, this work extended over a 30-year period, with Bourdieu taking up the analyses time and time again (see 1962b, 1972a and 1989a) in order to gather further insights into what they offered. As noted, in the case of Algeria too, reflections on his experiences and studies there were to become a bedrock for work for the rest of his academic life.

All this is to suggest that such a 'sociological gaze' was formed early for Bourdieu, and remained a constant with him throughout his professional activity. When it came to his initial work on education, there is a similar curiosity to understand 'what is a student' (see Bourdieu and Grenfell 1995) – what constitutes them and what meaning can be given to their lives? Here, Bourdieu's big 'discovery' was that the 'democratic school' was not very democratic! Rather than providing equal opportunities and a meritocracy, schools acted as a kind of cultural filter through which children passed. Those with the necessary cultural dispositions including language, gained from their family backgrounds, found themselves to be a 'fish in water', swimming with the current; those without such linguistic and cultural prerequisites had the opposite experience, and were themselves continuously ill at ease in the academic environment. And, of course, language was the medium for this implicit 'social selection'. The fact that it went on invisibly, and misrecognized, made it all the more effective. Those who were excluded even colluded in the process, accepting that their lack of academic success was due to lack of natural talent (see 1979a/1964: 71–2). Both *Les héritiers* and *Reproduction* include accounts of the literate practices of French students in the 1960s, which juxtaposes 'high' (academic) and 'low' (popular) culture. Bourdieu saw both a resonance and structural homology between 'bourgeois' culture and the ethos and character of French classical education.

Bourdieu was also active in dialogues with various political groups and individuals at the time, for example, his involvement with conferences such as the 'Week of Marxist Thought' (9–15 March 1966) and the *Cercle*

Noroit (June 1965) (see for example 2008a/2002: 34ff). This work sets out to address issues surrounding the social transformations which had taken place in France and elsewhere since the Second World War, in particular, the unequal distribution of profits and sharing which had resulted from these changes. The logical conclusion of these discussions was that education could be an instrument of change, if not liberation. However, Bourdieu's work on education also focused on the significant role that culture played as an implicit arbitrator of what was and was not acceptable and thinkable in scholastic discourse; hence, his other main topics of research in the 1960s – *culture* and language.

The idea of 'culture' as the vehicle for personal emancipation can be traced back to the Catholic 'non-conformist' intellectuals of the 1930s and beyond (see Loubet 1969), with writers such as the personalist Emmanuel Mounier (who incidentally founded the enlightened Catholic review, *Esprit*, in which Bourdieu published a couple of his first articles – see 1961, 1962c). Culture for this group was seen as both an antidote to the material, secular world, and in fact a vehicle to the spiritual realm. Culture, and its liberating potential, became a popular theme in Britain in educational writings in the 1970s and 1980s where alternative cultural forms were held up as equal, valid and valued, and (somewhat under the influence of Gramscian Marxism) as a challenge to a dominant culture which was seen as being hegemonic. Indeed, Bourdieu's academic profile in the UK rose significantly at this time through publications on education – *Reproduction* (1977a) and chapters included in the seminal publication *Knowledge and Control* (Young 1971), which highlighted the role that language played in the 'construction' of culture in general and classroom discourse in particular. In France, the immediate significance of culture can also be traced to the war years when intellectuals met with manual workers in the Resistance, an encounter which forged a new view of 'brotherhood' founded on education and culture (see Peuple et Culture 1945). Indeed, these ideas were at the core of social reconstruction in France, for example, with developed policies on *education permanente* and the creation of Malraux's *maisons de la culture* (see Grenfell 2004a: Chapters 3 and 4). Bourdieu's work on museums, photography and taste (1990a/1965, 1990b/1966) seems to be exploring and questioning the potential of culture as a force for liberation stronger even than that of education.

These themes are echoed in the major studies of the 1980s and 90s, including *The Weight of the World*. Here, there is the same preoccupation to examine the social forces shaping individuals, the socio-historic conditions of change, and the way that apparent 'liberating' institutions actually ensnare and trap those who go through them. For Bourdieu, nothing is as it seems. Much of his oeuvre can consequently be read as related to these themes; for example, the work on economics (2000b) shows how the discipline is institutionally constructed. This book, along with the *Contre-feux* publications highlights Bourdieu's analysis of the world of finance and the pernicious effects it has on everyday men and women. Culture and gender are also social constructions. In each case, Bourdieu develops a way of looking at the world which uncovers what is 'misrecognized' in social processes and its resultant repercussions. But, how to see the world in this way? To answer this question, we must return to issues of theory.

Theoretical Perspectives

As noted, Bourdieu undertook a classic academic training and emerged among the very top in his generation. He could only do this by imbibing a great deal of Western philosophical thinking. It is possible to find many strands of this in his work, but it is beyond the scope of this chapter and book to attempt such an undertaking. Nevertheless, it is important to appreciate something of these traditions and philosophical issues as a way of understanding the perspective, in theoretical terms, that Bourdieu arrived at, and why. In the country of René Descartes, who gave us the notion of 'Cartesian dualism', it is perhaps unsurprising that the intellectual tradition in France is one where metaphysical ideas have flourished. In contrast to the Anglo-Saxon academic world, where there has been a certain positivist and normative bias, French intellectuals have enjoyed a freer association with 'things of the mind'. So, even today, philosophy is taught to every school pupil, there is a strong literary industry and it is not unusual to see notions such as 'democracy' and 'society' openly discussed in a constructive way on television and in the press. This tradition began long before the Age of Enlightenment, but was given an accelerated twist by the writers of the time. The point is that the way in which writers such as Montesquieu (1689–1755) and Rousseau (1712–1778) debated the constitution of society founded an intellectual current which exists to this day, one in which it is not unusual to consider and even remake fundamental aspects of it. Montesquieu, for example, raised questions about the nature and possibility of equality in society at a time before the revolutionary period. Rousseau too contrasted the contemporary world with that of the 'pre-society' *noble savage*, who lived apparently unaware of the inequalities which have beset civilization. Despite this idealized vision of man as free of social differentiation, Rousseau too anticipated the worst aspects of revolution and feared what might happen when the 'general will' (*la volonté générale*) is given free reign in the world. De Tocqueville (1805–1859) continued in a similar vein in his work on American democracy, to address how to constitute an effective society. The Great Revolution and the subsequent instability of French social and political structures throughout the nineteenth and much of the twentieth century only heightened this French appetite to 'debate one's world'.

The point here is that Bourdieu was part of a radical tradition that was used to challenging the fundamentals of society. It is a radicalism that is shared across French life and history, including the political and intellectual spectrum. The first ingredient of Bourdieu's theoretical view is therefore a *critical perspective*.

In the introduction to this book, I described Bourdieu as a 'sociologist' but added that his was a special kind of sociology, perhaps much more like a social philosophy. Nevertheless, we should not overlook the sociological antecedents to Bourdieu's approach. The word 'sociology' was in fact first termed by a Frenchman, Auguste Comte (1798–1857). Comte's philosophy can be seen as a juxtaposition of value and fact. He argued that the ideas we hold of the world in effect shape it for us. For Comte, the past had been all about theology and militarism, but a new way of scientific and industrial thinking was displacing 'transcendent faith' in the old ways. 'Sociology' was part of this New World. In his law of three stages, Comte argued that man passes through stages in his intellectual thinking. In the first, phenomena are explained by association to aspects of man himself. In the second, metaphysics, abstract entities such as 'nature', are conceived in order to account for the phenomena. It is then in the third stage that men are happy to simply describe things as they are in terms of the relationship they hold with other things. This third stage is where transcendence is abandoned and things are described 'as they are' and in relation to the laws which underlie them. Of course, this latter account applied most immediately to the physical sciences – chemistry, biology, etc. – and Comte made the point that disciplines such as history and politics had yet to catch up. 'Sociology' was to be the means to do this, since it offered the possibility of discovering the 'laws' of society. Indeed, 'science' itself was defined in terms of 'knowledge' acquired to understand; in other words, a broader rather than a narrower view of the term.

In a similar manner, Bourdieu was intent on beginning with observation (empiricism) and discovering relationships between things. He understood that ideas – and in particular, the words we used to express them – could indeed alter the way we saw the world. Finally, 'science' for him was this broader perspective rather than a narrow nomo-thetical one. The second set of ingredients in Bourdieu's theoretical view therefore includes *observation, empiricism, relations* and '*science*'.

The third element of Bourdieu's theory of practice is constituted by the founding fathers of sociology: Marx, Weber and Durkheim. Bourdieu always made the point that he should not be closely identified with any of these three: 'for Marxists, I am a Durkeimian, for the Durkheimians, I am Weberian, for the Weberians, Marxist' (1995: 15). He also insisted that any commonality should be seen as much in terms of working *against* as *with* them. Consequently, it is possible to see many aspects of Bourdieu's theoretical view as a response to the work of these three. Marx, Weber and Durkheim were all concerned with the process of change in society. On a global level, this meant the evolution from feudal to capitalist society. Let us recall that Bourdieu began his academic career by exploring the relations between his own rural background and the local urban town, and the seismic shifts in Algeria which had opposed tradition and modernity. For Durkheim, such a transformation needed to be understood as the change from one form of *solidarity* to another: the traditional world was characterized by *mechanical* organization where small homogeneous groups and communities were made up of individuals with highly defined roles – almost self-sufficient. These were akin to Marx's feudal living or Tönnies *Gemeninschaft* (from where seemed to take this distinction between community and society). The modern world, on the other hand, constituted an *organic* form of living, where much larger numbers were connected in a form of interdependence; this was *Gesellschaft* or Marx's *capitalism*. It is clear that Bourdieu was highly dubious about the extent to which – as Durkheim suggested – the modern world could ever become a differentiated but mutually supported whole and, indeed, much of his work, especially *The Weight of the World*, was an attempt to show the way things really were – in effect, fragmented, isolated and biased towards the interests of various previously constituted groups, especially of the dominant elite.

There is also a 'moral' element to Durkheim's thesis, which is common to both Weber and Marx, and is one which Bourdieu shares. For Durkheim, the 'health' of organic society was dependent on the formation of a strong *collective conscience*, a kind of shared body of ideas, beliefs and values. The fact that this did not really exist in the modern world was, for Durkheim, a matter of concern; in fact, his view was that it was yet to form. The absence of its developed form was partly the result of changes in the 'division of labour' which had not yet stabilized. Many individuals existed in a world where the necessary *norms* were not sufficient to direct their action. A state of *anomie*, or normlessness, then followed – resulting in an increase in the suicide rate at its extreme. This state of the modern world, including its consequences was not far from Marx's view of capitalism and the inherent emergence of *alienation*, which in turn was echoed by Weber in his view of how contemporary living was being characterized by a state of disillusionment. Many aspects of this image are reflected in Bourdieu's work: for example, the poverty of experience that is the everyday lot of many Frenchmen and women; the *hysteresis* that results when individuals find that the world has literally 'passed them by' (what they once had, which was once valued, is no longer); and the numerous social and economic policies of government which in effect exclude individuals from full participation in society as a whole. Education implicitly raises a key question. For Durkheim, education could play an important role in forming the *collective conscience* through a 'pedagogy for the modern world'. In his writings on Algeria (1964a), Bourdieu too suggested that a 'rational pedagogy' could support the creation of a truly modern society. However, his subsequent work seems to argue that such a pedagogy somewhat goes against the logic of practice of the education field, which is at least in part to differentiate and to exclude.

It is also worth noting that sociology in France in the 1950s did not have the prominence that it does today. It was not taught in higher education. Durkheim was seen as a redundant thinker. At one point, Bourdieu describes being asked by Raymond Aron to teach Durkheim (Bourdieu and Grenfell 1995) – 'nothing could be worst'. In fact, sociology was for 'failed philosophers' and was 'lacking any theoretical or empirical inspiration' (1986a: 37). Yet, Bourdieu did embrace this discipline, perhaps out of necessity rather as a than career choice, but the ingredients of the sociological founding fathers can nevertheless be found in Bourdieu's developing theoretical point of view. These issues include a preoccupation with the way *society changes*, the *moral aspect* of human activity and the *positive* and *negative effects* these can have on the individual. More than this, each is concerned with the very *structure* of society. For Marx, such structure was essentially economic and class-based. Bourdieu shares something of this understanding, but structures for him exist in forms other than social class, and the economic is more than simply capitalistic activity. For Marx, the material *Infrastructure* of society manifested itself in its ideological *Superstructure*. Durkheim too developed a theory of knowledge which was based on understanding human thought as in some way shaped by the structures in which the thinkers lived. We shall see how significant this was for Bourdieu's own theory of practice and, indeed, his perspective on language.

However, before considering these in detail, there is one further ingredient to add to our list for understanding Bourdieu's theoretical view: that of the 'intellectual'.

I have already noted that Bourdieu emerged from one of the strongest global intellectual traditions. This tradition has been traced back to the writers and *philosophes* of the Age of Enlightenment and beyond. The kind of ideas outlined above offered a powerful framework for the men of letters who followed. However, the actual term 'intellectual' was not generally used until 1898, when Emile Zola (1840–1902) wrote and published *J'accuse* in response to the Dreyfus Affair, accusing the French government and army of collusion and corruption. This custom of directly addressing the populace on events of the day already existed in the habit of publishing pamphlets, essays and statements, as the only way of raising matters to public concern in an age before mass communications. It continued to be a popular form in the first half of the twentieth century, especially at times of war when there were restrictions both on printing materials and editorial policy (for example, during the time of Vichy France). In many ways the 1920s and 1930s were awash with the publications of the French intellectuals. This generation distinguished itself in two principal ways: first, by the fact that many were Catholic by persuasion; second, by their political affiliation. It was not assumed that Catholic was synonymous with 'conservative', and an 'enlightened' form of religious faith, dating back to the eighteenth century, had already developed a social policy to reach out to the people in the face of rising dechristianization.

In a way, Bourdieu's later activism mirrored this way of operating, as in the 1990s when he established small, published texts aimed at a general public, for example, the *Raisons d'agir* series, which included the *Contrefeux* publications. However, his own intellectual influences were more immediate.

Existentialism had already been a key influence for the Catholic intellectuals of the 1930s, inspired as they were by such writers as Karl Jaspers (1883–1969) and the Danish philosopher Søren Kierkegaard (1813–1855) before him. Existentialism is a broad philosophy, eschewing 'objective', 'scientific' knowledge and, instead, being set within a more Kantian tradition of metaphysics. 'Existence', for man, according to this view of the world, is defined by his actions and experience. Obviously, this kind of philosophy could in essence appeal to both the religious and the atheist, and it did. The chief exponent of humanist existentialism was, of course, Jean-Paul Sartre (1905–80) who, with his partner Simone de Beauvoir (1908–1986), was already active before the Second World War. At a time of war, when what someone did could literally be a matter of life and death, existentialism found a popular response among the educated classes, and, in fact, also captured something of the spirit of individualism which exploded in the 1960s (arguably, 1968 was a Sartrean event!). In our present context, it is important to realize that this form of subjectivism had no appeal for Bourdieu, who was more concerned with the way that the social, material environment shaped individuals, and what they did as a consequence. In fact, Bourdieu referred to existentialism as an 'insipid form of humanism' (1986a: 36). For him, classical philosophy was not much better, out of touch as it seemed to be with real-world problems – Algeria, Education, Béarn, etc. Michel Foucault (1926–1984) (who was of Bourdieu's generation and, like him, attended both the *École Normale Supérieure* and was elected to the *Collège de France*) wrote of the split at the time between a 'philosophy of experience, of sense and the subject, and a philosophy of knowledge and rationality'(see Pinto, 1998: 21). If Sartre represented the former, Bourdieu aligned himself with the latter view. Key writers here were the historians of the philosophy of science like Gaston Bachelard (1884–1962), George Canguilhem (1904–1995) and Alexandre Koyré (1892–1964). It is worth pausing again to consider just what we mean by 'science'. For these writers, it was not simply about discoveries and establishing physical laws – quite the contrary. They often saw science as a 'constructed form' of knowledge, which was shaped by a series of socio-historical conditions. For example, in Bachelard's view, the object of science was not a process of refinement and simplification through falsification, in a Popperian sense for instance, but the assumption of complexities in a greater understanding of the actuality of phenomena. 'Truth' is consequently never a single discovery but contingent, ongoing and partial. Such balancing of the relational and rational was termed *surrationalisme* by Bachelard, where the 'scientific fact' is something to be *captured* as part of a process of objectification. This is why we see in Bourdieu's work reference to the need to 'rupture' with the epistemological status quo and to focus on 'the construction of the research object' as it presents itself. In this way – 'applied rationalism' – social facts are 'conquered, constructed and recorded' (1968: 24). Writers such as Bachelard and Canguilhem can be seen as precursors to postmodernism. These individual also examined Foucault's doctorate. For both, falsity and truth were always relative to the ways in which they were constructed. However, although taking inspiration from these philosophers of the history of science, and embracing their main tenets, Bourdieu never followed the postmodern route in seeing all truth as a fiction, and all knowledge as an arbitrary event.

This section has outlined four key ingredients to Bourdieu's philosophy: first, its critical perspective; second, the major part that empiricism and observation play in his approach, and the importance of establishing relations between elements; third, the influence of the sociological founding fathers, in particular their moral concerns and theories of knowledge; and fourth, the role of the intellectual, both as an activist and the type of science he or she constructs. We have seen the personal and social contexts which influenced Bourdieu's thinking. It is time to consider his basic theory of practice.

A Theory of Practice

The last section focused on what could be viewed as the 'subjective' (existential) strand of French philosophical thinking up to the time of Bourdieu's coming of intellectual age, so to speak. This tradition can take various forms. Nevertheless, they all fall broadly into an area heavily influenced by what might be termed an 'idealist philosophy', perhaps best exemplified in the work of the German philosopher Immanuel Kant (1724–1804). However, there was another conspicuous strand to the French intellectual current which surrounded Bourdieu, and it is one to which we have so far given little attention – that of structuralism. The title of 'father' of modern-day structuralism is most obviously claimed by the founder of contemporary linguistics, the Swiss-born Ferdinand de Saussure (1857–1913). Details of Saussure's founding principles for linguistics will be discussed in the next chapter when we consider language per se. For the moment, it is enough to note that his approach was predicated on the notion that language was a formal system organized in terms of a structured set of constituents. It could thus be understood by analysing these elements and their functional properties. In his most famous work – the *Course in General Linguistics* (1907 and 1911) – he posited that a distinction should be made between language in terms of *langue* and *parole*: the former understood as the totality of the structure of language; the latter as individual acts of speech. There is a seminal idea here: that a formal base structure – which is finite – is the foundation for an infinite number of creative acts. Such acts are both individual and unique, but share common generative properties. In the Introduction, I described how the philosophy of man became the philosophy of language in the twentieth century and, we can see that linguistic theories such as those of Saussure offered metaphorically applicable terms for accounting for human activity. Thus, social systems are 'discourses' and cultural artefacts are 'signs' waiting to be deciphered and interpreted. Unsurprisingly, 'structuralism', as a philosophical system extended itself to such academic disciplines as anthropology, philosophy and sociology. Claude Lévi-Strauss (1908–2009) was the chief exponent of the first of these in France. In a series of books – *The Elementary Forms of Kinship* (1949), *Tristes Tropiques* (1955), *Structural Anthropology* (1959), *The Savage Mind* (1962) and *Mythologiques* – Lévi-Strauss presented a series of analyses which attempted to set out the 'ground structures' of human culture. His thesis was based on the notion that, although the surface structures of human society differed enormously across societies and cultures, deeper *structural relations* were universal, and could be understood as fundamental socio-biological exigencies; for example the incest taboo, the raw and cooked and totemic symbols. Such structures were 'objective'.

Given the prominence of Lévi-Strauss, and Bourdieu's own interest in anthropology following his investigations in Algeria and the Béarn, it would be surprising if Bourdieu had not engaged with this approach. For a while, he did write both *within* and *against* the Lévi-Straussian method. However, Bourdieu objected to the way that structures were interpreted as being both trans-cultural and rule-like in the way they directed human behaviour. Moreover, he questioned the static view that Lévi-Strauss took of such structural relations. As noted, Althusser (1918–1990) later developed a Marxist version of Lévi-Straussian structuralism. Here, the structures were invariably interpreted in terms of capitalist modes of production in which political, legal and cultural systems were all prior to individual action. But this interpretation was no better for Bourdieu because it suffered from a kind of fatalistic determinism – that we all follow rules which define what we do. Instead, Bourdieu was looking for something more dynamic where 'rules' were seen more as 'strategies' which *disposed* individuals to act in certain ways rather than determined them, and where change was a necessary aspect to the theoretical perspective. In short, it was what he described as 'a science of dialectical relations between objective structures and the subjective dispositions within which these structures are actualised and tend to reproduce them' (1977b/1972: 3). But what constitutes such a science in practice?

If the philosophies of Sartre and Lévi-Strauss can be seen respectively as representing the 'subjective' and 'objective' poles on offer in the human science in the 1950s and early 1960s, Bourdieu saw their direct opposition as disastrous for developing a truly authentic method, one that would take into account the ideas he had gained from the philosophers of the history of science mentioned above. In fact, at one point, he describes the duality of 'subjectivism' and 'objectivism' as they existed in the social sciences as 'fundamental', 'artificial' and 'ruinous' (1990c/1980: 25). The relationship between structure and culture is key to understanding how he sought to go beyond it.

For Bourdieu, there are two identifiable traditions in the study of culture, and both could be defined in terms of the way structure was interpreted. The first sees culture in its structuralist mode, as a set of signs making up systems of communication. This tradition can be seen in terms of the structuralism of Lévi-Strauss, and the trans-cultural structures which constructed meaning to be found in myths and language (again, this approach is akin to Saussurian linguistics). The second tradition sees culture in terms of its functionalist operations; in other words, as a product of the social infrastructure. Both Durkheim and Marx would share this second view since both were concerned with the ways ideas emerged as part of social organization, in particular, its material organization (albeit that Durkheim takes a positivist approach, while Marx is more critical/radical in intent). Bourdieu is critical of both traditions: the first for representing culture simply as a *structured structure* (the objectivist mode) and thus being simply too rigid, and static and underestimating the creative aspect of human facticity; the second for representing culture as just a *structuring structure* (the subjectivity mode) and therefore being idealist, for example, in seeing ideology as an imposition of the ruling class in the critical tradition, or as moral authority and social control in the positivist one. What Bourdieu is proposing as an alternative is to go beyond both traditions and, in so doing, arrive at a theory which will furnish us with a method to analyse 'symbolic systems (particularly language and myth) so as to arrive *at the basic principle* behind the efficacy of symbols, that is the structured structure which confers on symbolic systems their structuring power' (1971: 1255 my emphasis). It is worth emphasizing that this way of working requires a dialectical thinking of thinking, where identifiable structural relations are always seen as being both *structuring* and *structured*. Consequently, Bourdieu is looking to transcend the subjectivist/objectivist dichotomy, to constitute a new form of 'knowledge'. Later in this book, we shall consider just what this amounts to in terms of research into language and linguistics. For the moment, it is important to note that Bourdieu also presented this theoretical and practical position in terms of a series of 'breaks' from different forms of knowledge. Firstly, it is necessary to break with naive, empirical knowledge, as lived in everyday lives which proceed in a more or less un-reflexive manner. However, it is also necessary to break from dominant forms of 'scientific knowledge': for example, subjectivism as in phenomenology and existentialism, and objectivism as in structuralism and other forms of scientific thinking. If one could achieve this rupture, then there was the possibility of opening up a new space for enquiry and analysis. A further break is also needed – that from theoretical knowledge itself – but more of that later.

I have constructed this exposition of Bourdieu's theory of practice around the notions of 'culture' and 'structure'. Indeed, Bourdieu sometimes referred to his approach as 'structural constructivism' or 'constructive structuralism' in order to designate the dynamic two-way understanding of structure as outlined above (see 1989b). But what was 'structure' for Bourdieu? Clearly, he was interested in the structures of organization to be found in society – this was as true in his earlier works in the Béarn and Algeria as it was later in his analyses of education, art, politics and econom- ics. However, Bourdieu combined this 'objectivist way of thinking with a 'subjectivist' one. It is worth remembering that Bourdieu was trained in philosophy and was also a student of the French phenomenologist Merleau- Ponty (1908–1961). He had read the work of Edmund Husserl (1859–1938). In fact, an early thesis by Bourdieu was on 'a phenomenology of the affect- ive life'. Phenomenology is another philosophy of the Kantian tradition, and focuses on human consciousness as actively constituting phenomena as they appear *in themselves*. As a student of Merleau-Ponty and Husserl, it is not surprising (as evidence in his early study of the affective life) that his understanding of structure was essentially a phenomenological one. For phenomenologists, the primary act of consciousness and cognition arises from, generates and is generated by mental structures. In the very act of thinking, a structural relation of intentions is set up, essentially being structured because of their differentiating nature. For Husserl, there was a fundamental distinction to be made between *Noesis* and *Noema*, or between individual incidences of perception (an act of knowing) and background information (all that is known). The primary cognitive act initially occurs as a baby develops 'control' over its environment, and continues even into adult life. Of course, this interaction between the individual (a *tabula rasa* for a newborn) and the social environment does not happen in some Platonic realm of 'pure' knowledge. The *Noema* – the background know- ledge – is always formed in relation to a 'pre-given', coming with previously constructed ways of seeing the world, including values and interests. In this way, individual social agents are formed (structurally constructed and structured) according to the social context in which they find themselves. Just as one learns Chinese if one is born into a Chinese family, and English if born into an English family, one takes on the mores, customs, dispositions and modes of thinking of the cultural context in which one finds oneself, including socio-economic characteristics of position within the social hierarchy. In terms of the phenomenology of Husserl, this is the individual's encounter with the *habitualität* – the 'normal' way of thinking.

If this is the subjectivist side of the process, the objectivist side must not be overlooked. For Bourdieu, social space is itself structured, in that it is made up of entities positioned with respect to each other. These positions are often co-terminus with 'dispositions' to think and act in certain ways, associated with this positioning, but dispositions which exist in a 'virtual' state, that is, ready to be activated in response to particular occurrences within the field (see 2000a/1997: 149). The outcome of this reasoning is that a method is required which can integrate individual (cognitive) structures with social (spatial) structures – or the subjective and the objective; that is, structure as both a *modus operandi* (and thus generative of thought and action) and an *opus operatum* (and thus liable to objectification).

Such is the basis of the theory of practice which Bourdieu developed, doing so in the face of and in terms of the sorts of theoretical perspectives which surrounded him. Over the course of his work, Bourdieu developed two key concepts which respectively represent the subjectivist and objectivist levels of social activity: *habitus* and *field*.

Habitus is, of course, a term which can be traced back to Aristotle and beyond and, over the centuries of human thought, has been used in a number of contexts. Bourdieu defined *habitus* as:

Systems of durable, transposable dispositions, structured structures predisposed to function as structuring structures, that is, as principles which generate and organize practices and representations that can only be objectively adapted to their outcomes without presupposing a conscious aiming at ends or an express mastery of the operations necessary in order to attain them. Objectively 'regulated' and 'regular' without being in any way the product of obedience to rules, they can be collectively orchestrated without being the product of the organizing action of a conductor. (Bourdieu 1990c/1980: 53)

Here, we can see that Bourdieu captures something of the 'regulated' practice of individual human thought and activity, while escaping any notion of 'rule-governed' behaviour – a difficult balance to hold. Further, Bourdieu sets out a position to show how individual actions are mostly initiated at a level of mental process which is beyond the common dichotomy of conscious/unconscious. In this way, individuals can be 'disposed' to act and think in a certain way, but will only do so (or not) when in the particular social context (conditions) which 'fires' such predispositions. Such dispositions are themselves 'relational' and thus open to the theory of practice outlined above; in other words, they need to be read in terms of individual cognition and its background. *Habitus* then is both generative and structured (objectifiable) but, most importantly, it is also structuring (see 1977b/1972: 72).

Field, on the other hand, is defined as

> a network, or a configuration, of objective relations between positions. These positions are objectively defined, in their existence and in the determinations they impose upon their occupants, agents or institutions, by their present and potential situation (situs) in the structure of the distribution of species of power (or capital) whose possession commands access to the specific profits that are at stake in the field, as well as by their objective relation to other positions. (domination, subordination, homology, etc.) (Bourdieu and Wacquant 1992b: 97)

As I have emphasized, *field* is inherently structured from a Bourdieusian perspective because the entities of the world existed in a state of differential relations to each other. However, this degree of multidimensionality is hardly helpful as an analytic concept. An essential feature of the Bourdieusian *field* is therefore that it is identifiable and bounded; thus, for example, the *field* of education, the *field* of politics, the *field* of media, etc. Each of these would be ordered and structured in a certain way, and according to their function and purpose. As such, one of the inherent characteristics of a *field* is that it is constituted by a specific 'logic of practice': a logic that should be understood in terms of the principles which unpin the process through which what is found within a particular *field* is positioned by being valued according to a specific logic of distinction. These positions within *fields* can be occupied by various sizes of social grouping, as well as by individuals. So, while small groups have their place – as *microcosms* – within the *field*, large *fields* themselves exist in relation to other large *fields*. For example, the *field* of art is closely associated with the *field* of commerce. The principles and characteristics of the way *fields* behave are similar in both cases. They all need to be read against each other in terms of their positional and structural relationships to each other, as well as by their structural configuration (both as *intra-* and *inter-*field relations). Of course, if *fields* exist for a certain purpose, then they carry a certain *interest* with respect to their outcome, survival and growth. *Fields* are therefore never 'value-neutral' but saturated with *interests*. Indeed, part of Bourdieu's method is to uncover such *interests*. *Fields* are also always in flux, constantly transforming themselves in the course of social evolution. Change is essential to *fields*, therefore, and is often identifiable by internal dynamics which set current (and orthodox) ways of operating against new (unorthodox) ways: Bourdieu defines these as *doxa* and *heterodoxa*. *Fields* form, socialize, reward and punish those who pass through them – according to the logic of practice of the particular *field* – and offer the social conditions of existence for its 'members'.

Habitus and *field* must therefore always be seen as co-terminus; they must always be read against each other. In fact, Bourdieu calls the relation between the two one of 'ontological complicity' (1982b: 47):

> The relation between habitus and field operates in two ways. On the one side, it is a relation of conditioning: the field structures the habitus, which is the product of the embodiment of immanent necessity of a field (or of a hierarchically intersecting set of fields). On the other side, it is a relation of knowledge or cognitive construction: 'habitus contributes to constituting the field as a meaningful world, a world endowed with sense and with value, in which it is worth investing one's practice'. (1989c: 44)

However, there needs to be a medium for the operations of the *field*, one which connects it with *habitus* or, rather in this case, a possible multitude of different *habitus*. That medium is *capital*. *Capital* is defined by Bourdieu as an 'energy of social physics' (1990c/1980: 122). It is what is valued in the *field* and what 'buys' position. For Bourdieu, it exists in three principal forms (2006): *cultural, economic* and *social*. *Cultural capital* also exists in three forms: as official titles and designations (for example, positions and educational certificates); as physical entities (for example, books, paintings, etc.); and as sets of discernible traits (for example, accents, styles and ways of expressing oneself). However, all are symbolically powerful in buying power and prestige by defining one's position in the social hierarchy. *Economic capital* is simply money wealth and material resources – always a useful attribute in a capitalistic world. Finally, *social capital* is defined as the 'sum of resources, actual and virtual, that accrue to an individual or group by virtue of possessing a durable network of more or less institutionalised relationships of mutual acquaintance and recognition' (1992b: 119). In other words, knowing prestigious or powerful (well-positioned) individuals within a *field* can enhance one's own position within it by virtue of the fact of being 'sanctioned' by those in superordinate positions. Bourdieu makes the point that individuals, and indeed whole groups, can be identified and

characterized in terms of which form of *capital* they predominantly hold
and its volume.

It is clear that what is emerging here is a set of technical terms – Key
Concepts (see Grenfell 2008) – with which one can approach the analysis
of social phenomena. Bourdieu referred to these as his 'thinking tools', the
value of which could be assessed by the results they yielded. The practical
chapters of this book will be testament to them with respect to the study
of language and linguistics. But I wish to conclude with a few final remarks
about Bourdieu's theory of practice, the consequent research methodology
and how the resultant findings should be viewed.

Concluding Remarks

Bourdieu was a sociologist, albeit of a particular 'continental' kind. The
normal focus of study for sociologists are issues of social class, power,
gender and race, and most of these themes will emerge in the discussions
below. However, it is important at this stage to realize that Bourdieu would
begin any study of them by critically investigating how they were constituted, operationalized and presented in the actual academic field itself.
For example, many of Bourdieu's studies do include analyses, the outcome
of which utilize 'social class' as a defining category to present finding. Here,
there is an essential methodological issue at stake. It is common practice in
sociology simply to attribute social and individual practices to particular
designated classes so that 'social class' becomes an independent variable.
Bourdieu's intent is quite the contrary, and instead aims to construct a
model of a *social space* which accounts for a set of practices found there.
These practices need to be seen as differentiating themselves according
to observed differences based on the principles defining position within
that *social space*. So, what is at issue here, for example, is not so much the
similarities that classes share, but their differences. For Bourdieu, what we
need to do is 'construct social space in order to allow for the prediction of
the largest possible number of differences' (1990d/1987: 3). What he consequently offers is therefore less a sociology of 'social class' than a sociology
of distinction and differentiation, including its defining logic of practice,
and subsequent social classification. A simple acknowledgement of 'distinction' as a basic human instinct is therefore not sufficient. For example,
Bourdieu takes exception with Veblen's view of 'conspicuous consumption',
arguing that it is not enough to be conspicuous. Rather, it is necessary for
individuals to be noticed in terms of specific signs of signification within a

specific *field*. Social classes only exist, therefore, to the extent to which they are acknowledged as such in practical contexts governed by the particular principles of their position in the social space. The purpose of sociology is then to indicate the processes and consequences of that acknowledgement. Anything else is to confuse the 'things of logic with the logic of things' (1990d: 117). Naming a class, without this view, is tantamount to an insult as it acts as a form of *symbolic violence* in imposing a particular (absolute) perspectivism.

In researching social variation and differentiation, therefore, Bourdieu is drawing a distinction between the *actual structure* of the social system in its *multidimensional* stratification and the *symbolic products* which arise from it: 'In reality, the space of symbolic stances and the space of social positions are two independent, but homologous, spaces' (ibid.: 113). Bourdieu describes his consequent method as attempting to reconstruct the space of differences, or differential positions, and only then accounting for these positions as differential properties of the social space. Such properties would eventually be defined in terms of *capital*, or what is symbolically valued within a particular *field* context. Regions are then 'cut up' to see the operation and placing of a range of *social groupings*. These groupings may be of any kind – race, gender – although, at least in his work in education and culture, occupation was a major classifier, names and clusters of occupations being defined in terms of criteria and affinities, and the way they were distributed across the range of categories. Bourdieu further argues that in his empirical studies, the major 'primary' principles of differentiation need to be attributed to both the *volume* and the particular *configuration* of (cultural, social and economic) *capital*. In other words, individuals and groups define themselves by how much *capital* they hold and the profile of *capital* types within that holding. A further significant factor is the social trajectories of individuals and groups. In this way, social groupings 'on paper' can be related to what exists in reality. To the extent to which various individuals hold similar *capital* volumes and *capital* configurations (that is, share material conditions) in conjunction with others, they will constitute a homogeneous, and thus identifiable, group. They share similar positions in the overall structure of the *social space*, and thus also share similar *habitus*, and consequent dispositional characteristics.

This chapter has sought to interweave Bourdieu's theory of practice with his own biography, intellectual background and the socio-historic context in which he found himself. A number of influences can be discerned. Among these, Bourdieu's own language experience is worth noting. Clearly, his childhood in the Béarn, and the language he spoke there, led to clashes in his early years in schooling, especially in the distinction between his native language and accent, and that of education. In Algeria, he would have encountered diverse 'tribes', all speaking the dominant language, French, but in a different way according to social provenance and social standing. In his early writings on education and culture, it is therefore perhaps unsurprising that language featured as a carrier of knowledge, learning and distinction. But Bourdieu's own relation to language also changed. From writing for mostly an academic audience in the 1960s and 1970s, he increasingly adopted a popular style to address a general audience. This change of relationship itself needs to be understood in terms of an evolution in substantive intent. The issue of language use and intent needs to be kept in mind throughout this book. The latter part of the current chapter has outlined the key elements of Bourdieu's theory of practice, and the language – conceptual terms – associated with it. Part II offers practical exemplification of applications of this theory to a range of linguistic contexts. First, however, it is necessary to consider language and linguistics issues per se in connection with Bourdieu's theory of practice. The next chapter does this.

Chapter 3

Bourdieu, Language and Linguistics

Michael Grenfell

Introduction

This chapter gives an account of Bourdieu's writing on language and linguistics. It builds on Chapter 2 in that it takes his basic theory of practice and shows what this implies in terms of language. There are a number of key texts where Bourdieu explicitly addresses issues of language: for example, *The Economics of Linguistic Exchanges* (1977c), *Le fétichisme de la langue* (1975), *Ce que parler veut dire* (1982a), *Language and Symbolic Power* (1991c). These will form the core of the theoretical discussion of this chapter. I address Bourdieu's critique of the sciences of the study of language in general and modern-day linguistics in particular. There is exploration of the way in which words give meaning for Bourdieu and the signification to be attributed to the latter. *Habitus* and *field* are defining concepts, and the chapter addresses the way language features in these: for example, as *linguistic habitus* and *linguistic market*. The nature of *linguistic capital* and *legitimate language* is also considered. Bourdieu's perspective of language gives rise to further characterization of linguistic processes – *connaissance, reconnaissance, hypercorrection, hypocorrection, euphemization* – and these terms are also considered here. However, I begin with an overview of the way language features across the range of Bourdieu's writing as a whole.

Bourdieu and Language

This section considers the way language features in Bourdieu's work. Bourdieu was always interested in language. In the very earliest works in Algeria and the Béarn cited in Chapter 2, language formed a significant element of the ethnographies he constructed. For example, he noted the linguistic practices of the Béarnais peasant, most particularly, the oppositions set up between a largely rural population, who used local dialects, and the inhabitants of the nearby towns where French predominated. Many rural people, we are told, actually found it difficult to speak French. For Bourdieu, language was a form of 'objectivation': it substantiated something by 'naming it', or defined itself by taking on definitions corresponding to specific groups. The dominant discourse of the Béarnais contained words for the *patsanas empasanit* (empeasanted peasant) – *péquenot, plouc, péouze* – which only they spoke of. They also referred to themselves in these terms. Such *Francimandeja* also distinguished themselves by the clumsiness and heaviness with which they spoke French. This feature itself can be seen as indicative of their inability to operate in the modern urban world (see Bourdieu 2008a/2002: 198). As in the case of the 'working-class student' mentioned in the previous chapter, for Bourdieu, those who are imposed upon are partly complicit in that imposition because they adopt, implicitly at least, the same definitions about themselves that others have given them. One of the main objectives of schools in the Béarn at the time was to develop French literacy among the children of the area (pp. 74–5). Yet, Bourdieu argues that it was more the effect of the First World War, with large numbers of itinerant refugees, and the opening up of economic links with urban areas that seems to have acted as the main impetus to the way that French language eventually prevailed over local linguistic practices. Bourdieu made copious notes of such practices. Although these early analyses were never published by him, he has written of the way linguistic oppositions can strike the heart of rural life:

Between the last houses of the *bourg* (market-village) where French is spoken and the first isolated farms. Barely a hundred metres away, where Béarnais is spoken, runs the frontier between what might be called urban identity (*citadinité*) and the peasant identity (*paysannité*). So, at the very centre of his universe, the peasant finds a world in which, already, he is no longer at home. (p. 75)

Here, there is then a kind of social identification implied in the adoption of a particular form of language – that of the town or that of the country. In Algeria, as well, Bourdieu noted the way that the dominant use of French or Arabic by different sections of the populace correlated with entire dispositional attitudes towards modern and traditional life styles (1977b: 94–5). A 'visionary' attitude to the world – reference to God, fate, etc. – was consequently more frequent with those who generally spoke Arabic than with the French-speaking Algerians. This use of language also correlated with a whole social and political outlook. The French speakers seemed to be more 'realistic', 'revolutionary' and therefore politically engaged.

For Bourdieu, this phenomenon was not simply relative, but had as its base the socio-economic conditions of the time and place. French was the language of dialogue with 'the boss', for example, and therefore a means of expressing wants and needs. With language, so it seemed, comes the whole world viewpoint.

Given Bourdieu's own biography – bearing in mind his early experiences in the Béarn and Algeria and the fact that he grew up speaking Gascon – it is perhaps unsurprising that issues of language should also feature in the first of his major studies on education in the 1960s and 1970s.

Les étudiants et leurs études (1964b) *Les héritiers. Les étudiants et* **la** *culture* (1979a/1964) **and** *La reproduction* (1977a/1970).

As noted in Chapter 2, after the Béarn and Algeria, Bourdieu's first major study was on education, a sector with particular relevance at the time. Education was seen as contributing to the rebuilding of post-war France, and therefore of supplying the needs of the economy. However, it was also implicated in a philosophy of man shared by humanists and progressive Catholics alike. The notion of the 'democratic school' had been raised and educational policies developed to ensure equality of access. However, Bourdieu's analyses suggested that within this equity in provision, a further hidden selection was taking place in the way the culture of schooling was grounded on a particular dominant way of viewing the world – that of the dominant classes. Schooling could therefore operate according to its principles of open access, and the misrecognized systems of selection could do the rest. And, language was intimately involved in such systems as the medium of teaching and learning.

Both *Les héritiers* and *La reproduction* juxtapose the culture and attitudes of students according to their social background. They include accounts of the literate practices of French students in the 1960s which contrasts 'high' (academic) and 'low' (popular) culture. Bourdieu saw both a resonance and structural homology between 'bourgeois' culture and that implicitly characterizing French classical education. Schools were not simply places where individuals proved their innate talent and worth but provided a mechanism by which elites were perpetuated and transformed – in a word reproduced – themselves. Bourdieu and Passeron described the ideal French *homo academicus*:

The philosophy prizewinner in 1964 was the son and grandson of teachers, and intended to aim for the École Normale Supérieure, take the *aggregation* there, and become a philosophy teacher; while the winner of the first prize in Latin translation had 'read the whole of French literature by the age of 15 years 2 months,' and, 'fiercely individualistic' and 'astonishingly precocious'. Only hesitating between research and teaching. (1979a/1964: 43)

The title of the chapter in which this quotation appears is 'Games Students Play'. In brief, their argument went as follows: students were involved in a game of several facets. They read the latest 'avant-garde' writers of the time – Camus, Malraux, Valéry, Kafka and Proust – while asserting the 'values that are celebrated in orbituaries' (ibid.); in other words, a traditional outlook on the world . They involved themselves in the typical student game of 'distancing oneself from all limitations . . . (celebrating) difference for difference sake'. At the same time, they passed over in silence differences which derived from social origin (p. 47). All the while, differences deliberately expressed in opinions and tastes were manifest and manifested. This is a 'game' of signifiers, where what is signified is only partially explicitly acknowledged. Differences are therefore recognized but not the social derivation of which they are an expression. Such a phenomenon was omnipresent. Even where differences of economic background and its effects on scholastic outcome were indeed acknowledged, and even when this led to an overt political aim of rectitude, it did so in such a way as to mask the cultural processes which continued to ensure the social reproduction of privilege: 'The educational system can, in fact, ensure the perpetuation of privilege by the mere operation of its own internal logic' (p. 27) – this is its 'logic of practice'. That logic is one of 'differentiation' and it is operated by an entire system of strategies of exclusion and inclusion. Even the decisions which are made by representatives from different social categories are made in terms of the 'objective future' of that category. Bourdieu and Passeron write of the way in which the 'reality' of way students are studying is often 'denied', concealing 'self-interest' and thus disconnecting the present from the future, as a way of asserting an 'eternal autonomy', which is a valued prerequisite of the 'educated man'. The important principle here is that we need to distinguish between the function an educational system performs and the means by which it performs them (p. 66).

Academic success is often acknowledged in terms of 'talent' and inherent scholastic gifts. This 'charisma ideology' (p. 71) is even accepted by those from the 'lower classes' (sic.) in a way which directs them to a kind of academic and social fatalism; they fail because they are destined to fail due to lack of talent. And, by accepting how they are described – in language – they are complicit in their own subordination, and might even be considered to be 'consenting victims':

> When a pupil's mother says of her son, and often in front of him, 'He is no good at French', she makes herself the accomplice of three sorts of damaging influence. First, unaware that her son's results are a direct function of the cultural atmosphere of his family background, she makes an individual destiny out of what is only the product of an education and can still be corrected, at least in part, by educative action. Secondly, for lack of information about schooling, sometimes for lack of anything to counterpose to the teacher's authority, she uses a simple test score as the basis for premature definitive conclusions. Finally, by sanctioning this type of judgement, she intensifies the child's sense that he is this or that by nature. (pp. 71–2)

So the victims of what is being perpetuated in the name of democratic schooling collude (unknowingly) in the process by which 'what' they are is conflated to express 'who' they are in terms of scholastic talent. All the while, 'clumsy teachers' impose their 'essentialist definitions', imprisoning individuals as a result. But this 'imposition' does not operate in terms of a simple inculcation of knowledge and control. Rather, it is inherent in the practice of cultural transmission: *cultural capital*, of which *linguistic capital* is a core component. Moreover, it is not that *cultural capital* can be taken simply as 'cultural requisites' or content. Rather, imposition is expressed in the very forms and relations that culture takes on. Nowhere is this more evident than in the language of education. In *Rapport Pédagogique et Communication* (1994/1965), the issue of scholastic language is explicitly addressed. The currency of education is language and it is *the* medium of knowledge transmission. For Bourdieu, language has two basic levels of expression: form or structure, and content. Both form and content may exist in a way which favours certain ways of thinking and expressing that thinking. Moreover, they both may act as a mechanism for cultural transmission, which itself advantages and disadvantages those who encounter it depending on their background and the affinities (or not) this sets up when they enter a scholastic *field*. Bourdieu writes of the importance of language in the *academic discourse* and how it operates in education. If academic discourse is predicated on an assumption of communication between the teacher and the taught, this relationship is fraught with faulty signals:

> There are, in fact, two systems of contradictory demands that pedagogical communication needs to satisfy, neither of which can be completely

sacrificed: first, to maximise the absolute quantity of information conveyed (which implies reducing repetition and redundancy to a minimum); second, to minimise the loss of information (which, among other measures, may imply an increase in redundancy). (Bourdieu et al. 1994/1965: 6)

The paradox of language in the pedagogic relationship is consequently that it cannot satisfy these contradictory demands. Moreover, such demands are intensified by the social origins of learners and teachers, representing as they do, more or less, differing worldviews and ways of expressing them. Bourdieu argues that 'the aim of maximising the output of communication . . . goes directly against the traditional relationship to the language of teaching' (p. 6). He offers evidence of this 'misunderstanding' everywhere in his empirical studies of language in education:

> . . . the traditionalist professor can slide from the *right* to demand that his students learn . . . to the *fact* of making this demand when he has withheld from them the means of satisfying it. (ibid.: p. 8)
> The world of the classroom where 'polished' language is used, contrasts with the world of the family. (p. 9)
> . . . the teacher's self-assured use of professional language is no more fortuitous than the student's own tolerance of semantic fog. (p. 10)
> Student comprehension thus comes down to a general feeling of familiarity . . . . technical terms and references, like 'epistemology', 'methodology', 'Descartes', and 'sciences', shoulder each other up. He can quite naturally refrain from seeking clarification of each one of these . . . for his system of needs is not, cannot be, and up to a *point* must not be, analytical . . . the student is able to put together an essay which is apparently written in the same language of ideas, but in which the sentence 'Descartes renewed epistemology and methodology' can only be an impressionistic restoration. For outside this sentence, many students associate nothing with the word 'epistemology'. (p. 15)

Pedadogic authoritiy is hence defined and transmitted in language, and is carried in both the projection and reception of language in both form and content. The fact that this goes on in a way that is *misrecognized* – mistaken for innate talent and ability – makes it all the more powerful.

The State Nobility (1996a/1989) *Homo Academicus* (1988a/1984)

These various relations to language are also noted in Bourdieu's studies of Higher Education. In *Homo Academicus*, he analysed the structure and state of the Higher Education *field*. What he found was a shifting territory in the decades following on from the Second World War. Both the number of students in Higher Education and the subjects they studied had evolved considerably in response to the needs and socio-economic prospects of the modern world. Among a large number of other indicators, Bourdieu showed how it was possible to find strong relationships between identity, worldview and action in and through relations to language. For example, these patterns were manifest even in something as mundane as voting patterns to university elections. In subjects leading to a wide range of professional careers – such as the physical sciences, the arts, sociology and psychology – participation rates in elections were noticeably lower than where students were orientated towards clear 'tenured' posts, such as secondary school teachers. Language students were among this latter group. They therefore participated more fully in the elections – a participation which implied an already established pattern of social conformity.

The State Nobility is a study of the French *Grandes Écoles* (and let us recall that Bourdieu attended one of these – the *École Normale Supérieure*). Here, we find similar mechanisms of definition and imposition, the consequences of which are social selectivity. Language is again implicated in the way it is used to objectify individuals in the way they are described. The point revolves around the issue of the *verdict* (*judgement*). So, a statement such as 'you are common' or 'you are only a worker's son' would have no symbolic value and, moreover, would break a primary principle of legitimation, namely equality. A much more powerful and occluded strategy is therefore required: one of euphemization. Here, the same judgement is delivered, but it is done so in ways and phrases which fane objectivity; for example, in comments of written work, such as 'insipid style', 'OK', 'unimportant' (see 1996a/1989: 40–1). In this way, a taxonomy of values is created which has, at its base, the distinction between the mass and the few, the master and the novice, the refined and the vulgar, the authentic and inauthentic and, ultimately, the legitimate and illegitimate. These classifications are therefore not simply pragmatic terms for assessing students' work. They actually form and are formed by categories of thought which have, as their root, the type of phenomenology of experience and cognition outlined in the previous chapter; in other words, the categories are based on cognitive relations which are formed in childhood, reinforced in adulthood, and heavily laden with the values and *interests* of particular factions in the social hierarchy.

The *State Nobility* therefore begins with an analysis of the 'categories' of thought employed by academic lecturers in assessing students' work – for example, 'simple-minded', 'banal' 'vigorous', 'sincere', 'inspired' – relating

each to the social origins of the students to whom they are applied (p. 31).
In many cases, there is an opposition set up between 'one' and the 'other'.
However, this is not simply a process that applies at the extremes. Even
within the elite groups, there are noticeable oppositions which can be
understood as characterizing distinction. So, between the ENS (*École Normale Supérieure*) and the ENA (*École Normale d'Administration* – a high level
training college founded after the Second World War to train the new technicist elite required to drive the French economy) – there are differences
in the way scholastic competence is defined through language. For example,
in the oral exam of the ENA, mastery over complex situations is required,
such as the 'official interview' or the 'cocktail/dinner party'. At the ENS,
on the other hand, academic excellence is defined more in terms of the
presentation of written exams, which need to exhibit 'clarity', 'conviction'
and a certain 'presence of mind' (p. 420). There is a methodological point
to be made here about language in that any study of such a situation cannot
be made simply in terms of a discourse analysis of the text of the exams but
requires a 'methodological establishment of relations . . . between the
space of discursive stances and the space of the positions held by the
producers and recipients of the discourse . . . in the present case, in other
words, the entire field of the grandes écoles and its relations to the field
of power' (ibid.).

In 1976, Bourdieu also published an article which showed how the
contemporary political class in France adopted a certain language which
embodied the new technocratic state. *La production de l'idéologie dominante*
(1976) argues that the social changes described in the previous chapter had
led to a reconfiguration both within the intellectual *field* and between the
intellectual *field* and the *field* of power. Between the normal intellectual
class (deprived until then of temporal power) and the 'men of power' (politicians and leaders of commerce and industry), there had developed a
new generation of 'scientific administrators', the so-called *technocrats* of
the *École Normale d'Administration* (ENA), and 'professional researchers', the
graduates of the *Institut d'Études Politiques* (IED), both of whom were formed
to serve the interests of ruling administration. *La production de l'idéologie
dominante* opens with an 'Encyclopaedia' of accepted ideas drawn from
books, interviews and articles produced by powerful intellectuals of the day.
This Encyclopaedia included such words as ' Future', 'Happiness', 'Blocked',
'Change', 'Classes, ' Complexity', 'Dynamic', Discipline' etc. by writers of
the period, Servan-Schreiber, Giscard d'Estaing, Armand and Poniatowski
(2008c: 15ff). Bourdieu argues that these writers and their texts provide
those active in the dominant classes with themes to guide policy, and that

they do so by 'wiping out differences'. Words and language are then again implicated in the reproduction of society, at the level of culture, education and politics. Differences are nuanced and neutralized by the fact that those propagating them have all been through the same *Grandes Écoles* and administrative training institutions. These developments were particularly of note from the 1950s, but in fact could be traced back to the 1930s, when the Catholic 'non-conformists' began to converge with the economic power. As mentioned in Chapter 2, this convergence occurred through the discussion groups initiated in the 1930s, and was accelerated in the resistance movements of the Second World War. Here, Bourdieu argues, an 'antiparliamentary economic humanism, that sought to be neither right nor left . . . combined rejection of both capitalism and collectivism in a condemnation of the power of money and the power of the masses . . . (promoting) . . . a civilisation project based on asceticism of commitment and respect for hierarchical order based on competence' (2008c/2002: 89) – in a word, *technicism*. Language was central to this process since it acted as the mediator between various intellectual and power groups, but doing so in a way in which presuppositions implicitly rather than explicitly stated under the 'norms of good conduct' (p. 88) were carried in the terms of debate. In this way, an entire education and pattern of thinking were inculcated and routinized – another form of occult imposition.

La distinction (1984a/1979)

The idea that there are social distinctions across the social hierarchy coalesced for Bourdieu in his study of culture and taste. Culture, of course, featured in his early work in the 1960s and, as we have seen, was closely related to studies in education. However, his later work on taste dealt explicitly with likes/dislikes, cultural trends, behaviours and values within the French populace. The outcome of this study was a view of social agents as possessing, indeed being possessed by, cultural traits and generative matrices (*habitus*) that follow characteristic patterns as identifiable as the differences observed between the ENS and ENA students. By now, for Bourdieu, language, together with aesthetic sense formed an embodied state of being – *hexis* – which articulated entire cultural forms. These forms were observable in the very language employed by individuals: the outspokenness of the 'populaire', the self-censorship of the 'bourgeois' and the 'expressionist pursuit of the picturesque or the rhetorical effect of the choice of restraint and false simplicity' (1984a/1979: 176). Such oppositions also went to the very heart of language itself, for example, in the series of 'antagonistic adjectives' often used to describe the world: 'high (sublime, elevated, pure) and low (vulgar, low, modest), spiritual and material, fine (refined, elegant) and coarse (heavy, fat, crude, brutal), light (subtle, lively, sharp, adroit) and heavy (slow, thick, blunt, laborious, clumsy), free and force, broad and narrow, or, in another dimension, between unique (rare, different, distinguished, exclusive, exceptional, singular, novel) and common (ordinary, banal, commonplace, trivial, routine), brilliant (intelligent) and dull (obscure, grey, mediocre)' (p. 468). In this way, akin to a Durkheimian sociology of knowledge, language forms a homology with oppositions found within the social space which it therefore partly reflects.

The Weight of the World (1999a/1993) includes numerous examples of the way the 'language effect' operates in contemporary society. For example, there are the cases of Algerian women who, despite living in France, are still 'strongly integrated into their society of origin' (p. 79), rarely going outside of the home and so having few opportunities to learn French. In his discussion of *Masculine Domination* (2001a/1998), Bourdieu also notes the variation in linguistic usage between Algerian men and women. So, the phallus is connected with the *logos*: 'the public, active use of the upper, male part of the body – facing up, confronting (*qabel*), looking at another man in the face, in the eyes, speaking *publicly*' are all the preserve of men; while women 'renounce the public use of their gaze (they walk in public with eyes directed at the ground) and their speech (the only utterance that suits them is "I don't know", the antithesis of the manly speech which is decisive, clear-cut affirmation, at the same time as being measured and mediated' (p. 17). Once again, Bourdieu sees evidence of the way language is connected with, and symptomatic of, an entire cultural attitude, structural relation and lifestyle.

Elsewhere in *The Weight of the World*, there is the account of 'ghetto language' with its 'phonological specificities (the use of the suffix "s", the shift between is and are, the selective contraction or extension of syllables, etc.) and syntactical idiosyncrasies (especially the use of the invariant form "be", of the perfective "done" as in "he done got killed", or multiple negations, very common in informal conversation between social equals or acquaintances . . . not to mention continually refined lexicological innovations' (1999a/1993: 158). The observation is made that the way physical demeanour of the speaker is somewhat mirrored in language: 'irregular staccato', 'jerky', 'indolent', 'sprightly'. Again, embodiment – *hexis* – is linked with *habitus* and *cultural capital*, specifically *linguistic capital*.

Bourdieu also returns to the function of language itself, most specifically in the way it can be used to impose an entire worldview through its categories of thinking. Examples are offered in the use of such words as 'immigrant', 'native', 'we' and 'one'. For him, the philosophy of liberal economics is to be found present in the confrontational language used across the media to describe systems as the Market and State. 'Market language' includes such words as freedom, open, flexible, dynamic, moving, future, new, growth, individual, individualism, diversity, authenticity, democracy; while 'state language' is represented by such words as constraint, rigid, closed, fixed, past, passed, collective, archaic, uniform, artificial, autocratic, totalitarian (see Bourdieu and Wacquant 2000c: 7). En passant, it is worth recalling the issues of 'categories of thought' and 'antagonistic adjectives' referred to above; also the way these connect to both a phenomenological and cognitive theoretical understanding of human facticity outlined in Chapter 2, albeit seen through a critical/radical lens. Little wonder that Bourdieu at one point warns the would-be researcher to 'beware of words' because of the way they are the repository of all sorts of 'historical assumptions', silent confusions, impositions and academic interests (1989c: 54). The danger of misrepresentation through language is true everywhere. For example, at one point he responds to a letter from sixth-form students seeking support for their cause, by pointing out that they should be careful about being grouped together as a general class through the words used to describe them – 'youth', 'sixth-formers', etc. Such terms, he argues, overlook their true nature (2008a/2002: 181). 'Globalization', similarly, is a word which acts to construct its own myth: an *idée force* which 'ratifies and glorifies' its particular economic logic of practice, thus opposing itself to the principles of the welfare state (1998b: 35). 'Flexible working hours', 'night work', 'weekend work', 'irregular working hours', etc. are all secreted, in the manner of a Trojan Horse, once the globalization rubric passes into common, everyday parlance as a natural characteristic of progress. Bourdieu also criticizes journalists for an 'unreflexive' use of such words in their language (2008a/2002: 321). As we shall see, for researchers themselves, the very language of the constructed object of research must be scrutinized for embedded meanings.

This section has highlighted the way that language featured in a range of Bourdieu's major publications. It is time to look in detail at his critique of the science of linguistics itself.

Bourdieu and Linguistics

As noted in Chapter 2, the father of modern-day linguistics is Ferdinand de Saussure (1857–1913). Saussure famously proposed that the study of language should proceed in terms of its formal structural properties.

So words needed to be understood as signs (*signifiers*) of things *signified*. What constituted a sign/signifier could in fact be quite arbitrary; it was therefore necessary that a consensus be formed within a linguistic community to agree on which signs signified what. This approach to language gave birth to linguistic structuralism – for example, in the work of Leonard Bloomfield (1887–1949), which involved the study of the formal structure of language, that is, grammar and its underlying structures, rather than speech itself. The accent, coming from Saussure, was consequently on *Langue* (the totality of the linguistic system) rather than *parole* (individual speech acts) and on a synchronic (a-temporal) study of language rather than a diachronic (evolving) one.

Bourdieu was very critical of this 'formalist' approach to language, but he extends his critique back to the founding fathers of sociology as well as forward to contemporary figures in the field of linguistic study. Thus, he quarrels with Comte's view of language as a 'universal treasure' in which we all share. Here, language is a kind of social incarnation that is deposited in us and which we all carry in equal proportions – that is how we come to understand each other (see 1975: 27). For Bourdieu, this perspective overlooks differences between the 'common' and the 'private'. Cultural anthropologists commit the same error when they act as if a culture is common to all, rather than being differentiated and differential according to various social structures and groups, and the values and interests at stake within and between them. Critically, there are methodological issues at stake as a consequence. Saussure treated language as 'an object of study' rather than as 'a practice', thus constituting language as *logos* rather than *praxis*. Bourdieu notes the way that Saussure also uses the economic metaphor 'treasure' when talking about language. However, he then sidesteps the 'economic valuation' that language is given in symbolic systems, and ignores 'individual treasure' by stressing the sum of its parts – *langue*. Bourdieu argues that Saussure effects this approach by eliminating the physical part of communication, namely speech, and its individualization by particular people in particular contexts, in order to privilege the construction of language in itself. As such:

> (Saussure's work) reduces individual practice, skill, everything that is determined practically by reference to practical ends, that is style, manner, and ultimately the agents themselves, to the actualization of a kind of historical essence, in short, nothing. (Bourdieu 1990c/1980: 33)

In a way, the Saussurian view of linguistics, especially in its structuralist form, is now rather outmoded. The founder of contemporary linguistics – Noam

Chomsky (1928–) does not fair much better. In fact, Bourdieu sees Chomsky as following the same erroneous path by failing to see language as differential and differentiated. Again, there is the evocation of a 'universal competence', this time less as a 'deposit' than the discovery of a semi-biological 'Language Acquisition Device' (LAD), deep syntactical structure and *Universal* Grammar. For Chomsky, the Saussurian distinction between 'langue' and 'parole' is simply 'reinvented' as *competence* and *performance*. Competence as least has the advantage of positing language as a 'creative act', the product of which is an infinite number of utterances emerging from a finite form of structures. Analogously, *habitus* might be read as 'performance' based on a common cultural 'competence'. However, Bourdieu does not accept the Chomskyan precepts that linguistics should be solely concerned with an 'ideal speaker-listener', a 'homogeneous speech community' and 'perfect grammatical competence' (Chomsky 1965: 3). Such a position, argued Bourdieu, avoids the social and economic conditions of language acquisition and competence as an expression of legitimate, orthodox linguistic norms. Moreover, it ignores the way that linguistic usage is always sanctioned, and thus, shaped by imposition and censure. Bourdieu's alternative to Saussurian and Chomskyan linguistics can be summed up as follows:

> In place of *grammaticalness* it puts the notion of *acceptability*, or, to put it another way, in place of 'the' language (*langue*), the notion of *legitimate* language. In place of *relations of communication* (or symbolic interaction) it puts *relations of symbolic power*, and replaces the *meaning* of speech with the question of the *value* and *power* of speech. Lastly, in place of specifically linguistic competence, it puts *symbolic capital*, which is inseparable from the speaker's position in the social structure. (Bourdieu 1977c: 646 italics in the original)

Of course, behind these arguments again lies the philosophical distinction between fact and value, where a particular social phenomenon is an entity which holds specific symbolic power (value) in where and when it is deployed. Language is also a physical entity – a fact. But, one that exists as both in terms of process and product. The problem is that the former can only ever be surmised from the latter – the 'inside the black box' issue. Modern-day linguistics consequently aspires to be a 'science of language', and seeks to objectify its form as a system liable to study. However, it can only do this by conflating process with product and often completely ignoring the place of symbolic value in linguistic processes. There is a point of scientific principle at stake here, and one that leads us back to philosophies of science and ideas – Popper and Kant for example. Bourdieu lays the blame for this misleading perspective on language partly at the door of those writers – for example, the sociologist Max Weber – who argue that an interpretation of human activity can be considered to be true only if it is 'objectively valid' or, in other words, open to empirical verification. For Bourdieu, such 'objective' validity simply prioritizes the way the researcher sees the world, most often – as in the case of linguistic theory – by ignoring the economic and social conditions both of the object of study and the research process itself (see 1975: 30). In effect, such an approach falls prey to the same 'substantialist' trap mentioned in the previous chapter that others have fallen into in the social sciences, and which has so influenced the development of scientific thinking, and therefore knowledge. In effect, for Bourdieu, employing the words of Marx, this approach amounts to 'confusing the things of logic with the logic of things'; in other words, of confusing meaning or attributing meaning where there is none, and offering 'internal' readings of data in their own terms – as if the meaning of language can be found in language itself rather than in its social constitution and provenance.

Making Meaning

Such a debate on language goes to the core of how we are to regard it. How do we make meaning? What part does language play in that 'meaning making'? How are we to understand the relationship between thought and language? In Chapter 2, I described the 'primary cognitive act' as one that expressed a creative engagement with the world. Cognition describes how human beings manage the information that is presented to them. All social agents have a common set of fundamental schemes of perception, which can be objectified in language. But these meanings are neither static nor arbitrary; rather they are constituted within the structure of the social space from which they emerge. It is common in linguistics to acknowledge that thought and language are intimately connected. A Vygotskyan position on language sees thought being shaped by the language which expresses it, albeit that this language is an 'inter-psychological' product before it ever becomes an 'intra-psychological' one (see 1962, 1978).The Sapir-Whorf Hypothesis similarly draws attention to the way that language, and the meaning of language, can in fact structure thinking (see Whorf, 1940). This approach can also be related to Anderson's ACT-R (Adaptive Control of Thought-Rational) model (1983, 1993), where declarative knowledge (what is known) is contrasted with procedural (how we do things) knowledge. Here, language provides both the substance and form of thinking.

Mental processing is successful when action achieves a goal. However, for Bourdieu, such processes and successes are neither arbitrary nor simply accountable in terms of individual cognition, and always have to be understood with respect to their specific social context. In a seminal paper in 1966 – *Intellectual Field and Creative Project* (1971/1966) – Bourdieu builds on the discovery of the historian Panofsky that there was a link between Gothic art, for example in the design of cathedral architecture, and the mental habits of those involved in designing and making them. Each was symptomatic of the other. Bourdieu used this principle to argue that there was hence a *structural homology* between subjective thought and objective surroundings (*habitus* and *field*), the latter most noticeable in forms of social organization rather than cathedrals. Such homologies exist because they are both generated by and generate the *logic of practice* of the *field*, itself defined in terms of its own substantive *raison d'être*. The issue of successful cognition therefore also needs to describe the conditions necessary for success. Thinking itself is expressed in terms of the social conditions of the social *field* and the way these promote and inhibit the cognitive processes of *habitus* as two semi-independent, but mutually constituted, entities involved in knowledge construction and social action. In Bourdieusian terms, *Metacognition* – thinking about thinking – is also subject to the same pressures which, in effect, navigate between social and cognitive systems in terms of relations that can be either congruent or incongruent with respect to each other. The key point here is that defining what is and is not congruent – what is and is not thinkable – needs to be understood in terms of socially sanctioned degrees of relative orthodoxy and non-orthodoxy (itself subject to censorship) in relation to legitimate ways of thinking and speaking, and not simply to be found within the nature and form of language alone.

   In a similar way, the all-purpose dictionary is nothing more than a 'product of neutralization of the practical relations within which it functions' (1991a: 39), which in fact has no reality in itself outside of its use as an arbitrary artefact. In a very Wittgensteinian sense, Bourdieu argues that language only has meaning in terms of the situations within which it is immersed at any one time and place – literally, a game! The schemes of perception which individuals hold and the language which carries them are each homologously linked to social structures, which act as both their provenance and social destiny. Just as social agents exist in network relations, so do words also exist in networks of relations to each other – and partly acquire their meaning in terms of difference and similarity with respect to each other. Sense and meaning are always determined in the interplay between individual meaning and the social context in which language is being expressed. Words form a part of *fields* and can represent them. By entering a *field* (implying a semantic network), a word takes on meaning from that *field* through its position within the overall semantic *field*. The attribution of meaning is therefore always imposition (originating from the *field* context): a kind of transformation and transubstantiation where 'the substance signified is the signifying form which is realized' (see 1991c: 143) in practice. In other words, a specific meaning can be projected onto a word – signifying – prior to it being signified as a sign (word). Bourdieu's warning to researchers to 'beware of words' is therefore because such projections may carry field *interests* rather than the interests of science itself. These projections become literally 'more real' than the substance they implicitly claim to represent. For Bourdieu, language and words can therefore be the source of *symbolic violence* in that they impose one meaning over another, and thus one dominant worldview over another. This can be as true in scientific and research *fields* as it is in everyday life and the language that is used to mediate it.

Meaning itself, in words, is therefore a form of social construction, where *interests* are implied and carried in a way which goes *misrecognized*. Bourdieu's social universe is one where everything is symbolically valued. This view of language extends beyond words and may include any linguistic feature. Conventionally, linguistic study operates on a continuum: phonetics, phonology, morphology, syntax and semantics. Social differentiation and distinction can express themselves at any of these levels – all of them, one of them or any combination of them – according to the specific linguistic *field* conditions. However, in the study of language it is not enough to simply identify linguistic differences. There is, of course, phonetic variation across the social spectrum according to socio-economic stratification, for example, the difference between 'popular' and 'high' accents in speech. But Bourdieu is keen to point out that such differences should never be reduced to straight linguistic measures. Indeed, he sees a fundamental mistake in studies within the established *field* of the 'sociology of language' – when they put structured systems of socially pertinent linguistic differences in relation to structured systems of social differences – because (in a way which is very Saussurian) it 'privileges the relevant linguistic norms over significant sociological variation as if the capacity to speak was universally shared . . . (and) . . . identifiable with linguistic competence as a socially conditioned way to realize a natural potential' (see 1975: 14). In other words, an 'internal' reading is again prioritized over an 'external' one. Even in the use of grammar, variation is often studied against an implicit norm open to all, and to which all naturally converge. As such, the approach dissociates structure from function, and overlooks the fact that language is always a particular usage constituent of a particular situation.

The Linguistic Market

So, Bourdieu saw language usage as a specific form of *field* in the way that it was constituted and operated, and as following the kind of socio-cognitive processes outlined previously. However, language needs to be seen as a special kind of *field* since it could, of course, transverse many social *fields* at the same time. The educational *field*, the art *field* and the political *field* all have language as their core medium. In every *field*, the language that is used there has a specific value, defined in terms of the dominant forms – in this case, linguistic (terms, accents, ways of speaking, themselves constitutive of ways of thinking) – within it. Bourdieu extends the economic metaphor and coins the word 'market' to express these social processes, which he defines as 'a system of relations of force which determine the price of linguistic products and thus helps fashion linguistic production' (1989c: 47). So, 'systems of relations' are still central to this perspective on language. In fact, at one point, Bourdieu describes how a 'whole social structure is present in interaction' (1977c: 653). Linguistic variation itself can thus be explained in terms of the structure of social relations within the social space and the position of those within that space from whom the variation emerges.

All language has a value, therefore, and at every linguistic level. Linguistic utterances hence need to be understood as *dispositional*, that is, not based on perfect, invariant competence, but on individuals' linguistic competence and the 'linguistic climate' in which they find themselves. This climate derives as the social conditions at any one time and place which in fact set the value of linguistic exchanges. Pursuing the economic metaphor still further, any particular language use consequently always has an anticipated 'profit' according to the dominant forms within the particular *field*. For a value to be set, a 'base rate' needs to be defined: this is the *linguistic norm*. Such a 'norm' can be particular to a specific *field*, or indeed a microcosm within it, for example, the language of science, or culture, or politics. It can even be 'unorthodox', as deviant groups have their own (orthodox) ways of speaking. However, there is always a socially dominant linguistic form, which Bourdieu describes as *legitimate language*. He consequently argues both that no one ever acquires a language without also acquiring a whole social matrix, originating from the structures of society, and that such structures are not neutral, but have differential values according to positions within the *field* and/or *field* of power. Thus, normally (normatively!), the language of the dominant is consecrated and has a legitimacy which is not afforded to the dominated. The most obvious examples of this are 'standards' in national languages: for instance, RP English or *Academie* French. These forms of language – however imperfectly realized – set what is acceptable in terms of linguistic usage. Now, it is worth pausing to reflect on the view that *acceptability* is both arbitrary and relative. It is arbitrary in the sense that any linguistic form is equal to another, in theory at least. However, they are not equal when one form is valued differentially from another – a differential that is socially constituted and set according to (ultimately power) structures within the social space as a whole. The 'ideal norm' – as set in the dictionary and grammar books – is rarely realized in reality. Rather, there exist approximations, forms which define themselves implicitly in terms of their respective 'distance' or 'nearness' to the consecrated forms. Linguistic value is defined and determined with respect to this 'standard'. If what is 'legitimate' is defined according to a kind of transcendent *norm*, deviation from the norm is similarly set socially by objectively defined forms of acceptability; in other words, what is permissible in a particular context. Such a *linguistic market* can therefore be understood as a *field* condition.

Habitus, of course, makes up the other principal concept in Bourdieu's approach. So, a *linguistic market* represents the objective linguistic *field* relations, and *linguistic habitus* is the subjective element of *habitus* connected with actual language use. As always with Bourdieu, the two are in a constant state of dynamic interrelationship as well as evolving dynamically as a part of the transformation of social structures.

Bearing in mind that Bourdieu's method proceeds as an analysis of symbolic forms as immanent of the multidimensionality of the social structure, we therefore need to see any linguistic study as being concerned with variations in usage across groups and classes, as much as in the forms themselves. One of the most obvious examples of such variation is indeed the one found across socio-economic classes. Indeed, Bourdieu notes the differences in linguistic usage between what might be termed 'dominant' and 'dominated' social groups in, for example, the ways that the French 'r' is pronounced, or in the 'choice' of everyday words such as 'la bouche' and 'la gueule' for the mouth (1991c: 93). Each 'choice' arises dispositionally within social conditions which objectively set the limits of acceptability and normality for that particular context. However, each choice also defines and positions the user by situating use with respect to a set norm.

The analyst consequently has to be careful about the language that they use in studying language, as it can betray a whole set of relations to language. Bourdieu quotes the example of Bernstein (especially in his early work, which he then had to 'correct' later), who used a whole series of negative terms to refer to the language of popular classes and cultures – for example, ritualistic and particularistic (1975: 8–9). By doing so, he in effect stereotypes the linguistic characteristics of these groups in language, which is itself similar to that used by certain right-wing sociologists. Bernstein's original approach seemed to suggest that such characteristics were inherent from birth. He thus overlooked processes of 'inculcation' and 'dispossession', which are part and parcel of any academic discourse, and the way the latter consecrates certain ways of thinking and expression. In this way, 'linguistic deprivation' is conjured up to mean a handicap from birth rather than a social construction, and one that can be compensated for through offering special support to 'correct' difficulties seen as purely technical (see Bourdieu 1975: 27).

A similar error – but in reverse – is committed by the American sociolinguist, Labov, when he contrasts the apparent verbosity and verbiage of the American middle-class adolescents with the concision and precision of the children from the black ghettos. For Bourdieu, popular language is here 'canonized', that is idealized, without seeing that its value does not lie in the language form itself but in the social context in which it finds itself and the effects it has; in this case, of 'barring entry' to situations where only *legitimate language* is recognized (1975: 10). It is not unsurprising therefore that many individuals within the social structure invest considerable effort in gaining competence in the legitimate language forms, as this allows them an entrée into desirable echelons within the social structure. The defining issue is always the juxtaposition of levels of 'competence' between users. For Bourdieu, this competence constitutes *linguistic capital*: language – at all levels – which carries the authorized, sanctioned forms. *Linguistic capital* allows for the 'universalization' of legitimacy, as the 'official language, again defined as a result of processes of sanction and censorship. But, here, there is a kind of two-way process. Some individuals may be linguistically 'knowledgeable' (possess *connaissance*) by way of having practical mastery over 'legitimate' forms, while others recognize (*reconnaissance*) these without the mastery (see 1975: 27). There is consequently a kind of social dynamic perpetually being played out between those 'in the know', so to speak, and those excluded. For those with *reconnaissance* without *connaissance*, there is a constant effort to 'catch' up – to speak in the same way as the 'legitimate'. However, that effort itself betrays a lack of true competence, and is observable as a form of *linguistic insecurity*. Indeed, Bourdieu offers a picture of social agents who perpetually undertake a range of strategies in order to occupy the superordinate linguistic position, strategies which are demonstrable in an overly correct form of linguistic usage. For Bourdieu, this is the mark of those to be found at 'the maximum point of subjective tension through their particular sensitivity to objective tension' (1991c: 83), and is perhaps best exemplified by exaggerated correctness of the 'petits bourgeois' compared to the language of the 'lower classes' (sic.). The latter have, Bourdieu argues, no other choice (because of insufficient competence) than to use their own clumsy language or broken forms, or lapse into silence. The members of the dominant classes, on the other hand, those who represent the very realization of the norm, operate an inverse strategy. Here, their expressive competence is not enough. They assert still further their domination of linguistic forms by negating the sort of linguistic insecurity described above through strategies of *hypocorrection* – playing with the language, 'descending' into popular forms, even adopting vulgar forms as a way of providing a relief to their own supreme knowledge of the language. For Bourdieu, this can be seen as a *strategy of condescension*: a deliberate move aimed at creating a mark of distinction by the very way the anticipated is transgressed. The logic of practice of such strategies is one that creates a kind of *prise de distance* with the interlocutor, and places the speaker in a distinctive position. The fact that it occurs in a way which is misrecognized as such makes its results all the more effective. Nevertheless, a note of caution is needed: Bourdieu is not saying that all linguistic valuation needs to be seen simply as an opposition between the 'bourgeois' and the 'populaire' – although there are evident cases of this. Indeed, at one point he lists the oppositions – in language itself – which exist between the two groups in the social hierarchy: pretension and distinction; claimant and holder; riches and nouveau riches; aristocrat and bourgeois; established and parvenu; bourgeois and petits bourgeois; artist and bohemian; middle class and vulgar; or the middle class and the people. However, the whole point is that besides the highly objectified, publicly recognized styles of language, there is a multitude of forms which might each act as 'the legitimate language' for a particular social context: as noted, even unorthodox and dissident linguistic forms can be 'orthodox', 'consecrated' and 'legitimate' within a social microcosm, within a particularly bounded milieu. Ultimately, however, the power to define what is legitimate rests with the dominant, who thus have the means both to appropriate it themselves and impose it implicitly through sanctions (for example, affective approval and disapproval).

Language therefore has a *symbolic power* which is, in actuality, a violence, since it institutionalizes systems of dominance in line with established social structures. Nothing needs to be done to exert this *symbolic violence* – all it takes is for the logic of language to play itself out in its natural way, and its *misrecognized* function of social differentiation is performed (see 1991c: 170). Such misrecognitions can express themselves at any level of language, and even include the extra linguistic. I noted earlier that language for Bourdieu was not simply a social medium, but also a bodily and mental function. No one acquires a language without acquiring a relation to language, for Bourdieu. Such relations are then physical as well as mental; paralinguistic aspects of language – such as intonation, gesture and expression – are equally important in the operation of language as a symbolic power.

Fields and Language

Bourdieu saw the meaning of language as being other than what is to be found in words and linguistic structures themselves. Rather, that meaning was immanent within social structures and individual dispositions, and then expressed through language. All language, for him, involved forms of *euphemization*, that is, a kind of play-off between form and information, dictated by the social conditions of production. He uses the example of the British philosopher of language J.L. Austin (1911–1960), who had argued that what was important in language was the way it was used. For Austin, speech enacted a certain performative function and did this through what he called an *illocutionary effect.* Here, the actual language and its effect are separated – for example, the difference between declaring a meeting open and saying something like 'Ladies and Gentlemen', which has the effect of declaring the meeting open. Austin contrasts this phenomenon with the *perlocutionary effect,* which is defined in terms of the resultant action of language; in other words, the actual effect may be different from the intended illocutionary event. A successful perlocutionary effect must therefore by definition also be an illocutionary one. The point for Bourdieu, however, is that in both cases, the causes and consequences of these effects do not lie in the words themselves – as Austin seemed to suggest – but in the social conditions which surround them. In other words, illocution and perlocution are institutionally bounded. These effects are evident in the various social *fields* that Bourdieu examined with respect to language.

I now want to consider some examples of these *fields* with reference to a range of contexts and the part that language plays in these sites: religion, education, philosophy and literature. There are two principal points to bear in mind throughout this account: first, the specificity of each individual *field*; and, second, the way all *fields* – irrespective of their particularity – might be seen as behaving according to the same operative logic as set out above.

In considering the *religious field*, for example, Bourdieu's analysis presents language in terms of its inherent structures, in this case, two 'populations': the 'oblats', who are totally dependent on an institution to which they owe everything, and to whom they give everything; and the 'bishops', who are ordained later in life, thus entering the *field* pre-endowed with various *social*, *cultural* and *economic capital* (1982c: 5). For Bourdieu, there is thus a kind of paradox – he calls it a 'double consciousness'. On the one hand, the religious *field* presents itself as 'disinterested' in the material world, since it is based on principles of volunteering, offering and sacrifice. On the other hand, at least for Bourdieu, it is a *field*, just like any other, and is therefore seen as operating according an 'economy' of symbolic goods. Such a dilemma explains why the bishops laugh each time they are seen to refer to the church and their undertakings in the explicit language of economics: for example, 'phenomenon of supply and demand' (1998d/1994: 113ff). In this typical 'strategy of euphemization', the economic truth is denied, as a kind of taboo. The language used by the church operates a similar disguise: 'apostolate' is used instead of 'marketing', 'faithful' instead of 'clientele', 'sacred service' instead of 'paid labour'. Even 'promotion' of the clergy is euphemized to their 'recognition'. In this way, religious institutions work to establish and preserve an entire set of relations through the language it uses about itself and with the people who are involved with it: a classic case of mental structures and social structures operating homologously, which shows the complicity of *habitus* and *field* (subjectivity and objectivity) in recreating each other. As a result, exploitation is masked and constitutes a form of symbolic language resting on 'the adjustment between structures constitutive of the habitus of the dominated and the structure of the relation of domination to which they apply: the dominated perceive the dominant through categories that the relation of domination has produced and which are thus identical to the interests of the dominant' (ibid.: 121). For Bourdieu, religious language therefore functions as a kind of 'double language', and thus can be seen as a perfect instrument of such a strategy of euphemization – one which disguises true relations. Here, there is a kind of 'logic of self-deception' involved, one where individuals take on a language, and consequent worldview, which itself obscures true structural relations, in an act of collective collusion of misrecognition. So euphemisms, rituals, terms of address, and liturgy, in which language is the operating medium, all provide forms of mutual structuration of thought and action. Consequently, there is a powerful struggle over language and the terms used to describe social practice. For instance, the Church was historically the first to occupy itself with the 'public good', including education, care of the sick, orphans, the poor, etc. Therefore, Bourdieu argues, they were the first to build up a fund of 'public capital' which has never been entirely taken over by the State, despite a fierce struggle to do so on the part of the political bureaucratic machinery (ibid. 120, and 1998e).

Euphemization is also a key phenomenon in understanding the workings of the *philosophical field*; although in this case, such a strategy is also accompanied by a strong form of censorship, one which sanctions what can and cannot be uttered, and therefore thought. The most developed account offered by Bourdieu of the philosophical field would be that of the German philosopher Martin Heidegger (1991b/1988). *Field* structures are the base of the analysis: in this case, the way in which economic and political events had led to a crisis in the German university *field* in the 1920s and 1930s – for example, the rise of student numbers and the lack of career opportunities for would-be academics. This situation encouraged the formation of what Bourdieu calls a 'university proletariat', or 'free intelligentsia', who were forced to teach below the university level. In other words, again, a particular phenomenon can first be explained in terms of profound changes in the structure of the *field*, in this case, as so often, provoked by a large and rapid increase of *field* participants. Language was again intimately implicated in the response of these individuals to the world which surrounded them. On the one side was the secular world, described in terms of 'disintegration', 'decomposition', 'technicist', 'mechanization', 'automatic', the 'satanic'. On the other side was 'nature', 'myth', 'roots', the 'sublime'. However, the former was also associated with modernist, positivist thinking, and with everything that is low-minded, arbitrary and formless in the 'machine age'. Oppositions were consequently set up in language which structured people's thoughts: for example, culture versus civilization, Germany versus France (as a paradigm for cosmopolitanism), community versus the people (the incoherent masses), the Führer versus parliament, country/forest versus town/factory, peasant/hero versus worker, life/organism versus technology/the machine. Beyond these terms, there also existed oppositional concepts such as 'the total' versus the partial/disconnected – that is, integration versus fragmentation and, ultimately, ontology and true science versus godless rationality. The phrase 'total' or 'the whole' is again a classic case of euphemization. It is a term which does not need to be defined, other than by contrast with other words. It therefore acts as both a marker and 'an exclamatory shifter': for example, education for 'the whole student', 'whole insights' the 'whole nation', etc. (p. 24). For Bourdieu, Heidegger's work crystalized these distinctions by developing a philosophy which, in the very language it employed, implicitly separated the 'masses' from the 'elite'. He did this by being what Bourdieu called the 'master of double talk' – that is, 'of polyphonic discourse . . . (managing) to speak simultaneously in two keys, that of scholarly philosophical language and that of ordinary language' (1992b: 150). So, 'Being', 'care' and 'time' – everyday words – were all redefined by Heidegger outside of their normal usage, but in a way which allowed them, now-reconceptualized, to partly remain in everyday speech. Thus, their normal use is undermined and surplanted with reference to euphemized forms of philosophical dialogue which allows them to exist in the real world but in a transformed way. Such polysemic use of language hence has both ontological and political consequences. Bourdieu gives the example of Heidegger's *soziale Fürsorge* – 'social welfare' – a term which is subsequently used to refer to both the political context (protection) and the condemnation of assistance, health insurance, paid leave, etc., which was awarded to the masses. A similar philosophical distortion by association consequently also led to the degradation of such concepts as 'state aid' as being 'naturally right'. In this case, it is as if language itself is colonized by a different meaning and sent out into the public sphere to act like a semantic energy matrix, altering the way we think about the world. Here, what is signified is carried in the signifier, now 'transformed and transubstantiated' into a different meaning. For Bourdieu, the dangerous result of this process is that there is an implicit opposition set up between not only 'the mass' and 'the elite' but also 'them' and 'us'. These dichotomies are then ultimately accepted as a natural state of affairs. In a similar way, philosophical terms were established which seemed perfectly congruent with Fascist terminology: 'the essence of Being', 'human existence', 'the will to be', 'fate', 'dereliction', etc. (p. 4), allowing for an epistemological resonance between the specialist and the everyday – philosophy and politics – with all the consequences this had for subsequent social behaviour in its name.

I have already alluded to the *field of education* and the way that language is intimately implicated in its operations, and there is further discussion of this topic under a practical chapter in Part II. As noted, language is *the* medium of education. It transmits knowledge but, more importantly, it also represents a certain way of thinking – itself a product of social structures (themselves as constituted by specific logics of practice), which are then reproduced trans-historically to maintain patterns of dominance and domination, symptomatic of the evolution of society. These processes can be seen in curricula documents, pedagogy, classroom discourse, assessment materials and the principles underlying them. We have considered the way in which *linguistic capital* is a kind of subcategory of *cultural capital,* therefore representing certain dominant cultural values. As such, it is acquired in the family and then accentuated by the School. It also guides content and form in literary behaviour, both in terms of the subjects of literature and the ways in which they are discussed. In *Distinction* (1984a/1979: 116ff), Bourdieu also analyses how the different fractions of professional groupings could be ranked according to their notional quantity of *cultural capital* and their type of reading matter. So, higher volumes of *cultural capital* correlate with 'rarer' (more distinguished and distinguishable) types of reading. For example, teachers in higher and secondary education are more likely to read philosophical, political, economic and art books than any other professional category. They were also more likely to read novels than any other grouping, except public sector executives, with whom adventure stories were most popular. Behind these indices are issues of the aesthetic sense: the degree to which it is expressed differentially across social groupings, and the form of expression it takes. However, it is also about the way in which language is a medium for aesthetics. For the consumer of literature, it is a question of the extent to which a particular literary style resonates with an aesthetic sense permeating the whole of their life dispositions, including a relation of mind and body. For the literary artefact itself, there are questions of meaning content, degrees of ambiguity and linguistic form.

Language, of course, is also the substance of literary expression in that writers write with language. The issues here for Bourdieu are again the structure of the (in this case literary) *field*, the dominant linguistic (literary) forms to be found there, and how these two somehow mirror each other. The most extensive coverage Bourdieu gives to this issue is *The Rules of Art* (1996b/1992), where he analyses the *field* of artistic production in general, and *the literary field*, in particular, through a study of the nineteenth-century novelist Gustave Flaubert. His discussion is connected to the notion of the 'aesthetic sense' and how this is constituted within the literary *field*. Bourdieu argues that Kantian aesthetics did not occur at an arbitrary point in time, but rather when socio-structural shifts (in a phenomenological sense) were altering the boundaries of what was and was not 'thinkable'. The notion of the 'pure gaze' was therefore true in as far as it goes, but only as a phenomenology of the aesthetic experience of someone who is already distant from social and economic necessity – the privileged. This development implied a certain autonomy within the *field*. What Bourdieu saw in the changes of the art *field* during the nineteenth century was that a social structural shift had taken place which created a new space for art, one which possessed a degree of autonomy with regard to previous art–audience relations:

> Flaubert in the domain of writing and Manet in painting are probably the first to have attempted to impose, at the cost of extraordinary sub-jective and objective difficulties, the conscious and radical affirmation of the power of the creative gaze, capable of being applied not only (through simple inversion) to base and vulgar objects . . . but also to insignificant objects before which the 'creator' is able to assert his quasi-divine power of transmutation. . . . (This formula) lays down the autonomy of form in relation to subject matter, simultaneously assigning its fundamental norm to cultured perception. (1993a/1980: 265)

What Bourdieu is here describing is the separation of *form* and *function* – both in art and writing – as and within a product of the autonomizing of the *field* of artistic production (see Grenfell and Hardy 2007 for a more extensive discussion). It is in that separation – that 'art for art's sake' – that a *field* position analogous to the artistic process of the 'pure gaze' is born. There is then a mutually constituting relationship between the 'pure gaze' of the privileged consumer and the 'independent creative gaze' of the producer (writer). Both implicitly assert an independence and therefore uniqueness. In the eighteenth and nineteenth centuries, the changes in social structures led to the growth in a new bourgeois class. Art up to that point had performed a social function in positioning those who consumed it, and hence those who produced it, with regard to particular social, polit-ical and moral values of traditional elites – aristocratic and religious. The new bourgeois almost 'invented' a new morality which set it apart from the past. In the course of these developments, writers struggled to find a means of expression which gave them independence from the aesthetics of those they had previously served. Language forms had to be 'reinvented' and called to express different functions.

There is one final area which also needs to be touched upon in our consideration of the relationship between language and *fields*: that of politics. The *political field*, in the narrow sense of the word, would include a particular area of the *field of power*, that of political parties. However, following on from the above, it is also clear that there is a much broader definition which draws attention to the 'political' dimension of a very wide range of social phenomena. For Bourdieu, any social group can act in a 'political sense' and can be the site of *field* interactions. There is a paradox here: groups often exist in a virtual, unrealized sense and, in fact, cannot constitute themselves as a group, and, if they do, cannot 'act' as a group. There is therefore a tendency towards *delegation* and *representation* (1991e and 1991f). Indeed, both *delegation* and *representation* mark a stage in the formal coming together of a group, movement or party. But what happens at the same time is that in naming itself, 'the sign creates the thing signified' (ibid.: 207): the signifier not only represents the group, but signifies that it exists by mobilizing it. However, as noted, the group cannot speak *as a group*. Therefore, the right to speak for the group is 'delegated' to one or more individuals. For Bourdieu, this phenomenon is a 'veritable magical act of institution' (ibid.: 195) where a group invests someone with the authority *to speak in its name*. This instituting is not an arbitrary choice, however, but comes with a certain recognition of rank, position or the investment of someone in terms of the *field* in which the group is placed and the interests at stake there. Bourdieu also refers to the example of the *skeptron*, the Homeric device passed around in debates, conferring on individuals the authority to speak. Clearly, there is an almost totemic element to such a practice, in that it actualizes and ritualizes institutional power – a kind of act of moral magic that derives its power from the attributed power of the group. Political power itself is really the outcome of the struggles between individuals and parties to speak on behalf of others. Here, again, the real struggle is between signifier and signified – political party and party, party and class, etc. As always, what is at stake is a fundamental struggle of opposing ways of viewing the world as represented by different groups and expressed through language. There is therefore a kind of *illusion* in playing the game while not admitting to gamesmanship, or indeed that it is a game at all. The irony is that the group representative, the delegate, will not be representing the *interests* of the group at all but, in fact, their own interests. In this way, when power is endowed, the endower is dispossessed of power – to a greater or lesser extent.

Conclusion

What Bourdieu offers us is a kind of 'double critique' of language. First, there is the critique of the academic *fields* dedicated to the study of languages, the roots of which can be traced back to nineteenth-century writers such as Comte. However, his main attack is on Saussurian linguistics and all that has followed in its wake. Bourdieu's main objection is that the sciences of the study of language simply do not take account of the 'praxis' of language: the social conditions of its construction. Paradoxically, this objection would also apply to all those disciplines that seem to be concerned with the 'social' aspects of language, such as sociolinguistics and social psycholinguistics. The second part of Bourdieu's critique of language offers an application of its social dynamic in a range of *fields*. Language, it seems, is a source of power and, ultimately, *symbolic violence*. Nothing is as it seems in language once we view it through the lens of the *linguistic market*. Here, *linguistic capital*, acquired in the course of individuals' social trajectories, leads to valuations which result in a certain amount of symbolic profit. Such a profit 'buys' position in the *social space*. Unsurprisingly, therefore, a numbers of strategies – *euphemization, hypocorrection, hypercorrection* – are adopted as a way of capitalizing on linguistic behaviour. Every *field* has its own linguistic forms and practices and this chapter has drawn attention to some of these. Bourdieu's theoretical perspective also has something to say about the nature of language itself – the way it is constituted and its effects in shaping thinking about ourselves and the world. Caution is recommended for anyone who takes words at face value, as representations of fact. We have noted a critical point for researchers in terms of the very terms of research they employ. If we are to 'beware' of words for the social, historical and cultural impositions they may include, this is no less true for the researcher than the object of research.

At one point, Bourdieu talks about 'heretical discourse' as language which breaks with the *legitimate language* of the social world, and of the 'common sense' that it implies. Of course, such heresy is as present in the language of deviancy as it is in that of the artistic or literary avant-garde (indeed, by the same processes, the operations of these *fields* are almost identical). New language, heretical language, implies the construction of a new 'common sense', a new legitimacy. For such to occur, the *field* group must lend its recognition and acknowledge it, and, by so doing, endow it with the authority of the group. As this chapter has argued, the efficacy of such 'heretical' language does not reside in the words themselves or, as Bourdieu points out, in the charisma of its author, but 'in the dialectic between the authorizing and authorized language and the dispositions of the group which authorises it and authorises itself to use it' (1991c: 129). In other words, heretical language can become 'authorized', but only through the assent of the group. There is what Bourdieu calls a 'labour of enunciation' to be performed by naming the unnamed, and externalizing the internal, and, in so doing, objectifying the pre-verbal and pre-reflexive in ways which render them 'common and communicable' (ibid.). Such utterances always have to be sanctioned, and one must remember that a process of naming may well challenge and break with the established *doxa*. 'Naming the unnameable' can therefore involve the breaking with systems of censorship – both institutional and internal – which prevent what Bourdieu calls 'the return of the repressed'.

It is as well to keep these points in mind while reading the next part of this book, where a series of case examples are offered as applications of a Bourdieusian perspective to a range of language-based practical contexts. In each case, a conventional treatment to a particular research topic can be contrasted with a Bourdieusian approach. As such, we might view these examples as part of a project to establish a new way of looking at linguistic contexts in contrast to more conventional ones. We have seen the way that Bourdieu is offering a different language – encapsulated in his key theoretical tools – to describe language. That language itself challenges both the common sense orthodoxy of the areas covered – linguistic variation, language in education, language policy, language and ideology, and linguistic ethnography – and the academic disciplines dedicated to their study. Bourdieu's approach might then be offering a new potential authority and a new orthodoxy for the study of language and linguistics in the social sciences. Part III of this book will further consider many of the methodological issues raised from and across these chapters, and explore their potential for future applications and developments.

Part II

Practice

How any one individual researcher draws on Bourdieu's work and his theoretical approach itself is an issue, and there is no one methodological orthodoxy to which anyone can conform. Some use Bourdieu in an en passant fashion, while for others he is defining source. The aim of Part II of this book is to offer a series of chapters which demonstrate a selection of applications of Bourdieu's perspective to a range of language and linguistic contexts. The chapters themselves demonstrate a variety of approaches, and no one writer would claim to represent a definitive application. Rather, we see them as studies which can contribute to the debate on why language and linguistic researchers might use Bourdieu and how. Such issues 'towards a science of Bourdieusian linguistics' will be addressed further in Part III, which follows these practical chapters.

Part II begins with Chapter 4, which looks at 'language variation'. This study returns us to the basic components of language – phonetics, phonology and syntax – and considers linguistic variation in terms of *linguistic capital*. However, the chapter attempts to capture something of the dynamic of variation in use with reference to individual language users' backgrounds (*habitus*) and the context in which the language arises (*field*). The chapter shows how both quantitative and qualitative analyses are necessary to understand linguistic variation and why/how it occurs. Chapter 5 then addresses the topic of 'language and ideology'. The context here is Spanish and Catalan, and Robert Vann's analysis demonstrates the way a national language both imposes and impinges itself on a regional language. Bourdieu's notion of the 'linguistic market' is used to indicate the way certain languages are valued over others and why. Moreover, Vann shows how 'ideological' issues extend to researchers' own conceptualization of language, as well as what they choose to study and how. This chapter also makes use of detailed quantitative analyses within a Bourdieusian framework in order to offer empirical exemplification of the way language and ideology can be seen to be co-terminus.

Linguistic Ethnography is a new emerging field in the area of language study. Crudely, it is based on the coming together of two established academic fields – linguistic and ethnography – with a view of bringing the best out in each. Linguistics offers ethnography precise techniques for the analysis of language which can illuminate the qualitative data available to ethnographic studies; while ethnography provides linguistics with ways of contextualizing and understanding how a range of factors – social, cultural and economic – impact on language use. Chapter 6 is an example of Linguistic Ethnography in practice. Adrian Blackledge highlights issues of linguistic use and variation within a multicultural context, and shows how micro analyses of the individuals involved are necessary in order to understand structural relations to language, both within a linguistic group and in a broader community. We have considered Bourdieu's view on the relationship between linguistic orthodoxy and the nation state. Chapter 7 develops the issues involved in such a relationship by focusing on 'language policy'. Here, Stephen May develops the discussion to demonstrate how language manifests itself within a policy which reflects the interests of the 'field of power'. For Bourdieu, all social contexts are ultimately subordinate to the state and its power structures and, bearing this in mind, May addresses the existent implications and tensions for a more democratic, inclusive language policy. Chapters 6 and 7 take us in a qualitative direction, one which develops – from the perspective of both minority and majority linguistic groupings – issues concerning the link between socio-cultural forms of language, politics and power. Chapter 8 then returns us to a specific *field* context: that of education. This book has already highlighted Bourdieu's preoccupation with the role of language in academic discourse, and how it is complicit, through schooling, as the medium of reproduction for social hierarchies. However, Bourdieu himself never undertook analyses of classrooms and language in education. Chapter 8 takes us into the classroom and, through a series of excerpts of academic discourse, raises issues of *habitus, field* and *linguistic capital* in the very processes of teaching and learning to be found there. This chapter also employs a more systematic approach to the analysis by situating itself at three distinct levels, each of which brings out a particular feature of relations to language in the communication between individual microcosms, the larger *field* context and the role of national agencies.

As noted earlier, none of the authors in Part II would claim exclusivity or monopoly of approach in applying Bourdieu's perspectives on language to their individual topics. However, clearly, each has taken on board Bourdieu's 'theory of practice' in the belief that it offers insights about language and linguistics which are not normally present in conventional approaches in their respective research *fields*. These examples are an opportunity to consider practical exemplification of what those insights might be.

Chapter 4

Language Variation

Michael Grenfell

Introduction

This chapter addresses issues surrounding variation in language use. Of course, there is a long and rich tradition in recording the way language is actualized in the world through written and oral forms, as well as examining the ways in which meta- and para-linguistics aspects of language feature in systems of communication. It is impossible to go into great detail on each of these. However, the first section of the chapter revisits some of Bourdieu's linguistic theory of practice, as set out in Part I of this book, in the light of such academic fields as sociolinguistics and social psychology, and offers some exemplification of others' work on linguistic variation from a Bourdieusian perspective. The main coverage of the chapter, however, deals with a specific study of linguistic variation from a corpus of French collected in the town of Orléans. This study offers an exploration of the ways in which Bourdieu's conceptual terms with regard to language and linguistics – *habitus*, *field*, *capital*, etc. – can be used to elucidate a range of linguistic features. Both quantitative and qualitative analyses are provided in order to show how aspects of the 'linguistic market' operated in this town. The chapter concludes with some reflection on this methodological undertaking and projects forward in terms of a possible future research agenda for studying language variation in this way.

Objectivism, Subjectivism and Linguistic 'Groups'

The first two chapters of this book showed the way in which Bourdieu's theory of practice characterized itself by an attempt to go beyond 'subjectivist' and 'objectivist' modes of knowledge in the social sciences. The chapters also discussed the ways in which language located itself within this argument, both as an object of analysis and as a means of expression for linguistic studies. Clearly, the sciences of the study of language are many and various, and we might list linguistics, applied linguistics, sociolinguistics, psycholinguistics and social psycholinguistics among its many variations, not to mention particular methodological subcategories within each. Of course, many define themselves according to the type of questions that are being asked, but a common distinction identifies two principal approaches within these disciplines: quantitative linguistics and interactional linguistics. In terms of language variation, the quantitative tradition is probably best exemplified by the work of the sociolinguist, Labov (1972, 1977), while the interactionist mode was initiated by researchers such as Gumperz (1982) who studied the patterns of discourse strategies – how individuals modify their language and why – in spoken communications. Broadly, these two traditions can in turn be understood as representing the 'objectivist' and 'subjectivist' modes of knowledge referred to above. With sociolinguistics, there is the preoccupation to record the way that language variation exists in different forms across social groups, while the inter-actionists are concerned with showing individuals' local variation in use. To the latter 'subjectivist' mode, we could also add social psychologists of language and their accounts of the affective dimensions of language.

In effect, a Bourdieusian approach to language variation would be critical of both modes: first, for again taking an internal reading of the actualization of language – *logos* instead of *praxis* – and therefore looking for explanations of process in its product; second, for consequently collaps-ing the objective with the subjective, or indeed focusing on one at the expense of the other; third, for the way 'linguistic group' is defined in analyses, leading to all sorts of reductionism and essentialism which over-look the dynamic of language; and fourth, indeed, for the very language that is used in these approaches in talking about language (thus doing so with language which encapsulates misunderstanding, misinterpretations, historical impositions and misrepresentations).

Bourdieu was generally quite appreciative of the work of Labov, and even at one point published an interview with him (1983) where he comments that sociolinguists are ahead of sociologists in identifying and measuring the small modifications and variations that emerge in the course of social interactions. However, as mentioned in the previous chapter, he also accuses Labov of a simplistic – indeed somewhat originating in his own personal outlook – view of the linguistic group. For example, it is not enough to simply contrast the verbosity of adolescent offspring from middle-class Americans with the apparent 'precision' and 'concision' of the language of black children from the ghettos (1975: 10). Bourdieu accuses Labov's inter-pretation as an attempt at rehabilitating 'popular' language by awarding it value-based attributes derived from outside of the systems of usage, while what counts in fact is the practical use of certain features of speech relative to the linguistic contexts in which they are actualized. Furthermore, not only is Labov idealizing popular forms – itself a kind of scholastic fallacy – but he is also misrecognizing a key function of a characteristic of speech. For example, in the bourgeois use of 'filler phrases' ('some things like these', 'particularly', 'loosely speaking', 'let's say', etc.), it is not so much that these are unnecessary to communication, but the fact that 'their very redundancy bear witness to the extent of available resources and the disinterested relation to those resources which is therefore possible – (also) – they are elements of a *practical metalanguage* and, as such, they function as marks of the *neutralising distance* which is one of the characteristics of the bourgeois relation to language in the social world' (1992b: 85). In other words, features of language need to read off against a dominant (legitimate) form of language, and the relative proximity or distance a particular utterance displays, and at any linguistic level, with respect to it at a certain point of time and place. As also noted earlier, Bourdieu argues that Bernstein commits a similar error (if somewhat in reverse) when he uses value-laden terms such as 'restricted' and 'elaborated' to describe the characteristics of middle-class and working-class children's speech, seemingly attributing both to an accident of birth. In fact, both are only 'restricted' or 'elaborated' relative to a linguistic norm, and not inherent in themselves.

The 'subjectivist' perspectives of social psychologists do not fare much better from a Bourdieusian perspective. Writers such as Tajfel (1982), Giles and Powesland (1975) and Genesee and Bourhis (1982), for example, define linguistic variation in terms of cognitive, evaluative and emotional components, especially in the way individuals 'converge' or 'diverge' linguistically with respect to identifiable in- and out-groups. However, such groups are almost uniformly defined in terms of home-group ethnicity, identity modes and the subjective self-esteem. Their approach thus seems to be another form of interactionism, and therefore preoccupied with local interfaces rather than with reference to a base currency for linguistic variation.

To sum up, for Bourdieu, it is not enough to simply catalogue linguistic variation, but neither is it sufficient to make value judgements about language use without reference to dominant forms and therefore how they operate in defining social position. Indeed, from a Bourdieusian perspective, what is needed is something that will synthesize both approaches: to paraphrase Bourdieu, a science of dialectical relations between objective

linguistic structures and the subjective cognitive dispositions within which
these structures are actualized and tend to reproduce them. For Bourdieu,
such an approach would be through a study of linguistic *habitus* and *linguistic
market* (basically, the linguistic form of *habitus* and *field*), and the relationship between them. However, as we know, such relations will be expressed
in terms of *linguistic capital*, that is, the features of language which are
valued according to base 'currencies'. Such currencies can, in theory,
express themselves at any level, formally designated in linguistics as phonetics, phonology, morphology, syntax and pragmatics. It is also important
to remember that language for Bourdieu is above all a bodily function –
hexis – and acts as a kind of incarnate body of any one individual's whole
social and cultural background. Meta- and paralinguistic elements also play
a part in the totality of linguistic expression, and should consequently be
seen as equal to other levels.

This approach begins to look like a complex series of factors and levels,
and their interconnections with respect to individual agency and context
(socio-culturally expressed). The methodological issues are therefore similarly complex, numerous and interrelated. What follows in the empirical
study under consideration should only be seen as a beginning to tease out
these factors and relationships, and the grounding of a methodological
frame for approaching the study of linguistic variation from a Bourdieusian
perspective. Before looking at the study itself, there is one last factor which
needs to be considered: the issue of 'linguistic group'.

Chapter 1 made the point that what Bourdieu was interested in was
developing a model of *social space* that could account for the cause and consequences of positions within it in terms of underlying generative principles. Such principles are always 'to distinguish' – but in terms of which
capital? *Social space* is, of course, multidimensional; so much so that it is
impossible to fully represent it. However, what can be represented are symbolic systems arising from the *social space*, which will (in theory) display the
same differentiating logics of practice, and therefore the structure of the
social space which generated them. In other words, looking at linguistic
variation is not simply a case of considering similarities between individuals
and grouping these together, but rather accounting for differences – how
and why they distinguish themselves in terms of these variations – and to
do so in a way which will capture something of the dynamic of linguistic
usage. It is possible to work with socio-economic categories in exploring
these differences, and these are partly employed in the study below.
However, 'linguistic group' needs also to be considered in terms of other

cross-social-class clusters in order to take account of various features of linguistic *habitus* and *market*. I have argued with Bourdieu that any linguistic valuation presupposes a dominant *linguistic norm*, and this very often coincides with nationally recognized forms – *legitimate language*. However, within social microcosms and even deviant groups, *the* norm may be expressed in other ways, albeit 'imposed' through sanction and censure in the same way. In the course of the account, therefore, it will be necessary to have recourse to discussion of the French linguistic norm, as well as local variant forms, and to do so while considering a range of *habitus*-specific and *field* context factors.

The Linguistic Market and Orléans

The Corpus and Methodology

The linguistic corpus at the base of this study was collected in the French town of Orléans in 1969. In fact, any particular date is fairly arbitrary for the purposes of the study, since our interests are in actual processes of variation rather than in recording a particular historic form of French. Nevertheless, it is worth noting that Orléans is a town in the north-central part of France, about 130 km south-west of Paris. Its close proximity to the French capital means that it is an attractive satellite city, and has benefited both socially and commercially as a result. It is a medium-sized city of approximately 250,000 inhabitants. Linguistically, its central position also means that the spoken language of the populace there is free from the idiosyncrasies which mark some of the French regions.

(i) Collecting and Classifying the Corpus
The corpus was collected by a team of researchers under the Direction of Michel Blanc, and in association with Bourdieu. The research plan included the administration of three separate questionnaires:

1. An Open-Ended Questionnaire (Appendix 1)
This was designed as an introductory interview, inviting the interviewees to express themselves on a range of topics relevant to experience and life in Orléans: opinions, descriptions of work, leisure, etc. The language employed in responses therefore included a wide range of tenses, narrative/descriptive styles, the abstract and the hypothetical.

2. A Sociolinguistic Questionnaire (Appendix II)
The objective here was to ascertain precise views and detail about language and language practice.

3. An Open-Ended Questionnaire (Appendix III)
This questionnaire included a selection of personal details: age, gender, professional background, education, family, etc.

Questionnaires 1 and 2 were collected by taped interviews with the participants, while Questionnaire 3 was a written record only.

A sample of 600 inhabitants was initially selected, of which 147 were eventually chosen to make up the project group. Of course, this group could be classified according to a range of social factors: age, gender, etc. However, a preliminary classification was undertaken according to the socio-economic groupings used by the French social statistic agency, INSEE:

1. Patrons de l'Industrie et du Commerce (industrial and commercial directors)
2. Professions libérals et cadres supérieurs (senior managers)
3. Cadres moyens (middle management)
4. Employés (white-collar workers)
5. Ouvriers (blue-collar workers)
6. Personnel de service (service industry workers)

Of course, such a 'pre-classification' raises questions about the validity and reliability of the categories. Moreover, it is widely acknowledged that, in terms of tracking linguistic variation, occupational grouping is not necessarily the most sensitive factor. Some reasonably modest occupations are extremely linguistically sensitive, for example secretarial and Office work, while high economic standing in running successful businesses does not necessarily rely on language competence. *Linguistic capital*, as part of *cultural capital*, moreover, is developed as part of education. Consequently, it would seem important to utilize both *economic* and *cultural capital* indicators in approaching any study of linguistic variation. In discussing the sample, therefore, three distinct classificatory scales are consequently employed.

First, Occupation by analogy of the INSEE categories:
S(0)C 1 Higher Professionals

S(0)C 2 Lower Professionals

S(0)C 3 Non-manual workers

S(0)C 4 Skilled manual workers

S(0)C 5 Semi- and unskilled workers

Second, Education in terms of length of time in formal schooling/ training; this is expressed as age at the time of leaving (NB: in 1969, it was still possible that some of the remaining population had left school before 14 years of age):

S(E)C I 21+

S(E)C II 18–20

S(E)C III 17

S(E)C IV 15/16

S(E)C V 14 or under

The third category is then statistically calculated in order to combine both occupational and educational weightings (see Blanc and Mullineaux, 1982). For example, one respondent was in S(0)C category 1 because he was a bank manager, but in S(E)C category V because he had left school at 14 years, resulting in a S(0+E)C of C.

S(O+E)C A

S(O+E)C B

S(O+E)C C

S(O+E)C D

S(O+E)C E

There is then some attempt to combine different components of *habitus* as part of the analysis.

(ii) Methodology

Linguistic analyses of this sort are time-consuming and require expertise in undertaking detailed counts of variations of language. Each of the taped interviews/questionnaires was transcribed. These collected data then provided a source for answers to each of the questions directly posed. For the linguistic analysis itself, the 'open-ended' questionnaire was used, as it was here that respondents spoke most freely. The analysis focused on a range of linguistic features: phonology, syntax, semantics and discourse strategies. Of the full corpus, 14 respondents were used for the main study, offering a range of S(O+E) C categories. The answers to the 'sociolinguistic' questionnaire were then analysed on the basis of a selection of the questions. The results of these analyses are provided in the next section.

The Analysis

Quantitative Analysis

(i) Phonetics and Phonology

It is in the area of phonetics and phonology that sociolinguistics have been most active in analysing variation in language use. This tradition was developed on the basis of research conducted by such researchers as Labov and Trudgill. A number of findings somewhat resonate with Bourdieu's thesis on language: for example, that speakers perceive their own phonetics intentions differently from the actual sound produced (Labov, 1972: 132). Labov also demonstrates that linguistic variables can be correlated according to social factors such as age, sex, gender, etc. At the level of phonetics, linguistic variables are often constant in any context, although this increases as we descend the socio-economic categories – the opposite trend also being demonstrated. Guenier et al. have shown a 'linguistic norm' for French between a phonological pairing such as [e] and [ɛ]. [ɛ] is the norm of correct pronunciation: [tikɛ] rather than [tike]. They also were able to demonstrate that 'knowing' (*reconnaissance*) the correct form and being able to use it (*connaissance*) differed, and this pattern increased among respondents in lower socio-economic positions. Context was also important in their study, with the correct form appearing in 13% of cases for reading a French text out loud, compared to 53% for individual words. In a way, orthodoxy is lost as the linguistic exercise becomes more developed, rather than more difficult, when automatic patterns seem to take over.

In the Orléans sample, clearly, there were marked differences in the pronunciation of French, including regional accents from outside the area. For example, one respondent originating from Lorraine (S(O+E)C. B) unsurprisingly had a marked accent of the area: pronouncing [a] as [æ]. Another had a marked rolling of the French /r/; so that [ʁ] was pronounced [r]. Each of the interviews were assessed subjectively by the interviewers and described in terms of being '*legitimate*' or '*populaire*' where accents were particularly marked.

Variations extended to phonological differences. For example, the case of elision and liaison is particularly marked in French. Elision is the term used to describe a marked suppression of a phoneme:

/plus dɇ femmes/
/je sɥppose/

While liaison refers to the running together of two phonemes:

/mes_enfants/
/est_important/

The norm in French would be for liaison to be respected and for phonemes not to be suppressed; thus relatively fewer numbers of elisions and higher numbers of liaisons would be expected.

Table 4.1 and Graph 4.1 show the results of elision and liaison counts per 1,000 words for the sample. They indicate that elisions do indeed increase for lower social groupings, and decrease for higher social groupings. In a way, these differences can be understood as 'forces' of *legitimacy* and the *populaire*. In terms of the dynamic present in the graph, *legitimacy* will 'pull' respondents to the right and down, while *populaire* will pull them up and to the left. We can therefore identify an 'area of legitimacy', which seems to express the norm for this sample, and is mostly made up of respondents from S(O+E) C groups A and B. The dotted line is to 'standardize' positions, and to examine those who find themselves on each side of the line. Those in the area of the *populaire* on the graph, but to the right of the line, should show themselves to be relatively more *legitimate*, in the feature of liaison at least. Respondent 014 (Group E) was a stone mason/builder. However, it is necessary to read this relatively manual occupation against other features of his professional context. For example, he was also a union representative, and therefore quite used to using language as part of his daily activities. This could explain a relatively higher linguistic sensitivity, and therefore more inclined towards legitimacy. Yet, although he is more legitimate liaison-wise, his number of elisions is still quite high, probably a marked feature of his modest education (S(E)C. V). Elision and liaison seem therefore to have different values as *linguistic capital* and may be affected differentially according to social background.

Other examples follow this pattern. For example, respondent 001(D) had fewer elisions and comparatively more liaisons. As a butcher, he was relatively modest in terms of socio-economic occupation (S(O)C. 3). However, he too had 'ascended' socio-economically, as he was now the owner of a string of supermarkets – and therefore aspiring. Respondent 087 had a high number of elisions and fewer liaisons, and was judged to be the typical *français populaire*. Respondents 006 and 106 are both in the area of the *populaire*, with fewer liaisons and increased elisions; however, these measures need to be interpreted comparatively, as they are reduced with

Table 4.1 Counts of elisions and liaisons/1,000 words together with elision/liaison ratio set out according to S(O+E)C, age, gender and profession

SUBJECT NO.	OCCUPATION	EDUCATION	EDUCATION AND OCCUPATION	PROFESSION	AGE	SEX	NO. OF LIAISON/1000 words	NO. OF ELISION/1000 words	ELISION/LIAISON RATIO	
058	1	I	A	Prof. en retraite	63	M	35	48	1.4	*
012	1	I	A	Ingénieur	54	M	33	43	1.3	*
019	2	IV	B	Comptable retraite	72	F	43	59	1.4	*
059	3	II	B	Employé Bureau	25	M	59	57	0.9	*
094	2	III	B	Directrice	40	F	29	40	1.4	*
066	2	IV	B	Restaurateur	30	M	20	84	4.2	**
010	3	IV	C	Couturière	59	F	14	27	1.9	*
001	3	V	D	Boucher	57	M	34	79	2.3	**
087	3	V	D	Agent EDF	39	M	25	142	5.6	**
135	3	V	D	Employé Bureau	39	F	34	53	1.5	*
140	3	V	D	Vendeuse	19	F	21	101	4.8	**
006	5	V	E	Chauffeur	52	M	18	85	4.7	**
106	4	V	E	Sans Activité	60	F	25	77	3.0	**
014	4	V	E	Maçon – Syndical	34	M	33	93	3.0	**

Key
'Légitime' = *
'Populaire' = **

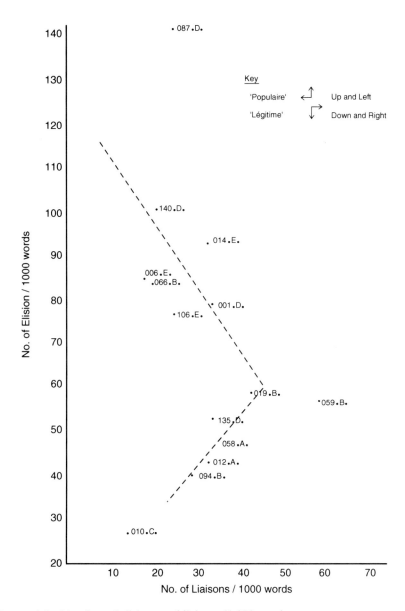

GRAPH 4.1 Number of elisions and liaisons/1,000 words

respect to the typical *populaire* respondent. It is again necessary to read such results against other factors and *field* context. For example, Bourdieu argues that women are symbolically more sensitive. It might therefore be expected that sociolinguistic features are accented towards the legitimate for them. This is true for respondent 106 who had had close contact with *les familles bourgeoises* (upper-middle class families), although he is now unemployed. Respondent 006 also is a chauffeur and is therefore used to being linguistically active with servicing clients etc. By contrast, respondent 066 is a restaurant owner (S(O+E)C B) but spends most of his time in the kitchen, thus not engaging with the clientele. It is therefore possible to surmise that being in the *populaire* zone means that he has not shaken off the effects of his modest education (S(E)C. IV). Respondent 135, on the contrary, is in the zone of legitimacy, even though, as a secretary she is judged to be socio-economically quite modest: (S(E)C. 3). But, her position is not really surprising, given the fact that manipulating and representing language is her job, and is thus sensitive to the correctness of language. Of note also is the case of respondent O59, who has a very high incidence of liaisons and rather more elisions. Her young age (25 years) may suggest a relaxation on liaisons for her generation, although this does not extend to elisions.

(ii) Syntax

For the purposes of this chapter, I shall take syntax to include specific lexical alternatives as well as their utilization in the structure of language. Implicit on Bourdieu's approach to language is a certain 'freedom' to act; in other words, to make 'free choices' about that language we use (all the while bearing in mind, of course, that this 'choice' is always relative as we are all predisposed to act in certain ways in response to certain times and places). Structural dispositions in the usage of oral French are well catalogued. For example, Sankoff and Laberge (1978) analysed the use of *être* and *avoir* verbs deployed in the perfect tense; *Qu'est-ce que/ce que* in headed constructions; and *on/ils* variations. In each case, they found that the former of the pair is used increasingly by individuals with a high socio-economic index – and thus penetration into the linguistic market. Similarly, Rouvière (M.S.) examined specific structural sequences in French, such as 'nominal reduplicated phrases', where, for example, both a noun and subject pronoun are employed:

Monsieur Bailletot, il m'a dit

In corpus studies, she found that this feature of French was particularly sensitive to such variables as social level, education, age, etc. Ashby (1982) designates this feature in terms of topic/anti-topic sentences:

Topic Sentences	Anti-topic Sentences
moi, je dors	je dors, moi
lui, il dort	il dort, lui
cet enfant, il dort	il dort, cet enfant

In topic/anti-topic sentences, the disjunctive pronoun or subject noun phrase is phonologically set off from the rest, involving a left or right dislocation (in rare cases, both may occur). In contrast, 'pure' subject sentences do not do this:

Subject Sentences
Je dors
Il dort
Cet enfant dort

Ashby found that the probability of topic rather than subject sentences for old referents was twice as high in upper social categories compared with lower groups.

A range of topic, anti-topic and subject sentences was found throughout the Orléans corpus. For example:

Le patron, il nous a dit (topic)
Il a dit, lui (anti-topic)
Elle est professeur (subject)

In the current study, a topic/anti-topic ratio was calculated in terms of absolute numbers of counts across the recorded questionnaire of each respondent; a high ratio indicates a popular disposition, and a low ratio is a marker of legitimacy. Phrases such as 'moi, je trouve' were excluded from this calculation since they featured extensively across the corpus. Indeed, this type of phrase has become normalized as a discourse strategy to manage oral conversations. The ratios are given in Table 4.2.

These figures show a consistent pattern between upper and lower social categories (Kendalls T = 0.75, significant at $p < 0.05$). It is interesting to note the high ratio (and therefore topic usage) of respondent 087, earlier described as the 'ideal type' *langue populaire*, thus confirming that this

Table 4.2 Topic/anti-topic ratio according to S(O+E)C

Corpus Number	S(O+E)C Group	Ratio
058	A	0.8
012	A	0.4
019	B	1.0
010	C	1.0
001	D	2.3
087	D	8.25
006	E	4.8
014	E	6.0

feature is characteristic of a less legitimate form of French. Despite coming respectively from S(E)C. V and VI, respondents 001 and 010 both show a reduced use of this feature within their own speech, but this needs to be read in terms of the trend set within their elision/liaison patterns – both of which were marked in the direction of legitimacy.

iii) Discourse Features

Sociolinguists and social psychologists often overlook this feature of language, intent as they are on respectively identifying specific linguistic variations and affective responses. Yet, there are marked differences across the corpus. Bourdieu notes the relative degree of verbosity among the 'middle classes', and certainly contrasting just two in the sample, this aspect of language does indeed feature in the corpus. For example, when asked to explain the events of May 1968, the *chauffeur* (S(E)C. E) manages to sum them up in 250 words, while the *ingénieur* launches into a detailed analysis of some 3,500 words, somewhat confirming what was said about a certain characteristic of French education.

Labov also noted a high number of 'filler phrases' in middle-class speech. These are the phrases that are used in discourse to mark a pause, hesitation, repetition, etc.: for example, in French, 'disons', 'bien', 'puis'. Consequently, Table 4.3 sets out the number of filler phrases used by the respondent per 1,000 words.

In this case, there is clearly no clear opposition between social categories (Kendalls T = 0.043). This finding is perhaps unsurprising if we take the number of filler phrases to be indeed particularly accented in middle groups – as a marker of linguistic insecurity in aspiring to a higher level

Table 4.3 Number of filler phrases/1,000 words according to S(O+E)C

Corpus Number	S(O+E)C	Number of Filler Phrases
012	A	23
058	A	23
019	B	45*
059	B	65*
094	B	14
066	B	46*
010	C	27
001	D	58*
087	D	28
135	D	23
140	D	20
006	E	21
106	E	28
014	E	30

*respondent judged as using *Langue populaire.*

of oral literacy. Membership to middle categories does not necessarily suppose a high incidence of filler phrases. However, inordinate usage of these does seem to be a characteristic of certain individuals within these groups: for example, the *butcher* – (S(O+E)C. D) – whose upward mobility aspirations might result also in this accented need to appropriate what are perceived as signs of educated expression.

However, it is also necessary to be sensitive to both the quality of filler phrases as well as their incidence. So, there is a marked distinction between the range and sophistication of filler phrases of someone coming from (S(O+E)C. A) compared with (S(O+E)C. E):

(S(O+E)C. A) (Ingénieur)

Dans la mesure	en ce qui concerne
On doit dire	d'une façon générale
D'ailleurs	étant donné

(S(O+E)C. E) (Boucher)

Ben	hein
Quoi	donc
Puis	quand même

Bourdieu calls these phrases a 'practical metalanguage' (1982a: 89) which acts to create a 'neutralizing distance'. For him, such features are part of a general attitude that upper groups have towards language, as 'an affirmation of a capacity to keep one's distance from one's own speech', as opposed to those who 'abandon themselves without reservation or censor to the expressive impulse' (ibid.). It need only be added that this type of 'distancing' is part of an entire outlook on the world, including a relation to one's own body. This feature acts as a kind of substitute for the performative ease, so important to *legitimate language* users – in French at least. It is therefore mastered by those in upper groups. The middle categories, on the other hand, have 'penetrated' this feature as a linguistic marker of symbolic value (*reconnaissance*), but then either over-state it, or betray their own *habitus*-based lack of familiarity with its use (*connaissance*) in the range of phrases employed. Indeed, such linguistic insecurity literally speaks for itself, and is applicable across the social spectrum: 'the linguistic "norm" is imposed on all members of the same "linguistic community", most especially in the educational market and in all formal situations in which verbosity is often *de rigueur*' (see Bourdieu 1992b: 53).

What emerges is a complex picture of the usage and effects of various linguistic features and, clearly, the above are only a selection of the possible levels in which *linguistic capital* expresses itself in language. Biographical background – *habitus* – is clearly an important indicator of linguistic usage. However, *field* context is also an important context factor in understanding the salient characteristics of any one individual's language and why they follow certain patterns. It is not simply an opposition between *the* norm and the rest, and yet the latter seems to act as a defining symbolic system against which the dynamic of the *linguistic market* operates. The legitimate forms of language are consequently represented but are also open to manipulation. However, any deviation from the norm is still site-specific, and defined in terms of what is perceived (affectively and as a result of implicit signals) as permissible. Even in this small sample, there have been examples of *hypercorrection* from individuals within 'lower' groups, and the marks of distinction within the 'upper' groups. Such patterns of *legitimacy* and the *populaire*, linguistic conformity and deviance, are highly complex. For example, it seems that the 'deeper' the linguistic level, the less the feature is prone to manipulation. Certainly, *hypocorrection* rarely seems to extend to the phonetic. Before exploring these issues further, let us consider the content of the qualitative analysis.

Qualitative Analysis

The same sample of respondents was used as the basis for the analysis of the sociolinguistic Questionnaire. For the purposes of this discussion, and to give a broad range of coverage, a selection of the questionnaire questions was used. These were sub-classified to cover various aspects of language use, attitudes, practice: Self (practices) – personal language background and habits; Self (opinions) – views on linguistic issues; Others – judgements of others' speech; Objects – material supports to language use, paper, pens, etc.

1. (a) Self (Practices) : Did your parents correct you when you were a child?
   : Do you do crosswords?
   : What was your best subject at school?
1. (b) Self (Opinions): Would you be favourable to a reform of French spelling?
   : Is the French language deteriorating?
   : What do you think of 'franglais'?
   : Is it important to have good handwriting?
   : Is it important to have good spelling?
2. Others : Are there differences in speaking according to social classes?
   : Of the people you know, who speaks best?
3. Objects : Do you have/use a fountain pen?
   : What type of writing paper do you use?
   : Do you have dictionaries at home?

The results to these questions are given in Table 4.4.

With such a small sample, it would be impossible to generalize on the basis of systematic differences. Also, the questions were administered orally on the spot, often in the homes of the interviewees; as a result, the occasional question was omitted in some cases. Nevertheless, there do seem to be trends across the group according to social positioning within the sample. We can sum these up as follows.

Upper groups are disposed:
–to be against a spelling reform
–to see less social class differences
–to be against franglais

Table 4.4 Response to sociolinguistic questionnaire according to socio-economic groupings

SUBJECT NO.	OCCUPATION	EDUCATION	OCCUPATION AND EDUCATION	SEX	AGE	PROFESSION	REFORM OF SPELLING	SOCIAL CLASS DIFFERENCES	FRENCH SPOKEN BETTER OR WORSE	FRENCH GETTING BETTER OR worse	PARENTS CORRECTED	CROSS-WORDS	FRANÇAIS	BEST SPEAKER	fountain-pen	WRITING	SPELLING	BEST SUBJECT	TYPE OF PAPER
058	1	I	A	M	63	Prof.	NO	YES/LESS	WORSE	WORSE	YES	NO	AGAINST	TEACHERS	YES	IMPORTANT	V. IMPORT.	science	NEVER SQUARE
012	1	I	A	M	54	Ingénieur	NO	YES/LESS	WORSE	WORSE	YES	YES	AGAINST	LAWYERS	YES	IMPORTANT	USELESS	ALL	NEVER SQUARE
019	2	IV	B	F	72	Comptable	NO	YES/LESS	WORSE		YES	YES	NOT AGAINST		NO	IMPORTANT	IMPORTANT	SPELLING	WHITE NOT LI
059	3	II	B	M	25	Employé Bureau	NO	YES	BETTER		YES	YES	AGAINST	HE DOES	YES	IMPORTANT	VERY IMPORTANT	FRENCH	NOT LI

ID							YES		WORSE	WORSE	NO	YES	NOT AGAINST	DOCTORS	YES	READABLE	VERY IMPORTANT	MATHS	NEVER LINED
094	2	III	B	F	40	Directrice	YES		WORSE	WORSE	NO	YES	NOT AGAINST	DOCTORS	YES	IMPORTANT	VERY IMPORTANT		NEVER LINED
066	2	IV	B	M	30	Restaurateur	YES IMPORT.	YES	WORSE	WORSE	NO		INDIFF.	OLD TEACHER	YES	IMPORTANT	VERY IMPORTANT	GEOGRAPHY	NEVER LINED
010	3	IV	C	F	59	Couturière	YES	YES	SAME	WORSE	YES	NO	NOT AGAINST	DIRECTOR	NO	IMPORTANT	IMPORTANT	COMPOSITION	NEVER SQUARE
001	3	V	D	M	57	Boucher	YES		BETTER	BETTER	NO	NO	AGAINST	COLONELS WIFE	YES	IMPORTANT	IMPORTANT	SPELLING	USES
087	3	V	D	M	39	Agent EDF	YES	NO		SAME	YES	NO		CENTRE CHIEF	NO	LITTLE	IMPORTANT	SPELLING	LINED
135	3	V	D	F	39	Employé Bureau	NO	NO	BETTER		NO	NO	NOT AGAINST	DOCTORS	YES	IMPORTANT	IMPORTANT		
140	3	V	D	F	19	Vendeuse	YES	YES	SAME	SAME	NO	NO	INDIFF.	STUDENTS		NOT IMPORTANT	QUITE IMPORTANT	SPELLING	LINED
006	5	V	E	M	52	Chauffeur	YES	YES	BETTER	WORSE	NO	YES	FOR	LAWYERS	YES	NOT IMPORTANT	IMPORTANT		LINED
106	4	V	E	F	60	Sans activité	YES	YES	BETTER		NO	NO	FOR		YES	IMPORTANT	VERY IMPORTANT		LINED
014	4	V	E	M	33	Maçon – Syndicaliste	YES	YES	BETTER	WORSE		NO	NOT AGAINST	TEACHERS	YES AGAIN	IMPORTANT	IMPORTANT	CALCUL	

–to do crosswords
–not to use lined or squared paper
–to think that French is spoken less well than in the past

Lower social categories, on the other hand, are disposed:
–to be favourable to a reform of spelling
–to see greater social class differences
–to be for franglais
–not to do crosswords
–to use lined paper
–to think French is spoken better now than in the past

The next part of this chapter comments on these trends with reference to actual views expressed by the respondents in the sociolinguistic Question- naire which are taken from the transcripts of the interviews.

(1) Self (practices)

The practices concerned with 'self' show various behaviours with respect to language. So, parents seem more likely to correct their children's lan- guage in upper categories compared with the lower groups, representing a kind of 'opposition of practice' between the two. However, even here, it is necessary to be circumspect: the respondents 'remember' their parents correcting – that does not mean that they actually did. Various individuals do crosswords – a pastime which represents both an intellectual game and a 'playing with language'. Unsurprisingly, perhaps, some of the groups find them 'irritating' while others enjoy them: this phenomenon itself reveals a certain relation to language, for example as an '*exercise intellectuel*' (012, A). When recalling 'best subjects' at school, individuals in the middle to lower categories seem disposed to choose language-related subjects like French, Spelling and Composition; while the upper group representatives select sci- ence and maths. This contrast between disciplines may be explained in terms of 'linguistic insecurity': in the upper echelons of the hierarchy, 'linguistic competence' is assumed. Passing over 'language subjects' is therefore a kind of hypocorrection, while the reverse is true lower down the scale.

(2) Self (opinions)

Most in the group seemed to feel that French was deteriorating, although there were marked differences between written and spoken forms. Lower groups felt it was actually spoken better. Clearly, spoken and written language are two different forms and perceived differently. In a way, written language is a more 'objective' phenomenon, and can be objectified more easily, while perceptions of the spoken form are rather more subjective – thus, impressionistic, attitudinal and affective. It could be that for upper groupings, the written and spoken forms are seen as being much closer, while lower groups experience them as distinct. In interviews, lower groups certainly expressed the view that spoken language was improved by education, upper groups being much clearer about an 'objective norm' which was being violated. Similarly, upper groups were against both a reform of French spelling and franglais, the reverse trend being present among lower group respondents.

All respondents clearly recognized (*reconnaissance*) the importance of writing in a language. However, there were interesting differences in attitudes. So, the *Ingénieur* (012, A) simply states that handwriting is only important in order to be legible. For Bourdieu, this position is a kind of *strategy of euphemism* where the symbolic value of something is understated as a form of *hypocorrection*, and therefore, of course, asserting an expression of linguistic dominance. In fact, the *Ingénieur* goes on to state that 'spelling is useless' but, as such, it is also 'precious like a jewel'. This can be read as similar to the aesthetic sense analysed by Bourdieu in *Distinction* – a kind of Kantian 'pure gaze', and so reminiscent of the upper groups in society as an expression of their transcendent (thus justified) dominance. This relation to spelling is very different from that of the *Chauffeur* (006, E). For him, spelling is so much more important than writing, knowing that slips of spelling can be symbolically devastating for him and that presentational style is rather less important. But these are nuanced features of attitudes and opinion, and it is important to appreciate the complexity of the interlinking aspects of language, opinion, background, biography and context.

(3) Self and Others

Most of the respondents are aware of the differences in language use between people. The *Ingénieur* – somewhat of an ideal type for his group – acknowledges how central family background is in avoiding spelling errors and writing correctly. A lower group individual like the *Directrice* (094, B) sees her own background as having some 'tics'. The significance of family is expressed well into the middle-area groups. The lower groups, however, see education as being the most significant influence on social class differences in the use of language. When asked about differences in the way people speak, practically all respondents recognize them, although they offer differing views of how they manifest themselves. The restaurant owner (066, B) sees differences as 'big and important', while others underplay them. This phenomenon of 'occultation' is most clearly marked among the upper groups. The *Ingénieur* (012, A), for example, interprets social class differences in terms of regional accents, the disappearance of which he regrets because of their 'character. Worker/middle-class differences are denied. These attitudes, shared with others in the upper groups, are themselves a kind of idealization which combines the strategies both of occultation and euphemization – again, as attitudinal marks of superiority (albeit understated) and dominance. The linguistic norm itself is therefore interpreted in terms of an idealized heritage, thus implicitly denying the very real symbolic value it has as a marker of social distinction.

The way other language users are perceived is also present in views expressed concerning 'best speakers' of French. Among these, individuals from the 'educated professions' are mostly represented – for example, doctors, teachers, lawyers – demonstrating again that the *linguistic norm* is interpreted as representing the most prestigious social activities. The *Couturière* (010, C) describes such individuals as being 'proud' and 'polite', and then contrasts these attributes with her husband, who is 'impulsive'. Superior language traits are therefore associated with a whole set of values concerned with manners and behaviour. However, such values can also position individuals 'on the outside'. The *Agent EDF* (087, D), although admitting that the language of such individuals is impressively correct, describes such individuals as being 'cold', and complains that people like these 'understand you better than you understand them', referring to a deep sense of social insecurity expressed through *linguistic insecurity*.

As we descend the group, there is a tendency for respondents to personify their best speaker: that is, name an individual rather than a generic group. The *Directrice* (094, S(E)C. III) names her daughter's teacher, but then adds that she 'intimidates her', indicating again the insecurity that can be provoked when confronted with a style of language with which they feel little sympathy. The picture is evoked of the symbolically valued, relational structures that are set up when individuals encounter one another and in the moves to accommodation and differentiation that operate in one-to-one situations. The *Maçon-boiseur* (014, E) is someone with a relatively low occupational status, but has shown himself to be sensitive to language in his linguistic features. He explains how he has to change his language according to whom he speaks to; when he speaks to the 'bosses', it is he who has to change: 'I try to think about what I am going to say . . . I try to speak precisely . . . I speak less than when I speak with a worker'. This restraint again marks a certain *linguistic insecurity*, as well as contrasting the 'at-ease' verbosity of this group with the 'educated' language group representative seen as being in a superordinate position to him. The freedom of choice in linguistic use is therefore always partly constrained, and determined by the specific *field* context.

(4) Symbolic Objects

This section of the questionnaire deals with the 'hardware' of language: pens, dictionaries, paper, etc. These objects themselves each hold a symbolic value, and the type of paper one uses or the colour of ink all express a certain *cultural capital*. So, for example, upper and middle groups know that squared paper ('commonly' used in France) is not 'correct'. Unlined paper rather exhibits a certain mastery and control over writing; so much so, that this is mimicked by the insertion of a 'lined guide' under unlined paper, which itself is again a form of *hypercorrection* betraying *linguistic insecurity*, and which also backfires by resulting in an over-correct line formation. Many of the respondents have a fountain pen – admittedly, often a relic of their first communion – but do not use it. Use, however, is highly sensitive to social position and profession. The *Professeur* (058, A) admits that he was shocked when he was told he could use a biro. The above *Maçon-boiseur* (014, E) states that he is trying to take up the fountain pen again because it is more 'fine', thus again demonstrating his sensitivity to what is symbolically valued in language.

Such differences can also be seen in attitudes and practices with relation to the use of dictionaries etc. The *Chauffeur* (006, E) claims to have four or five dictionaries in the home – 'fat ones!' – stating also that they have 'replaced the bible'. The *Syndicaliste* (014, E) also refers to 'large books' – a treasury of language – although his use of them is mainly for crosswords. Compare this practical use of such books to the *Ingénieur*, who has the Larousse (the standard French dictionary) in ten volumes, and frequently consults them – although not for spelling but for the 'exact sense – the etymology of words'.

Conclusion

This chapter has offered a basic approach to an analysis of language variation based, in this case, on a corpus of French collected in Orléans.

In fact, the actual form and context of the corpus is incidental, as the exercise was to explore language in use from a Bourdieusian perspective and to use a selection of concepts for such an approach. Paramount to the discussion has been the notion of *linguistic market*, which itself presupposes an orthodox norm, or *legitimate language*. Indeed, *linguistic capital* – what is valued linguistically – is the medium through which the market operates. If such a *norm* can act at an official, national level, there are clearly also local variations of form and/or the way various features of language are evaluated with respect to it. So we might see both national and local linguistic markets, which again define themselves relative to each other. In the quantitative study of the Orléans corpus, it was possible to identify a range of features – at the levels of phonology, syntax and discourse – which showed variation, and to express these in terms of the directional forces of legitimacy and the *populaire*. It is important to emphasize that these latter are never absolute terms: one individual is never one or the other, and for all time. Rather, there is variation both across linguistic level and in actual usage. In this respect, language is always defined in terms of its immediate context. So these forms were the language used by these individuals *in such a particular context*. One further methodological point to be made is, therefore, that it is impossible to analyse actual language use – whether quantitatively or qualitatively – without taking into account the form of the dialogue: where it took place, when, why and the language of all interlocutors. One of the weaknesses of the Orléans corpus is that there is no information on the interviewers. Furthermore, the differences emerging from the analysis have also been tabulated and discussed according to predefined social categories; while it is a hazardous and misleading undertaking to use substantive terms such as 'social grouping' without the caveat that these are simple indicators of social background and not real in themselves. The construction of the research object terms of analysis is critical here. Adjectival descriptors such as 'upper' and 'lower' can themselves be interpreted in a value-judgemental, even pejorative, way. And yet, some form of words is necessary to express the hierarchical nature of *social space* with respect to the individuals involved. What is clear from this small sample is that linguistic variation does not follow simple derivative patterns and, if there are tendencies and dispositions, there are also exceptions. Indeed, this observation is critical to any appreciation of the operations of the linguistic market, and indicates the way it is always necessary to read variation against other contextual factors: for example, the actuality of professional jobs and, in these cases, the extent to which language concerns feature in them. Such operational mechanics raise questions concerning the definition and designation of a linguistic group and how these constitute and differentiate themselves from other social category factors – gender, profession, age, culture, education, etc. Yet, throughout it all, there is a clear demonstration of a *linguistic norm* and variance from it.

This objective variation was extended and compared with an analysis of the sociolinguistic Questionnaire from Orléans. The analysis indicated that indeed there were also subjective differences in attitudes, beliefs and practices in language. Some group representatives acknowledge and respect standards and correctness in language use, but both knowledge (*connaissance*) and recognition (*reconnaissance*) of legitimate norms are highly variable, with particular patterns being set up both within individuals and across them. Even when normative linguistic practice is acknowledged, it is possible to see these as expressing other aspects of such practice than simply observing *the norm*: for example, in establishing power relations and asserting social positions. Control – of self and others – in language can consequently be understood in terms of both security and insecurity, which are constantly being renegotiated and played out with respect to each other, implicitly at least. And, here, it is worth noting that language matters are rarely *of themselves* but exist in *fields* – education, commerce, politics, science, culture – where other forms of *capital* are at stake. In this sense, language can be brought to the service of other *field* operations.

At base, though, language is able – in itself – to establish patterns of dominance and domination, and hence the chance of social ascendancy and demotion. Once such patterns are set, the licence to judge and act on language becomes the prerogative of the dominant – a position which itself allows for its own autological legitimation. But, the actuality of such processes is often misrecognized since there are a range of strategies – *hypercorrection, hypocorrection, euphemization* – which implicitly deny the differentiating practical logic of the linguistic market and therefore occult what is occurring. Again, it is important to note considerable individual variation, both within individuals and across group members, and a similar necessity to read differences off against other *habitus-* and *field*-based factors. In this respect, the quantitative and qualitative are both necessary for any understanding of language variation.

This study has highlighted the way that language often operates according to a range of dichotomies: moreover, in addition to the obvious differences between written and spoken language, and 'popular and 'legitimate' forms, we have raised such oppositions as relaxation and tension, deviance and conformity, *connaissance* and *reconnaissance*, censor and sanction, self-control and the automatic, the mastery and the amateur, *hypocorrection* and *hypercorrection* – all of which could be reinterpreted in terms of such Saussurian oppositions as the signifier and the signified, and, ultimately, langue and parole. For Bourdieu, the reconnection of any 'norm' within social activity implicitly creates competition for and against it as a mark of distinction. Such competition can be seen in the strategies which develop between individuals and the contexts that surround them, remembering that success or failure will always be determined in terms of the mismatch or fit between individual *habitus* constituents and the valued products – *capital* – of the *field*. Indeed, change in language overall needs to be understood as a product of this pressure on those with linguistic marks of social distinction to further distinction themselves in the face of challenges to that distinction. What is linguistically recognized therefore is constantly being confronted by everyday variation, which itself requires an institutionalized norm to act as final arbitrator – in the final analysis. The dynamic between the orthodox – legitimate – and the unorthodox finally provides the motor of change, but language, at any linguistic level, is only part of a much more pervasive social practice which, operating as it does in both the mind and the body, determines the structure of social space (albeit in its generally particularized but particularly generalized forms). The point of a Bourdieusian approach to the linguistic elements of such social processes is therefore to draw out the connections between language and social practice as they are interwoven: in other words, 'one must submit social and epistemological conditions to a critical objectification which makes possible not only the reflexive return to subjective experience of the social world but also the objectification of the objective conditions of this experience' (1990c/1980: 43) – something which sociolinguistics and social psychology rarely succeed in accomplishing.

Appendix 1

The Open-Ended Questionnaire

a. Preliminary Questions
   1. How long have you been living in Orléans?
   2. What brought you here?
   3. Are you happy here? Why?
   4. Do you intend staying here? Why?
b. Work
   1. What is your work?
   2. Could you describe to me a typical day's work? What is the most important aspect of your work? Are you happy with it or not?
   3. If you were not a . . . . what would you have liked to have been?
   4. More and more women work these days. Are you personally for or against this? Why?
c. Leisure
   1. What do you do with your free time? Evening? Saturday and Sunday?
   2. How did you spend last Sunday?
   3. What are you doing for your summer holidays?
   4. If you had 2 hours extra free time each day, what would you do with it?
d. Education
   1. In your opinion, what should children be taught at school? Why?
   2. What do you think of Latin at school? Which subjects would you like your children to be strong in?
   3. How is it that children succeed or not at school?
   4. Until what age should children continue their studies? Why? Is it the same for girls and boys?
e. Orléans, Social Classes, May 1968
   1. Is enough done for those living in Orléans?
   2. Who has the most influence in Orléans?
   3. Can you explain the events of May 1968 to me?

Appendix II

The Sociolinguistic Questionnaire

1. Do you have a dictionary/encyclopaedia? How often do you use it? Why? Where did you get it?
2. Do you have a book on 'the art of speaking/writing'?
3. Do you do crosswords?
4. Do you think that children should learn Latin at school?
5. What do you think of 'franglais'?
6. Are there differences in speaking according to social classes?
7. Do people speak better or worse these days?
8. Of the people you know, who speaks best?
9. Is there an organization in France who decides if a word is correct or not?
10. Is it an idea to make journalists on TV, radio, etc. speak good French?
11. Is French taught better or worse these days?
12. In which subject were you strongest at school?
13. Do you normally have something to write with?
14. Do you have a fountain pen?
15. When did you last write?
16. Do you write for your job?
17. Do you think that it is important to have a good 'script'?
18. Is it important to spell properly?
19. Would you be favourable to a reform of French spelling?
20. Do you or your wife/husband normally do the writing at home?
21. When you write to friends, do you make a rough copy first? Do you re-read the letter, and are you careful about making spelling mistakes?
22. With what do you write?
23. What type of paper do you use?
24. Do you change any of this when you write to your child's teacher?
25. And for an official letter?
26. Are there things about your wife's/husband's language that annoys you?
27. Who normally fills in official forms in your home?

28. Who writes/speaks best? You or your husband?
29. About how many letters do you write each month?
30. Do you keep personal letters that are sent to you?
31. Could you describe how you make an omelette?
32. Did your parents correct you in matters of speech when you were a child?
33. Is the French language getting worse?

Appendix III

The Close-Ended Questionnaire

1. Date of birth?
2. Sex?
3. Married/Single/Divorced?
4. Date of arrival in Orléans?
5. Number of children?
6. Profession?
7. Original nationality?
8. Information on family plus education.
9. Education of children?
10. Is there someone in the family studying (a) Latin, (b) Greek?
11. Level of education?
12. Private education in the family?
13. Years of study?
14. Did you study Latin/Greek?
15. Type and conditions of education?
16. Do you listen to the radio? Number of hours? Favourite programmes?
17. Do you watch TV? Number of hours? Favourite programmes?
18. Do you go to the cinema? How often? Films preferred?
19. Is the TV or radio an instrument of culture?
20. Do you do photography? Frequency?
21. Do you paint? Visit art galleries? Favourite painters?
22. Do you like music? Favourite composers?
23. Do you go to the theatre? Preferred authors? Frequency?
24. What newspapers, magazines, reviews do you read regularly?
25. How many books do you read each year?
26. Is there a political party that represents your opinions?

Chapter 5

Language and Ideology

Robert E. Vann

1 Introduction

This chapter, as one of the five chapters on specific practice, aims to exemplify how Bourdieusian thought can illuminate our understanding of linguistic data pertaining to particular *field* research. The previous chapter related seemingly disparate instances of liaison, elision and syntactic variation in the French town of Orléans by means of the common thread of *legitimate language* and local dialect. The present chapter explains how Bourdieusian thinking tools can also be used to relate seemingly disparate levels of research on language and ideology.

On one level, language ideological research can focus on the ideologies reproduced through individual practice of a language in a particular speech community. On another, quite distinct level, language ideological research can focus on the ideologies reproduced through linguistic investigations about individual practice of a language in a particular speech community. This chapter focuses on both of these levels of research with regard to the Spanish of Catalonia, Spain. In particular, the chapter concentrates on (1) the ideologies reproduced in practices of Catalan ways of speaking Spanish in Barcelona and (2) the ideologies reproduced in linguistic research that describes Catalan ways of speaking Spanish in Barcelona.

Given its multiple potential applications at various levels of analysis and its concomitant interdisciplinary functionality, a Bourdieusian perspective offers a significant advantage over traditional approaches to these seemingly unrelated language ideological phenomena. No traditional language ideological research has simultaneously attempted a joint explanation of the language ideologies associated with Catalan ways of speaking Spanish and the language ideologies reproduced in linguistic analyses of such ways of speaking, that is, metalinguistic analysis. In fact, the latter may be seen as contributing to the element of reflexivity inherent in Bourdieu's approach. This chapter demonstrates how Bourdieusian thought consolidates in a unified way what traditional language ideological research has previously considered separately or not at all.

The framework for this chapter is as follows. Traditional language ideological research concerning the Spanish of Catalonia is surveyed in Sections 1.1 and 1.2. Section 1.1. reviews conventional investigations of language ideology and linguistic practice in Barcelona. Section 1.2 reviews conventional investigations of language ideology and linguistic research in Barcelona. Illustrative examples are given throughout Section 2 to contrast Bourdieusian approaches to the study of language ideologies relating to the Spanish of Catalonia with conventional approaches such as those cited in Sections 1.1 and 1.2. Concluding remarks and directions for future research are given in Section 3.

Theoretical and practical issues pertaining to research on language ideologies relating to the Spanish of Catalonia that are addressed in this chapter include *why 'Catalan' Spanish may be practised* as well as *why there has been such a lack of linguistic documentation of such practices.* From a Bourdieusian perspective, these issues are clearly related theoretically in a way that is not readily apparent in more conventional approaches: the ideologies associated with ways of speaking Spanish in Catalonia and the ideologies associated with linguistic descriptions of Spanish in Catalonia can all be seen as products of *habitus/*market interaction. The value added of such an analysis is apparent in so far as the Bourdieusian model accounts for, under one umbrella, language ideological practices in what Woolard and Schieffelin (1994: 58) called 'different arenas of language ideology'.

1.1 Previous Work on Ideology and Linguistic Practice in Barcelona

In their seminal article on the matter, Woolard and Schieffelin (1994: 58) identify several arenas of language ideology including literacy studies, public discourse on language, the politics of multilingualism and linguistic structure. Indeed, language ideologies in Catalonia have played out in all of these arenas (see Vann 2004), especially fuelled in the last three decades by the socio-political context of Spain's highly successful transition to democracy, which has been described as a period of intense political and ideological debate both in Spain and within Catalonia itself (DiGiacomo 1999: 109–13).

Much of the research concerning language ideologies in Barcelona has had to do with linguistic identities (cf., e.g. Boada 1986, Boix 1993, among others) and language choice (cf., e.g. Doyle 1996, Woolard 1989, among others), both of which are undoubtedly related to the progressive normalization of Catalan (cf., e.g. Fishman 1991). In particular, the choice to speak Catalan versus Spanish in Barcelona has been seen as a clear statement of ideology in such research. In a series of publications beginning with Vann (1995), the author's own research has nuanced this established division, suggesting that Catalanist language ideologies in Barcelona might be expressed not only through the choice to speak Catalan, but also through particular ways of speaking Spanish. A few others have occupied themselves with this niche, most notably Sinner (2002, 2004).

In a pilot study with seven Catalans from Barcelona and five monolingual Spanish speakers living in Madrid, Sinner (2002) examined individual practice of language ideologies concerning the Spanish language in Barcelona. Based on Kremnitz (1995), Sinner argued that ideologies are a main building block of individual identities. Therefore, his analysis considered language attitudes towards, and linguistic stereotypes of, the Spanish of Catalonia. Noting a strong orientation of Catalans towards the Spanish language standard (p. 160), Sinner's analysis in this paper focused on language ideologies of correctness and purism.

The data used by Sinner for his analysis of ideology-based identities consisted of hearsay opinions about language use elicited from 'self-conscious language specialists' such as linguists and translators who had been sought out for linguistic interviews. Still, when seen as primary data themselves, the Spanish recorded in Barcelona and transcribed by Sinner for his investigation revealed interesting ways of speaking that were clearly language ideological. One such way of speaking involved the use of the term *castellano* 'Castilian'. Sinner (2002: 169–74) described the ideological practice in Barcelona of using this term to refer to individuals in Catalonia whose native or dominant language was Spanish, or to Spanish speakers who were not from Catalonia, regardless of Peninsular origin.

Another such way of speaking concerned the expression of ideologies through pragmatic reference. First and second person plural reference in discourse was analysed as an ideological practice used to construct social inclusion whereas third person reference in discourse was analysed as a practice used to construct exclusion. Such references were ideological when it came to metalinguistic commentaries. Participants in Sinner's study revealed their language ideologies through their practice of inclusive pragmatics when assessing standard forms and, conversely, their practice of exclusive pragmatics when talking about innovative language use in Catalonia that they viewed as broken Spanish.

Though ideologies such as those described above appear to be linguistic on the surface, Sinner (2002) concluded (pp. 180–1) that such ideologies might well be politically motivated. He suggested, for example, that such ideologies might have stemmed from historical rejections of Catalan Spanish and the rejection of this variant in Spanish lessons in schools and universities. The actual construction of such ideologies was not measured quantitatively or qualitatively.

From a Bourdieusian approach, analyses such as the approach taken in Sinner (2002) can be found lacking in so far as such work makes no attempt to relate language ideologies that individuals may practise through ways of speaking in particular speech communities to language ideologies that academics who describe such communities may practise in their professional research. In other words, Sinner (2002) did not recognize that academic research in Spain that describes Catalan Spanish is inescapably a product of the same school and university system that it informs, and so are the language ideologies it reproduces. If, in fact, Spanish lessons in schools and universities contributed to the development of the ideologies associated with individual linguistic practice in Barcelona as Sinner (2002) claimed, then investigation of the language ideologies reproduced in the academic texts used in such lessons would seem to be warranted, as would any potential relationship between these two different levels of language ideology. As will be discussed further in Section 2 and throughout Section 3, a Bourdieusian perspective might well seek and develop a unified, multilevel understanding of such clearly related phenomena, with explicit recognition that the language ideologies that individuals may practise through ways of speaking in particular speech communities and the language ideologies that academics who describe such communities may practise in their professional research are all obvious products of the interaction between *habitus* and the *linguistic market.*

In a follow-up to his earlier study, Sinner (2004) included a statistical analysis of language attitudes in the same community investigated initially in Sinner (2002), though the construction of ideologies was still not measured quantitatively. The 2004 study aimed to uncover what Catalans might know about the Spanish spoken in Catalonia and how such metalinguistic knowledge might affect their attitudes towards the linguistic features of this variety. Twenty language professionals in Barcelona were interviewed, as were 20 language professionals from Madrid. Two related goals of the research were to ascertain what these informants thought of the Spanish of Catalonia and what they thought of their own way of speaking Spanish based on their subjective assessments of the acceptability of different linguistic forms.

The informants' grammaticality judgements concerning different stereotypical features of Catalan Spanish were compared and contrasted in each group and across groups. Sinner (2004) found statistically significant differences between judgements in the Barcelona group and judgements in the Madrid group concerning a number of lexical expressions. Qualitative analysis of the informants' comments during the interviews complemented these statistics. Sinner claimed (p. 567) that such comments suggested the strategic ideological use and avoidance of certain linguistic features in the Spanish of Catalonia.

Unfortunately, however, as Sinner himself admitted (2004: 168), his investigation did not examine 'real' linguistic practice. Despite his affirmation cum quotation that, in sociolinguistics, very rarely can we believe our informants (2004: 132) – a position that is generally taken as axiomatic in sociolinguistics – Sinner's investigation relied mostly on what his informants said they would or would not say in real life. By measuring statistical differences between the judgements of a small group of informants from Barcelona and a small group of informants from Madrid, the analysis in Sinner (2004) can thus, at best, be taken to reveal linguistic attitudes and aspirations, not linguistic norms and usage, in spite of Sinner's claim to have identified a 'minimum nucleus' of constituent linguistic forms of the Spanish of Catalonia (p. 563).

The approach taken in Sinner (2004) can again be found to be lacking, particularly where a Bourdieusian perspective might well develop a *habitus*-based understanding of linguistic practice and language ideologies. Stated simply, research that attempts to quantitatively relate linguistic practice directly to language ideologies with no regard for a potentially underlying common source fails to capture the elegant generalization that both linguistic practice and language ideologies are, or can be, mere expressions of habitus. This issue is discussed further in Section 2.3.1.

Some frequency analysis of spoken linguistic forms in Spanish was undertaken in Sinner (2004) based on the language used by informants at the end of the interviews, and statistically significant differences were found in the frequency of use of certain grammatical constructions in the Spanish spoken by the Barcelona informants versus the Spanish spoken by the Madrid informants. Given the methodology of the investigation, however, such language must be regarded as interview talk, by design of the most formal register (Sinner 2004: 146). Furthermore, due to an unconventional and somewhat questionable selection of informants that purposely focused on so-called 'multipliers of linguistic usage' (p. 186), no direct measure was conducted of the practices pertaining to any natural or representative group of Spanish speakers in Barcelona. Consequently, no direct measure of the language ideologies associated with such linguistic practice could have possibly been conducted either. Quantitative analysis with a representative sample or a naturally pre-existing social group would be needed to credibly measure such issues.

In summary, Sinner's research on language ideologies in Barcelona focused on language attitudes towards particular ways of speaking Spanish and revealed language ideologies of Spanish speakers in Barcelona and Madrid concerning linguistic stereotypes of Catalan Spanish. Though no natural or representative social groups were sampled in either study, frequency differences were uncovered, and discourse analysis of metalinguistic comments made during linguistic interviews did suggest potentially language ideological ways of speaking Spanish in Barcelona.

As noted, a Bourdieusian approach to language ideologies as practised in particular speech communities such as those in Barcelona, Spain, would need to consider language ideological ways of speaking as a form of practice born of *habitus*–market interaction. Furthermore, Bourdieusian thinking tools can allow for the construction of ideologies to be accounted for in a quantitative model for such *habitus*–market interaction. This model would empirically demonstrate support or the lack of qualitative analyses such as Sinner's unsubstantiated analyses of the language ideologies associated with linguistic practice in Barcelona. Given the broad applicability of these tools, in contrast to Sinner's research, Bourdieusian analysis of the language ideologies that individuals might practise via particular ways of speaking Spanish in Barcelona could also simultaneously account for the ideologies reproduced in academic descriptions of these ways of speaking. Such analysis is illustrated throughout Section 2. Section 1.2 first reviews previous work on the ideologies reproduced in linguistic research that describes Catalan ways of speaking Spanish.

1.2 Previous Work on Ideology and Linguistic Research in Barcelona

The arena of language ideology that Woolard and Schieffelin (1994: 58) identified as the 'politics of multilingualism' includes doctrines of linguistic correctness, standardization and purism, which are tied to writing and its associated hegemonic institutions. In this vein, conventional approaches to the study of the Spanish of Catalonia in the last two decades have portrayed much of the linguistic practice of Spanish in Catalonia as the product of active or nativized processes of linguistic interference and language acquisition errors (cf., e.g. Atienza et al. 1997, 1998, Badia i Margarit 1969, 1975, 1980, Boix et al. 1997, Casanovas Catalá 1996a, 1997, García Mouton 1994, Hernández García 1998, López del Castillo 1984, Marsá 1986, Payrató 1985, Sinner 2004, Wesch 1997, 2002, among others). Some of these investigations considered this linguistic variety to be a broken form of Castilian Spanish, while others held that the Spanish of Catalonia should be classified not as Castilian Spanish at all but, rather, as a dialect unto itself. Sinner (2002: 160) dismissed the omission of Catalan Spanish from the majority of Spanish dialectology manuals as a direct consequence of 'past prejudices against the Catalan language, and, consequently, against Catalanisms and Catalan Spanish'. Many of these prescriptive investigations paid little attention to the sociolinguistic documentation of the linguistic practices of this variety.

Some recent investigations such as those by Blas Arroyo (2004), Sinner (2004) and Sinner and Wesch (2008) have described and lamented the state of linguistic documentation regarding the Spanish of Catalonia. Nevertheless, such investigations have not put forth any comprehensive ideological analysis rooted in well-grounded social theory to explain the dearth. This is an area in which there is a notable gap in previous research. The author's own research (cf. e.g. Vann 2002, 2009a) has attempted to address this void through Bourdieusian analysis.

Blas Arroyo (2004: 1065) also suggested that specialists might be distracted from analysing Catalan Spanish due to their preoccupation with the many sociological and ideological issues of language contact in Catalonia. Among the issues he cited were language attitudes, language functions and usage contexts, diglossic relations and linguistic conflict. While this observation may well be true, it remains an observation and not an analysis. By way of contrast, a Bourdieusian perspective might well develop a phenomenological understanding on these points to explain, as a logical function of *habitus*–market interaction, the existence of the language ideologies reproduced in academic discourse about Catalan ways of speaking Spanish in Barcelona.

The ideologies reproduced in linguistic research that documents Catalan ways of speaking Spanish in Barcelona were treated more directly in Sinner (2004), which, as discussed above, investigated language attitudes in Barcelona. The review of the literature included in this investigation (pp. 21–51) described at length the historical disregard for dialectal recognition and description of the Spanish of Catalonia, as well as the lack of consideration of Catalan Spanish in encyclopaedias, histories of the language, manuals of dialectology, dictionaries and grammars. Though the word *documentation* does not even appear in the lengthy index to Sinner (2004), the author did

mention (p. 25) the lack of scientific objectivity in linguistic descriptions of
Catalan Spanish in the latter part of the twentieth century that gave rise to
more recent corpus projects, and he did offer brief ideological explanations
(p. 38) as to why the Spanish of Catalonia might have been treated as it
was in encyclopaedias, histories of the language, manuals of dialectology,
dictionaries and grammars of the twentieth century. The content and even
the discourse of such works were evaluated and criticized, though not
analysed within any theoretical model of language and ideology. The few
pre-theoretical explanations offered had to do with unity in the Spanish
language, potential variability in linguistic classifications and the value of
written versus oral Spanish. Mostly, Sinner (2004) expressed surprise for, as
opposed to ideological analysis of, the treatment (or lack thereof) afforded
Catalan Spanish in such works.

   Here again, as discussed in Section 1.1, the treatment of language ideologies in Sinner's research can be found to be lacking precisely where
a Bourdieusian perspective might well develop further the underlying
reason(s) why such language ideologies might exist. As illustrated later in
Section 2, Bourdieusian thinking tools, grounded in a solid social theory,
can be used to contextualize the deconstruction of the textual ideologies
of academic discourse within their political contexts as simple products
of *habitus*–market interaction, not unlike individual ways of speaking or the
practices of language ideologies that may accompany individual ways of
speaking. In other words, the same basic Bourdieusian thinking tools
can help us understand linguistic practice, the ideologies reproduced in
linguistic practice and even the ideologies reproduced in linguistic research
that describes linguistic practice. As we will see below, one compelling
advantage to a Bourdieusian approach to language and ideology is the
ability of a single unified sociological theory to so successfully and elegantly
bridge such seemingly disparate areas of research via a single set of basic
thinking tools.

   Though clearly Sinner (2004) did not approach language ideologies in
academic discourse from a strictly Bourdieusian perspective, his research
into language attitudes towards the Spanish of Catalonia did reference the
roles of what Bourdieusian scholars might call *authorized* and *legitimate*
language in reproducing language ideologies in academic research. He
noted, for example, the tendency for pejorative labels such as *barbarismo*
(barbarism) and *vulgarismo* (vulgarism) to mark Catalan Spanish usage in
Spanish language style manuals, grammars and dictionaries, including
those produced by the Spanish Royal Academy (pp. 48, 608). Sinner questioned the intent of such terminology and suggested, as he had already

implied in Sinner (2002), that such academic practices likely influenced speakers of Spanish in Catalonia, given that classroom language use likely reflected the terminology used in such books on language. Furthermore, Sinner noted (p. 615) that the influence of academic criticism of the Spanish of Catalonia played out in the mass media, in particular the press, the radio and television, in spreading the perception that the political imposition of Catalan in Catalonia contributed to the slow impoverishment of the Spanish of Catalonia.

An updated description of the still poor state of linguistic documentation regarding the Spanish of Catalonia appeared in Sinner and Wesch (2008), who themselves continued to discuss the characteristics of the Spanish of Catalonia in terms of linguistic interference while lamenting the lack of oral and written corpora to appropriately document the Spanish of Catalonia. No ideological analysis per se was offered in this article; however, as in Sinner (2004), there was a focus on the lack of scientific objectivity in linguistic descriptions of Catalan Spanish in the latter part of the twentieth century that gave rise to more recent corpus projects. Indeed, Sinner and Wesch went so far as to claim (p. 17) that there has been a long tradition in Spain of the academic prejudice of considering the linguistic features of Spanish in Catalan-speaking areas to be indications of the impoverishment of the Spanish language.

As in Sinner (2004), the descriptions given in Sinner and Wesch (2008) regarding ideologies in academic research concerning the Spanish of Catalonia were *pre-theoretical* in nature. That is, no attempt was made to advance any unified theory-based analysis of language ideologies as much as there was explicit reporting and cataloging of examples of academic bias. Reasons offered for how Catalan Spanish has been treated (p. 19) included brief mention of the progressive democratization of Spain as well as a language pedagogical agenda. Sinner and Wesch (2008: 25) explained that the didactic nature of much of the late twentieth century research on Catalan Spanish justified its ideological purism.

In contrast to Sinner and Wesch (2008), as mentioned above, a Bourdieusian approach to analysing the ideologies reproduced in linguistic research about Catalan ways of speaking Spanish in Barcelona would seek to understand and explain in terms of a model of practice why such language ideologies might exist in academic discourse. As I have argued, ways of speaking Spanish in Catalonia and ideologies associated with ways of speaking Spanish in Catalonia can both be analysed as products of *habitus*–market interaction, as well as the ideologies associated with linguistic descriptions of ways of speaking Spanish in Catalonia. The advantage of such an approach is apparent in its simplicity. The Bourdieusian model deconstructs not only linguistic practice but also seemingly unrelated ideological practices (those associated with individual ways of speaking in a particular speech community and those associated with academic discourse concerning such ways of speaking) and reveals their similar sociological nature and raison d'être in a political economy of language.

2 Examples

This section reviews Bourdieusian approaches to the study of language ideologies relating to the Spanish of Catalonia and contrasts such approaches with the more conventional research cited above. Examples are given to illustrate how the application of Bourdieu's thinking tools illuminates research on language and ideology. We shall see how adaptations of several of Bourdieu's thinking tools have proven useful in addressing these issues, in particular his thinking tools regarding *linguistic habitus, symbolic capital, linguistic markets, legitimate language, symbolic domination* and the power of naming. These tools are discussed below.

2.1 Operationalizing the Linguistic Habitus

The author's early research into language and ideology involving Spanish in Catalonia (Vann 1996, 1998a, 1999a, 2000a) involved the methodological operationalization of Bourdieu's notions of linguistic *habitus* in an empirical project that quantitatively related the *habitus* variable to the use of certain ways of speaking Spanish in Barcelona. The project involved participant observation and linguistic interviews with 58 individuals: 32 members of a pre-existing social network in the historical neighbourhood of Sant Andreu and 26 members of a pre-existing social network in the historical neighbourhood of Pedralbes. Detailed information about the networks and the network members is given in various previous publications, most recently in Vann (2009a).

Operationalization of the *linguistic habitus* was mapped off from Thompson's definition of the *linguistic habitus* in his introduction to Bourdieu (1991c: 17). Background data about the participants were obtained in three particular contexts: the family, the peer group and the school. It was reasoned that, for individuals in Catalonia who grew up speaking both Spanish and Catalan to varying degrees, dispositions of *linguistic habitus* acquired in the course of learning to speak in familial, social and educational contexts would depend heavily on the language used in these particular contexts. To gauge this experience, relative exposure to both languages was measured on a continuum. A relative exposure variable was statistically constructed for each individual from smaller extralinguistic variables that measured language use in each context. The self-report data used to create each of these component variables came from background questionnaires.

As reported in Vann (1999a, 2000a), the data from the background questionnaires were coded with 1, 0 and −1 in additive scale models. An answer was coded 1 if it was either 'Spanish language' or 'no'. An answer was coded −1 if it was either 'Catalan language' or 'yes'. All other answers were coded 0. The coded values were summed up in each acquisition context to create three indices per person. After Cronbach's alpha test indicated that the three indices measured 84% of the same underlying construct, the three indices were later combined in a superindex called relative exposure to Catalan and Spanish. The theoretical range of this variable was −25 to +25, whereas the observed range was −24 to +21. Increasingly negative values represented more exposure to Catalan during a speaker's formative years, whereas increasingly positive values represented more exposure to Spanish during those same years.

2.2 Relating Habitus and Linguistic Practice

The author's earliest work to operationalize the linguistic *habitus*, cited above, quantitatively related the relative exposure variable to linguistic practice, specifically practice of deixis in the Spanish of Catalonia. The variable in question concerned the use of motion verbs, locative adverbs and demonstrative adjectives in the Spanish of Catalonia, all of which demonstrate innovative pragmatic scope when compared to usage among monolinguals in Spain outside the contact zone of Catalan (Vann 1998b). Many individuals in Barcelona use *venir* (to come), *traer* (to bring), *este* (this) and *aquí* (here) whereas Spanish speakers outside the contact zone of Catalan use *ir* (to go), *llevar* (to take), *ese* (that) and *ahí* (there). Such usage is illustrated in example (1).

(1a) *Ya   voy (/*vengo)!*
       already *go*-PRES-1s (/*come)
       'I'm *going*!'

(1b) *Ya   vengo!*
       already *come*-PRES-1s
       'I'm *coming*!'

Example (1a) illustrates a typical response to a doorbell in varieties of Peninsular Spanish outside the contact zone of Catalan. Example (1b) illustrates the innovative use of motion verb deixis in the Spanish of Catalonia. The main difference between *ir* and *venir* in Spanish is directionality of movement with respect to the *origo* or deictic centre. In varieties of Spanish outside the contact zone of Catalan, the deictic centre includes only the speaker such that *ir* represents movement away from the speaker whereas *venir* represents movement towards the speaker. In the Spanish of Catalonia, however, the influence of Catalan has led to the rise of innovative linguistic norms governing the pragmatic scope of the deictics under investigation (Vann 1998b). The innovative norms allow for the expansion of the deictic centre to include the addressee as well as the speaker. Therefore, movement towards the addressee outside a door can be expressed in Barcelona as in (1b).

The other deictics mentioned above all pattern in a similar fashion. For example, *traer* expresses motion with an object towards the deictic centre in Spanish, which, outside the contact zone of Catalan, includes the speaker but not the addressee. In such areas, therefore, movement with an object in any direction other than that of the speaker is expressed with *llevar*, which expresses motion away from the deictic centre, rather than *traer*. In the Spanish of Catalonia, due to the pragmatic innovation of expanded deictic centres, *traer* can express motion towards the addressee as well. These uses are illustrated in example (2), in which the speaker and addressee are in two different locations.

(2a) *Si quieres,   te   llevo   el documento personalmente.*
        if want-PRES-2s DAT-2s *take-PRES-1s* the document personally
        'If you want, I'll *take* the document to you personally.'

(2b) *Si quieres,   te   traigo   el documento personalmente.*
        if want-PRES-2s DAT-2s *bring-PRES-1s* the document personally
        'If you want, I'll *bring* the document to you personally.'

Example (2a) represents typical usage of motion [+ carry] deixis in Peninsular Spanish outside the contact zone of Catalan. In contrast, example (2b) illustrates the innovative usage of motion [+ carry] deixis in the Spanish of Barcelona. Expanded deictic centres are also used with the locative *aquí* in the Spanish of Barcelona, as in example (3) in which the addressee is in Madrid and the speaker is not.

(3a) *Aquí en Salamanca bien; ¿Qué tal   ahí/allí/allá en Madrid?*
        here in Salamanca well   what such *there*   in Madrid?

'All is well here in Salamanca. How are things *there* in Madrid?'

(3b)   *Aquí en Barcelona bien; ¿Qué tal   aquí en Madrid?*
here in Barcelona well what such *here* in Madrid?
'All is well here in Barcelona. How are things *here* in Madrid?'

Example (3a) illustrates typical usage of locative deixis in Peninsular Spanish outside the contact zone, in which *aquí* is not used because the locational reference is not where the speaker is. Example (3b) represents the innovative usage of *aquí* that at times occurs in the Spanish of Catalonia, in which the scope of *aquí* has been extended to include the location of the addressee.

Expanded deictic centres occur with the demonstrative *este* in the Spanish of Barcelona as well. Consider (4a), which illustrates typical usage of demonstratives in Peninsular Spanish outside of the Catalan contact zone, as well as (4b), which illustrates usage of *este* with an expanded pragmatic scope in the Spanish of Catalonia.

(4a)   *No me   gusta   este   aquí,   ni   ese   allí.*
not DAT-1s   please-PRES-3s   *this.one* here   nor *that.one* there
'I don't like *this* one here or *that* one there.'

(4b)   *No me   gusta   este   aquí,   ni   este   aquí.*
not DAT-1s   please-PRES-3s   *this.one* here   nor *this.one* here
'I don't like *this* one here or *this* one here.'

Though both (4a) and (4b) are heard in Peninsular Spanish outside of the Catalan contact zone, they are not interchangeable. (4a) is used to distinguish distinct relative proximities to the speaker whereas (4b) is used when both items are relatively proximal to the speaker or when proximity itself is not at issue. That is, in Peninsular Spanish outside of the Catalan contact zone, *ese allí* is clearly further from the speaker than *este aquí*. In the Spanish of Catalonia, (4b) may be used to reference items that are proximal to either the speaker, the addressee or both.

In the Spanish of Barcelona, practice of the various deictic expressions explained above clearly represents a distinctly Catalan way of speaking Spanish. This Catalan way of speaking Spanish can convey symbolic capital, generating profits of cultural distinction in social markets by revealing patterns of cultural and linguistic Other (Vann 2000b). Regression analysis published in Vann (1999a, 2000a) revealed that innovative usage of Spanish deictics increased with more relative exposure to Catalan ways of speaking in social, familial and educational contexts ($p < 0.0001$, Rsq = 0.49). In other words, Bourdieusian analysis was able to distinguish empirical language

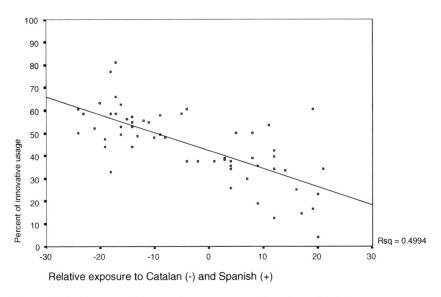

FIGURE 5.1   Percent of innovative usage as a function of relative exposure to Catalan and Spanish

differences between individual speakers based only on a construct of *linguistic habitus*. This relationship is illustrated in Figure 5.1.

As noted in Vann (1999a, 2000a), the seemingly minor variations in the pragmatic considerations of the Spanish words discussed above can be seen to reflect the sociolinguistic conditions present during language acquisition for the participants in the study. In other words, the intersection between an individual's relative exposure to Spanish and Catalan in familial, social and educational contexts in Catalonia and his or her use of deixis on the *linguistic market* can be articulated as a matter of practice of the *linguistic habitus*. Based on the linear relationship found between the relative exposure variable – itself a construct of *linguistic habitus* – and the innovative usage of the target deictics, these investigations concluded that variable usage of the innovative pragmatic norms observed in the Spanish of Barcelona can be seen to represent differing practices of the *linguistic habitus* in Catalonia.

The studies cited above, as well as others such as Vann (2000b, 2003, 2007), have demonstrated that Bourdieu's notions of *habitus, market* and *symbolic capital* are crucial to understanding different ways of speaking Spanish in Barcelona. These investigations concluded that practising Catalan Spanish in some *linguistic markets* expresses a certain *symbolic capital* and contributes to the development of linguistic *norms* concerning social contexts of language use. Such practice is clearly associated with language ideologies in the Spanish of Catalonia. The particular association between language ideologies and innovative practice of the deictics, as illustrated in examples (1b), (2b), (3b) and (4b), is discussed in Section 2.3.1.

2.3 Habitus and Linguistic Ideology

This section explains applications of Bourdieu's thinking tools in the area of linguistic ideology. Two distinct levels of ideology are considered. Section 2.3.1. concerns language ideologies that individuals may practise in particular speech communities, in this case the two neighbourhood networks in Barcelona discussed above. Section 2.3.2. concerns language ideologies that linguists who describe such communities may practise in their very research.

2.3.1 Habitus and Individual Practice of Linguistic Ideology

At first glance, the discussion of *habitus* and linguistic practice in Section 2.2. may not appear to be germane to a chapter on language and ideology. In-depth sociolinguistic investigation of the speech community discussed in Section 2.2. revealed, however, that the same construction of *habitus* also predicted linguistic ideologies in this community at statistically significant levels (Vann 1998a, 1999b). The present section discusses how the quantitative association between linguistic practice and language ideologies in this community was found to be spurious, in so far as the *habitus* variable was found to predict both of them.

As explained in Vann (1998a), questionnaires were used to obtain self-report data concerning the language ideologies of participants in the project. Questions were asked to gauge Catalanist viewpoints, based on attributes previously demonstrated to be ideologically important in studies such as that of Woolard (1989). A measure of language ideologies was constructed using additive scale models from the ideology questionnaires. Cronbach's alpha test on the indicators of ideology returned a value of 0.9315, confirming that the indicators of ideology very strongly measured the same phenomenon.

When the ideology variable was entered as an independent variable into a multiple regression along with an independent variable that measured the degree of integration into Catalan social networks, only the ideology variable ($p < 0.0001$) was revealed to be a significant predictor of innovative practice of Spanish deixis (Vann 1998a). In other words, Catalanist ideological views were found to contribute significantly to variation in the deictic usage, but density and multiplexity of relationships within Catalan society were not. When the relative exposure variable representing *linguistic habitus* was included in the model, however, the ideology variable was no longer significant at all. This relationship is apparent from the statistics given in Tables 5.1 and 5.2, adapted from Vann (1998a).

The correlations given in Table 5.1 suggest that the relationship between Catalanist ideology and innovative practice of Spanish deixis in the community under investigation was basically spurious. Essentially, it was concluded that both variables were related by sharing the common effect of a third variable: the construct of *linguistic habitus*. This relationship was invetstigated further by Vann (1999b). The theoretical relationship between *habitus* and ideology was empirically measured in a case study to determine if individuals educated in Barcelona during the Franco years could come to value the dominant ideological forms that were imposed upon them as children through the official use of Spanish in school and in public life. Indeed they could; indeed they did.

Table 5.1 Correlations, 1-tailed significance T-test

	Innovative practice	Relative exposure	Ideology	Integration
Innovative practice	1.00			
Relative exposure	−0.71/0.00	1.00		
Ideology	0.58/0.00	−0.80/0.00	1.00	
Integration	0.35/0.00	−0.47/0.00	0.62/0.00	1.00

Table 5.2 Independent variables in the multiple regression on innovative practice

Variable	B	SE B	Beta	T value	Sig T: $p <$
Relative exposure	−0.78	0.18	−0.69	−4.26	0.0001
Ideology	0.02	0.32	0.01	0.05	0.9615
Integration	0.10	0.61	0.02	0.16	0.8708
(Constant)	41.52	3.75		11.07	0.0000
R square	0.50				
F statistic	17.99				
Significant F	$p < 0.0000$				

Working with the same sample as the studies cited above, Vann (1999b) found that individuals in Barcelona who were exposed to Spanish more than to Catalan in academic environments during their youth tended towards more pro-Spanish and less pro-Catalan ideologies as adults, indicating the effects of *habitus* influences. A Bourdieusian approach illuminated this statistically significant relationship through an account of *legitimate language* and *symbolic domination* in Catalonia. The investigation was significant because previous research in the Bourdieusian paradigm had found that in 1980 despite 40 years of coercive institutional domination of Spanish in Catalonia during the Francoist dictatorship in Spain, the linguistic hegemony of Spanish in Catalonia was not authentic (Woolard 1985).

Expanding on the quantitative analysis published in Vann (1998a), Vann (1999b) published the results of regression analysis on ideology as the dependent variable with three independent variables: (1) the *linguistic habitus* variable; (2) the variable that measured degree of integration into Catalan social networks in society; and (3) a variable representing membership in the Sant Andreu neighbourhood network versus the Pedralbes neighbourhood network. The results of this multiple regression analysis are summarized in Tables 5.3 and 5.4, adapted from Vann (1999b).

Table 5.3   Correlations, 1-tailed significance T-test

	Ideology	Relative exposure	Integration	Neighbourhood network
Ideology	1.00			
Relative exposure	0.80/0.00	1.00		
Integration	0.62/0.00	−0.47/0.00	1.00	
Neighbourhood network	0.70/0.00	−0.48 /0.00	0.57/0.00	1.00

Table 5.4   Independent variables in the multiple regression on ideology

Variable	B	SE B	Beta	T value	Sig T: $p <$
Relative exposure	−0.36	0.05	−0.57	−7.76	0.0000
Integration	0.43	0.22	0.15	1.94	0.0581
Neighbourhood network	6.09	1.38	0.35	4.42	0.0000
(Constant)	−8.06	1.98		−4.08	0.0002
R square:	0.79				
F statistic:	69.17				
Significant F:	$p < 0.0000$				

As indicated in Table 5.3, the ideology variable was very strongly correlated with the relative exposure to Catalan and Spanish variable ($r = 0.80$)
as well as the network membership variable ($r = 0.70$) and the integration
variable ($r = 0.62$). Furthermore, all three independent variables were
found to contribute significantly to person-to-person variance in ideology,
with the greatest contribution coming from the relative exposure variable
($T = -7.76$), which, as described above, was a construct of *linguistic habitus*.
The amount of variation in ideology explained or accounted for by the
entire model approached 80%, and the amount of variation in ideology
accounted for by the *habitus* variable alone exceeded 64%. Figure 5.2,
adapted from Vann (1999b), represents the exact amount of person-to-
person variance in ideology accounted for by the *habitus* variable operationalized through relative exposure to Catalan and Spanish.

As indicated in Vann (1999b: 200), 'those more exposed to Spanish in
educational and social settings generally display a more pro-Spanish ideology

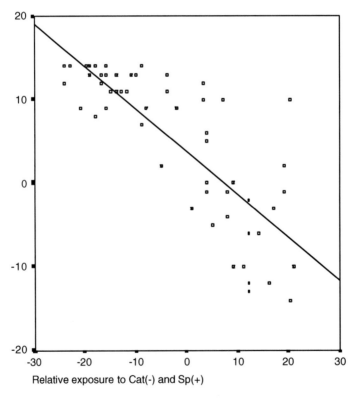

FIGURE 5.2   Effect of relative exposure to Catalan and Spanish on ideology

than their peers who were more exposed to Catalan'. Thus, the *habitus* variable, as operationalized through relative exposure to Catalan and Spanish, was found to explain a great deal of person-to-person variation in ideology in the community studied. Additional analysis presented in Vann (1999b) was able to nuance this conclusion further. Because the neighbourhood network variable had also been found to be a significant predictor of ideology ($p < 0.0000$) in the regression model given in Table 5.4, Vann (1999b) presented split sample analysis as well.

In split sample analysis, both the measures of ideology and the measures of *linguistic habitus* continued to be reliable within each neighbourhood network (Cronbach's alpha tests > 0.82 for each index). Mann-Whitney tests revealed that these variables patterned significantly differently over the two groups ($p < 0.000$ for ideology, $p < 0.0003$ for relative exposure). Members of the Pedralbes neighbourhood network had significantly more exposure to Spanish than members of the Sant Andreu neighbourhood network; their ideologies are also significantly more pro-Spanish. Regression analysis performed on each network separately indicated that relative exposure continued to be the most significant predictor of ideology in each network ($p < 0.0000$). Interestingly, while integration in Catalan life was not at all significant in predicting ideology in Sant Andreu, it was in Pedralbes ($p < 0.0351$). This finding underscored the significance of ideological indoctrination in the young, implying that adult involvement in Catalan life is more important in the formation of Catalanist ideologies if one is not exposed as much to Catalan in the early years.

The analyses given in Vann (1998a, 1999b) exemplify how Bourdieusian thought can illuminate our understanding of linguistic data pertaining to particular *field* research, in particular, the ideologies reproduced in practices of Catalan ways of speaking Spanish in Barcelona. The novel operationalization of *linguistic habitus*, often considered to be a thinking tool of qualitative analysis, in quantitative variationist analyses demonstrated clearly that research on bilingualism and ideology is an area where a Bourdieusian approach complements traditional statistical methods of sociolinguistic research.

Aside from bridging a gap between two major schools of thought often practised independently in sociolinguistics, these investigations revealed an important link between relative exposure to *legitimated language* and the development of certain political and linguistic philosophies in this particular bilingual situation. With few exceptions, previous research in language and political economy has not addressed these issues through empirical case studies. As Vann (1999b) concluded, 'at this time, more investigations

are warranted to further elucidate the ideological ramifications of pro-
tracted linguistic domination'.

2.3.2 Habitus and Practice of Linguistic Ideologies in Linguistic Research

In an article that highlights the lack of legitimate linguistic description and
linguistic documentation of the Spanish of Catalonia, Vann (2002) built on
the analysis in Vann (1999b) with a Bourdieusian discussion of academic
discourse as a context in which language ideologies have been and continue to be challenged and contested in Spain. He analysed the ideologies
reproduced in linguistic research about Catalan ways of speaking Spanish
in Barcelona in an attempt to explain why, rather than being objectively
studied by linguists in Spain, this variety and its ideologies have so often
been academically trivialized. The analysis concluded that it was precisely
due to hegemonic linguistic ideologies that the Spanish of Catalonia was
poorly described in linguistic treatises, unrecognized as a legitimate dialect
of Spanish and unanalysed from a social perspective.

Works from the Spanish dialectology canon, such as Zamora Vicente
(1989), and the few investigations actually written in Spain about the
Spanish of Catalonia, such as Badia (1980), were considered in light of
the cultural, political, linguistic and geographic contexts in which they
were written. The professional 'overlooking' of the Spanish of Catalonia
in descriptions of Spanish dialectology and sociolinguistics in Spain was
analysed in the context of power relations and larger socio-economic, socio-
historic and socio-political processes. The language ideologies apparent in
works such as those cited above were deconstructed based on Bourdieusian
thinking tools. They were consequently considered to be functions of the
socio-cultural and political processes of the times, that is, in more theoretical
terms, functions of *habitus*–market interaction.

The specific thinking tools of *legitimate language* and *symbolic domination*
were very useful in understanding how Franco's official linguistic policies
contributed to language ideologies in research about the Spanish of Catalonia. After the Spanish Civil War, first and foremost in Franco's programme
was that all divisive tendencies had to be repressed and persecuted in the
name of the explicit goals of the nationalistic and administrational unity of
Spain. Castilian Spanish was declared the sole authorized language for all
Spaniards, and use of other languages was strictly prohibited. The Francoist
attempt to impose Castilian Spanish as the (only) legitimate language
throughout Spain led to predictable ideological practices, including the
institutionalization of Castilian and concomitant propaganda to undermine
the other languages of Spain, in particular Catalan.

As discussed in Vann (2002: 231), such language ideological practices, typical in the linguistic policies imposed upon colonized societies (Woolard & Schieffelin 1994: 63), led to the symbolic domination of many people in Catalonia. Due to practices of institutional *linguicism* (De Beaugrande 1998), many Catalans grew ashamed of their own language and culture. Repetition of the authorized argument that the Catalan language itself was not actually a language but merely an inferior dialect of Spanish and that the Spanish spoken in Catalonia was not even a locally evolved dialect of Spanish but rather a bastardization of the imposed authorized language, Castilian Spanish, led to the instantiation in discourse of such beliefs.

Catalan Spanish was left out of mid to late twentieth-century academic discourse on Spanish dialectology, in part because such practices led many academics to simply not perceive the objective dialectal reality of Catalan Spanish at all. Those who did perceive Catalan Spanish as a dialect were likely to view it as less salient and less worthy of study during that period as well. That is, the *symbolic domination* of the professoriate itself contributed to the academic construction of the illegitimacy of Catalan Spanish. Further-more, as noted in Vann (2002: 231), what limited academic documentation of Catalan Spanish there was during the period would have been subject to the *Normas para investigaciones lingüísticas* (Norms for linguistic investigations) – official instruments of government-authorized censure intended to consolidate what Althusser (1994) termed a 'repressive state apparatus'.

Linguists who grew up during this period were indoctrinated with such beliefs precisely through the hegemonic presence of Castilian language ideologies in schools and universities throughout Spain. As Woolard and Schieffelin have noted (1994: 64), 'codified, superposed standard languages are tied not only to writing and its associated hegemonic institutions, but to specifically European forms of these institutions'. Universities, in particu-lar, have been said to reflect and reinforce the experiences of the dominant class by privileging certain cultural practices and linguistic forms on the academic market, which in turn has social, economic, political and aca-demic repercussions (Vann 1999c). The imposition of authorized linguistic practices is a matter of cultural hegemony that can easily lead to the cul-tivation of ideological discrimination.

Given that academic investigation in Spain is a product of universities and as such reflects the linguistic ideologies that such institutions repro-duce (see Vann 2002: 242), students of Spanish philology during the late twentieth century, for example, would not have had textbooks of Spanish language dialectology that included the Spanish of Catalonia among the other named, and therefore academically authorized, dialects in Spain. Bourdieu's thinking tool about the power of naming was key to the conclusion in Vann (2002) that, for contact dialects such as the Spanish of Catalonia to be scientifically investigated, described and subsequently documented, they must first be recognized as legitimate in the academic literature that is at once a product and (re)producer of the existing power relations in Spain.

In sum, the practice of language ideologies in linguistic research to describe and document the Spanish of Catalonia can be seen as the product of the complex interaction of *linguistic habitus* and academic market in a political economy of language. Bourdieusian thinking tools are highly useful in fleshing out the mechanisms of this interaction, which, in turn, help us to understand how and why such language ideologies exist. This understanding provides a significant advantage over more traditional research that has noted such research bias with no comprehensive, theory-based account of its socio-cultural etiology.

Conclusion

Taken together, the alternative analyses in Section 2 reveal how, in terms of Bourdieusian theory, the same notions of *habitus* and market interaction relate language ideologies to both use and description of the Spanish of Catalonia. In contrast, more conventional approaches to the investigation of Spanish in Barcelona, even those that have qualified and catalogued the linguistic practices of this variety as dialectal (cf., e.g. Sinner 2002, 2004, Wesch 1997, 2002, Sinner and Wesch 2008), have not been able to relate language ideologies to linguistic practice and sociolinguistic description in terms of any single, unified theory. Indeed, they have not even tried.

The need for future research to document Catalan Spanish through the publication of linguistic corpora is now well recognized in the literature (cf., e.g. Boix et al. 1997, Sinner 2004, Vann 2001, Wesch 1997). More recently, in their outstanding review of the current state of research on Spanish in Catalan-speaking lands, Sinner and Wesch (2008) clearly identified (pp. 28–30) that the most important lacuna in the field today remains the lack of publicly accessible oral corpora to enable appropriate linguistic documentation of Spanish in Catalan-speaking areas such as Catalonia. Vann (2009a) constitutes a small step towards starting to fill this lacuna. In addition to several chapters on language use and the political economy of language in Catalonia, this book provides actual transcripts of colloquial spoken language from two social networks in Barcelona to facilitate the long overdue legitimate linguistic documentation of Catalan Spanish.

Projects for the future include the creation of a linguistic archive of the sort described in Vann (2006) and Vann (2009b). Given that Catalan Spanish remains overlooked due to persistent ideologies of illegitimacy, its future documentation will depend on both continued linguistic practice and increased recognition of the legitimacy of this variety. Due to a growing market, perhaps with higher visibility in the public eye since media coverage of the 1992 Olympics in Barcelona, the Spanish of Catalonia now receives more attention in research on language description than it did a few decades ago. Ultimately, however, future research documenting linguistic practice in Catalan Spanish will be a function of the reproduction of academic recognition of this variety in scholarly works of authorized language in Spain. Bourdieusian approaches to the study of the Spanish of Catalonia are very useful in this regard, in so far as they provide a common foundation for understanding and relating the language ideologies associated with ways of speaking Spanish on the streets of Catalonia to the language ideologies reproduced in the documentation of such linguistic practices in the academic literature.

The specific case of the Spanish of Catalonia, however, is just one particular instance of the value of Bourdieusian thinking tools as they relate to questions of language and ideology more generally. These tools can and will be related to language and ideology in many different ways in the study of many different languages. As the Bourdieusian paradigm continues to develop, desiderata emerge for new techniques and new methodologies to be developed to best practise Bourdieusian theory.

On the quantitative side, future research will need to develop new and different procedures to operationalize the various different aspects of a Bourdieusian approach, building on the author's pilot research in this regard. The initial quantitative research in this area, illustrated in Section 2, looks promising and warrants further development. There are likely many ways to quantitatively measure the position that each individual occupies in a multidimensional social space. In addition to statistical models of *habitus*, the actualization of Bourdieusian agency theory through multidimensional mathematical models, for example, or a way to reliably and objectively measure the amounts of the different kinds of *capital* that we each possess or the dynamic rate of reproduction of language ideologies in given social and linguistic markets could lead to fascinating research in the area of language and ideology and in other areas of research as well.

Likewise, additional qualitative techniques will need to be developed to facilitate future Bourdieusian approaches to analysing the many facets and levels of language and ideology. On the qualitative end of things, future language ideological research in the Bourdieusian paradigm would certainly benefit, for example, from the development of new and informed techniques of reflexive sociology. Furthermore, future Bourdieusian research on language ideological issues could benefit as well from the development of qualitative techniques to better study issues of participant knowledge.

As demonstrated above, a Bourdieusian approach to language and ideology can use both quantitative and qualitative methods to analyse and account for various forms of linguistic and ideological practice, bridging seemingly disparate areas of research (as well as distinct levels of analysis) by means of a single set of basic thinking tools. Given this breadth and depth, a Bourdieusian approach should, in principle, be able to build on diverse yet complementary methodologies practised in anthropological linguistics, sociolinguistics, the sociology of language and other disciplines that might also investigate similar subject matters. Undoubtedly, future Bourdieusian projects devoted to the study of language and ideology will benefit from techniques inspired by interdisciplinary knowledge and collaborative practice.

Chapter 6

Linguistic Ethnography

Adrian Blackledge

Introduction

This chapter offers an account of how Bourdieu's writing on language contributes to ethnographic work which takes a linguistic focus, and linguistic research which works from an ethnographic approach. In particular, the chapter introduces recent developments in 'linguistic ethnography', and brings a Bourdieusian critical perspective to the analysis of micro-interactions in the multilingual marketplace.

Linguistic Ethnography

Linguistic ethnography is a recently emerging academic research field. It has been shaped by developments in linguistic anthropology, including ethnography of communication (Hymes 1968, 1974, 1980), interactional sociolinguistics (Gumperz 1982, 1999), and micro-ethnography (Erickson 1990, 1996). Hymes criticized both linguistics, for not making ethnography the starting point for the analysis of language use, and anthropology, for insufficiently drawing upon linguistics to understand and describe culture and context: 'it is not linguistics, but ethnography, not language, but communication, which must provide the frame of reference within which the place of language in culture and society is to be assessed' (Hymes 1974: 4). For Hymes, what was needed was a general theory and body of knowledge within which diversity of speech repertoires, and ways of speaking, take primacy as the unit of analysis. Hymes' argument was that the analysis of speech over language would enable social scientists to articulate how social behaviour and speech interact in a systematic, ruled and principled way. This view became articulated in the ethnography of speaking (Hymes 1968) and later the ethnography of communication (Hymes 1974), and even impacted on communicative language teaching.

Interactional sociolinguistics, on the other hand, focuses on discursive practices in social contexts and considers how societal and interactive forces merge. The goal of interactional sociolinguistics is to analyse how speakers read off and create meanings in interaction. Because language indexes social life and its structures and rituals, language use can be analysed to understand how presuppositions operate in interactions (see Creese 2008). Moreover, interactional sociolinguistics has looked at how speakers use language to create contexts. Interactional sociolinguistics is also often concerned with intercultural encounters and the systematic differences in the cultural assumptions and patterns of linguistic behaviour which are considered normal by those involved. A main purpose of interactional sociolinguistic analysis is to show how diversity affects interpretation, and in this respect it has much in common with micro-ethnography (Erickson 1990, 1996).

Erickson's work has been influenced by Goffman (1959), whose concern with the presentation of self in daily life has done much to demonstrate that in any encounter speakers produce signals which reveal aspects of identities. Erickson, like Goffman, has emphasized close detailed observation of situated interaction. The approaches described here, with their emphasis on close observational and textual analysis interpreted through an ethnographic understanding of the context, have all in some way shaped the work of scholars of linguistic ethnography. Like the early work in the ethnography of communication which argued that linguistics had wrongly occupied itself wholly with the structure of the referential code at the expense of the social (Hymes 1974, 1980), linguistic ethnography's argument is also for a socially constituted linguistics (Creese 2008).

'Linguistic ethnography' has a relatively young history. The UK Linguistic Ethnography Forum (UKLEF) was initially constituted in 2000 by David Barton, Angela Creese, Janet Maybin, Ben Rampton and Karin Tusting. In 2001 the *British Association of Applied Linguistics* provided an infrastructure for meetings (Rampton 2007). This led to a position paper published on the UKLEF website in 2004 (UKLEF 2004), and a special issue of *Journal of Sociolinguistics* in 2007. Since then other publications have begun to consolidate the position (e.g. Creese 2008, Blackledge and Creese 2010), as has a series of seminars, conference presentations and an ESRC-funded research development initiative. Oriented towards these particular epistemological and methodological traditions in the study of social life, linguistic ethnography argues that ethnography can benefit from the analytical frameworks provided by linguistics, while linguistics can benefit from the processes of reflexive sensitivity required in ethnography. In linguistic ethnography, linguistics is said to offer an ethnographic analysis of a wide range of established procedures for isolating and identifying linguistic and discursive structures. In contrast, in linguistic ethnography, ethnographic analysis is said to offer linguistic analysis a non-deterministic perspective on data. Because ethnography looks for uniqueness as well as patterns in interaction, it 'warns against making hasty comparisons which can blind one to the contingent moments and the complex cultural and semiotic ecologies that give any phenomenon its meaning' (Rampton et al. 2004: 2). A linguistic ethnographic analysis then attempts to combine close detail of local action and interaction as embedded in a wider social world. It draws on the relatively technical vocabularies of linguistics to do this. Linguistic ethnography situates the study of language as action within a methodology – ethnography – that is very widely shared not just in anthropology but also in, *inter alia*, sociology, education and management studies. At the same time, 'it specifies the linguistics of discourse and text as the primary resource for our efforts to contribute in a distinctive way to the broader enterprise of social science' (Rampton 2007: 600). Rampton suggests two tenets which underpin the development of linguistic ethnography: (i) 'meaning takes shape within specific social relations, interactional histories and institutional regimes, produced and construed by agents with expectations and repertoires that have to be grasped ethnographically'; and (ii) 'meaning is far more than just an "expression of ideas", as biography, identifications, stance and nuance are extensively signalled in the linguistic and textual fine-grain' (2007: 585). The linguistic and textual fine-grain resonates with Bourdieu's (2008b: 5) call for 'attention to the most trivial data' as fundamental to research in the social sciences.

Linguistic ethnography's current interpretive stance is shaped by a disciplinary eclecticism. It is the interdisciplinary nature of linguistic ethnography that allows us to look closely and look locally, while tying our observations to broader relations of power and ideology. Rampton argues that linguistic ethnography is 'a site of encounter where a number of established lines of research interact, pushed together by circumstance, open to the recognition of new affinities, and sufficiently familiar with one another to treat differences with equanimity' (2007: 585). Recent research into linguistic interaction has begun to emphasize the advantages of combining analytical approaches, rather than relying on only one approach or framework (Rampton et al. 2002, Stubbe et al. 2003, Zuengler and Mori 2002). As Rampton et al. argue, a range of approaches to analysing classroom interaction 'offer more to the analysis of classroom discourse in combination than they do alone' (2002: 387). Stubbe et al. (2003) also consider the benefits of utilizing different discourse analytic approaches to interpret professional talk. They conclude that each approach provides 'a different lens with which to examine the same interaction' (2003: 380), noting that different approaches are not necessarily in conflict with each other, but may be used in complementary ways. Tusting and Maybin (2007: 576) argue that linguistic ethnography particularly lends itself to interdisciplinary research, and offers a practical and theoretical response to 'the turns to social constructionism and to discourse across the social sciences', in its ability to probe in depth the interrelationship between language and social life. According to Blommaert the autobiographical–epistemic dimension of ethnography lends itself to interdisciplinary engagement. This dimension allows ethnography to be inserted in all kinds of theoretical endeavours, to the extent that such endeavours allow for situatedness, dynamics and interpretive approaches. Thus, 'there is no reason why ethnography cannot be inserted, for example, in a Marxist theoretical framework, nor in a Weberian one, nor in a Bourdieuan or Giddensian one' (Blommaert 2001: 3). In what follows I will demonstrate that the theory and practice of Bourdieu can usefully illuminate understandings of phenomena observed in a linguistic ethnographic framework.

A Critical Perspective

In Chapter 2 we saw that the first ingredient of Bourdieu's theoretical view is a *critical perspective*. I will argue that a critical perspective is crucial to an understanding of language in social life. I will further argue that Bourdieu's 'thinking tools' have made a considerable contribution to the development of a critical perspective in research on language. I will make this argument through a recent example of linguistic ethnographic research. However, in doing so I will attempt to resist an approach which brings Bourdieu's tool kit to fine-tune or repair an analysis situated in another, 'flawed' paradigm. Rather than viewing Bourdieu's thinking as a useful add-on, I propose that it is an integral feature of language research at the levels of planning, fieldwork, analysis and representation. Instead of proposing 'this is what Bourdieu can do to improve existing social and linguistic research', I will suggest that Bourdieu's thinking is central *throughout* the processes of investigating the social world.

The particular example I will take here is a linguistic ethnographic investigation of multilingualism in four cities in England. We need a 'critical' perspective on multilingualism because public discourses and language policies in the UK, as elsewhere in the developed, English-speaking world, are frequently out of step with the plural linguistic practices of its population. More than 300 languages and varieties are spoken on a daily basis in England. Yet in recent times the discourse of public elites has proposed that minority languages other than English are associated with, and even responsible for, problems in society. Although this notion has previously been implicit in debates about immigration and multiculturalism in the UK, the first decade of the twenty-first century has seen a noticeable shift. The discourse of politicians and media commentators has frequently characterized the use and visibility of minority languages other than English as problematic. This public discourse has made associations between the use and visibility of minority languages and societal problems such as civil unrest, social segregation, family breakdown, educational failure and financial burden to the state. Furthermore, the discourse of elites has argued that speakers of these languages must be required to demonstrate that they are able to understand English, as a failure to do so constitutes a threat to national unity, British identity, social cohesion and democracy itself (Blackledge 2005). These political arguments are not simply about language, however. Rather, debates about language become emblematic of debates about immigration and multiculturalism. They are arguments not about minority languages but about the speakers of those languages. They are also arguments about the kind of society the UK wishes to become. In practice, the UK is multilingual, multicultural and pluralistic. In the beliefs and attitudes of the powerful, however, debates about multilingualism have become a means of constructing social difference, as the privileging of English (and a certain variety of English) above minority languages is evermore insistently imposed.

Crawford (2008: 1) argues that language-minority communities have limited power and resources to fight back against 'a growing paranoia and intolerance toward speakers of other languages'. Research which is concerned with access to linguistic resources, and with control of the circulation of linguistic resources, is inevitably research which is concerned with the construction and reproduction of social difference. The social construction of distinction based on 'ethnicity', 'race' and 'class', goes hand in hand with the social construction of distinction based on linguistic practice and ideology. A critical perspective on multilingualism is needed because debates about minority languages and linguistic minorities have become embroiled in the construction and reproduction of social difference. Another reason we need a critical perspective on multilingualism is because it enables us to interrogate the notions of 'multilingualism' or 'bilingualism' themselves (Heller 2008: 252).These are notions which are constructed historically and socially, and which have different meanings across different spaces and times. Questions about multilingual practices must always be situated in relation to major forms of social organization. That is, in order to understand access to, and use of, a range of linguistic resources, it is necessary to take a critical view of the ways in which discourses represent those resources. A critical ethnographic approach allows us to make connections between the politics and practice of multilingualism.

The Multilingual Marketplace

As we saw in Chapter 3, when one language dominates the market, it becomes the norm against which the prices of the other modes of expression are defined (Bourdieu 1977c: 652). Bourdieu's metaphor of the 'market' puts relations of symbolic power in place of relations of communication, and so replaces the question of the 'meaning' of speech with the question of the 'value' and 'power' of speech. Throughout this volume we are guided by Bourdieu's argument that political domination goes hand in hand with linguistic domination, and that integration into a single linguistic community is a condition for the establishment of relations of linguistic domination (Bourdieu 1991c). In Chapter 7 Stephen May demonstrates this clearly through a historical account of the increasing power of the French language in France, and in Chapter 4 Michael Grenfell provides a persuasive account of the linguistic market of Orléans. The present chapter extends the debate by considering relations of symbolic power in the multilingual marketplace in urban settings in England.

Debates about language use and choice have become increasingly prevalent in political and media discourse in recent times. These debates cannot be treated as simply 'linguistic' or 'cultural heritage' issues, but are 'important political questions that may affect the social and economic position of the social groups of a given territory' (Pujolar 2007: 144). That is, debates about language are often debates about immigration, and about 'pluralist' or 'assimilationist' policy in relation to immigrant groups. In public discourse language often becomes inseparably associated with a territorially bounded identity in a relationship that takes language, territory and identity to be isomorphic (Freeland and Patrick 2004). One implication of this is that ideally the nation should be monolingual, with adherence to another language often misrecognised as a lack of loyalty to the national identity. However, it is not sufficient to say that speakers of the same language belong to the same nation state. This common-sense understanding of the relationship between language and nation ignores the diversity and variety of the language(s) spoken within many states. Bourdieu argues that the official language is bound up with the state, both in its genesis and in its social uses: 'It is in the process of state formation that the conditions are created for constitution of a unified linguistic market, dominated by the official language' (1991c: 45). In order for one language to impose itself as the only legitimate one, the linguistic market has to be unified and the different languages (and dialects) of the people measured practically against the *legitimate language*. The goal of the state is often integration into a single linguistic community, which is 'a product of the political domination that is endlessly reproduced by institutions capable of imposing universal recognition of the dominant language, and the condition for the establishment of relations of linguistic domination' (Bourdieu 1991c: 46). This linking of language, literacy and national identity happens in a number of sites which include language planning, standardization, educational policy, citizenship testing and language instruction for immigrants (see Blackledge 2005, Stevenson 2006). Recent work on language testing, for example, for citizenship has demonstrated that in a broad range of national contexts particular languages and language varieties become gatekeeping devices to determine who is permitted to become a member of the community of citizens (see Blackledge 2005, Mar-Molinero 2006, Maryns and Blommaert 2006, Stevenson 2006). Another way that governments may seek to impose national identities is through educational policies that decide which languages are to be employed – and thus legitimized – in the public school system. Recent research has clearly documented the interpenetration of the ideological with the local, in institutional, nationalist and political dimensions. When a language is symbolically linked to national identity, the bureaucratic nation state faced with a multilingual population may exhibit 'monolingualising tendencies' (Heller 1995: 374).

In many Western countries a dominant ideology is constantly produced and reproduced which positions the majority language (often English) as the only language of communication in institutional and other public contexts. Hornberger (2007: 179) argues that 'The one-nation-one-language ideology, the idea that a nation state should be unified by one common language, has held sway in recent Western history'. In this ideology minority languages associated with immigrant groups are 'rejected into indignity' (Bourdieu 1998a/1994: 46). Minority languages which have historically been associated with particular ethnic identities often continue to be important for particular groups (May 2004), but have little *capital* in majority-language markets. Very often, multilingual societies which apparently tolerate or promote heterogeneity in fact undervalue or appear to ignore the linguistic diversity of their populace. An apparently liberal orientation to equality of opportunity for all may mask an ideological drive towards homogeneity, a drive which potentially marginalizes or excludes those who either refuse, or are unwilling, to conform (Blackledge and Creese 2010).

Heller (2007) argues that rather than treating notions of 'community', 'identity' and 'language' as though they were natural phenomena, they should be understood as social constructs. Specific or single categorizations therefore cannot be attached to an individual based on their 'ethnicity', or 'language'. Heller refers to the work of Giddens (1984) to consider language as a set of resources which are socially distributed, but not necessarily evenly. This uneven distribution of resources is the product of political and economic processes, enabling us to ask questions about what linguistic resources are assigned what value, and with what consequences. Furthermore, some discourses inscribe value (or its lack) to particular linguistic forms and practices. Linguistic practice can only be understood in relation to histories, power and social organization. Bourdieu (1977c: 653) makes this point concisely: 'The whole social structure is present in the interaction.' At the same time, structural analysis must include accounts of actual linguistic practices, which at times may differ from those we might expect.

In his discussion of Occitan, Bourdieu proposed that 'language is itself a social artifact invented at the cost of a decisive indifference to differences which reproduces on the level of the region the arbitrary imposition of a unique norm' (1991c: 287). That is, a language may be called into being through the process of naming it as a language, but this 'act of social magic' (Bourdieu 1991c: 223) which creates a new social division, and consecrates a new limit, is proportional to the authority of the person doing the naming. A language may be invented when the inventor has the authority to authorize its invention. Makoni and Pennycook (2007) argue that the notion of languages as separate, discrete entities, and 'countable institutions' (2007: 2) is a social construct. They propose a critical historical account which demonstrates that, through the process of classification and naming, languages were 'invented' (2007: 1). They add that, in direct relation with the invention of languages, 'an ideology of languages as separate and enumerable categories was also created' (2007: 2). Thus languages cannot be viewed as discrete, bounded, impermeable, autonomous systems.

If languages are invented, and languages and identities are socially constructed, we nevertheless need to account for the fact that some language users, at least some of the time, hold passionate beliefs about the importance and significance of a particular language to their sense of 'identity'. It is now well established in contemporary sociolinguistics that one 'language' does not straightforwardly index one subject position, and that speakers use linguistic resources in complex ways to perform a range of subject positions, sometimes simultaneously. However, while accepting this, May (2001, 2005: 330) argues that 'historically associated languages continue often to hold considerable purchase for members of particular cultural or ethnic groups in their identity claims'. While it is certainly an oversimplification to treat certain languages as 'symbols' or 'carriers' of 'identity', we are obliged to take account of what people believe about their languages, to listen to how they make use of their available linguistic resources and to consider the effects of their language use – even where we believe these 'languages' to be inventions. Heller (2007) suggests that if we tend to understand linguistic resources as whole, bounded systems which we call 'languages', it is because nations and states have found it necessary to produce powerful discourses which constitute language ideologies in the process of national belonging. Makoni and Pennycook (2007: 36) further argue for language policy in education which focuses on 'translingual language practices rather than language entities'. Garcia (2007: xiii) suggests that if language is an invention, we must observe closely how people use language, and base pedagogical practice on that use, and not on what the school system says are valuable practices.

The Multicultural Habitus

The degrees to, and the ways in, which today's migrants maintain identities, activities and connections linking them with communities outside their places of settlement are unprecedented (Vertovec 2009: 66). This has led some researchers to refer to the 'bifocality' of dispositions and propensities (Guarzino 1997, Mahler 2001), as migrants live their lives in relation to their homeland and/or diaspora. Guarzino (1997) proposes the notion of a 'transnational *habitus*', which incorporates the social position of the migrant and the context in which migration occurs. Aspects of life 'here' and life 'there' are thus perceived as complementary (Vertovec 2009). Vertovec summarizes research which refers to an ongoing 'sense of double belonging', 'a *habitus* of dual orientation' and 'a *habitus* re-oriented to more than one locality' (2009: 68), and argues that by conceptualizing transnational experience through the metaphor of *habitus*, we might better appreciate how dual orientations arise and are acted upon. Vertovec proposes that the notion of *habitus* illuminates the ways in which transnational life experiences may give rise not only to dual orientations but also to personal repertoires comprising varied values and ways of being drawn from diverse cultural configurations. Gardner (1995) describes the dynamics of the notions of *desh* (home) and *bidesh* (foreign settings) for Sylhetis in Britain and Bangladesh. While *bidesh* is associated with migration and economic improvement, *desh* is redolent of group identity, spirituality and family.

However, research further indicates that there is also interplay between the migration generation's 'transnational *habitus*' and the 'multicultural *habitus*' of the second and subsequent generations (Levitt 2002). Bourdieu points out that *habitus* changes constantly in response to new experiences, as new dispositions 'are subject to a kind of permanent revision, but one which is never radical, because it works on the basis of the premises established in the previous state' (Bourdieu 2000a/1997: 161). Maira (2002) argues that second-generation youth culture becomes a site of struggle to define the authenticity of the heritage in relation to local and global practices. Vertovec further points out that a reorientation of *habitus* takes place in the course of any person's relocation and integration into a new social system, and the reorienting of first-generation *habitus* conditions that of second and subsequent generations (2009: 83). Transnational dispositions and practices have an impact on individual and family life course and strategies, individuals' sense of self and collective belonging, the ordering of group memories, patterns of consumption, collective practices, child-rearing practices and so on. Vertovec concludes that even though transnational orientations and practices of communication and exchange may not be sustained strongly by second and subsequent generations, 'the process of being socialized within a milieu of such transnational orientations and practices will often have a substantial influence on longer-term configurations of outlook, activity and – perhaps especially – identity' (2009: 76). An important element of such orientations and practices relates to language use.

Multilingualism in the New Linguistic Economy

In the remainder of this chapter I will suggest that Bourdieu's metaphor of the *linguistic market* is fundamental to the investigation of linguistic practices and ideologies, and is of particular value in understanding the ways in which access to resources is negotiated in multilingual settings. I will do this in relation to a recent research project (ESRC RES-000–23-1180, 2005–2006) which examined linguistic practices and identities of multilingual children, young people, parents, teachers and administrators in and around 'complementary schools' in four cities in England. Complementary schools, also known as 'supplementary schools', 'heritage language schools' or 'community language schools', provide language teaching for young people in a non-statutory setting. The research project consisted of four interlocking case studies with two researchers working in two complementary schools in each of four communities – Gujarati schools in Leicester, Turkish schools in London, Chinese schools in Manchester and Bengali schools in Birmingham. The present chapter focuses on data collected in and around the Bengali schools in Birmingham. Bengali complementary schools in Birmingham are managed and run by local community groups on a voluntary basis, usually in hired or borrowed spaces, with few resources. They cater for children between 4 and 16 years of age, and operate mainly in the evenings and at weekends. One of the specific aims of the research project was to investigate how the linguistic practices of students and teachers in complementary schools are used to negotiate young people's multilingual and multicultural identities.

Each case study identified two complementary schools in which to observe, record and interview participants. After 4 weeks of observing in classrooms using a 'team field notes' approach, two key participant children were identified in each school. These children were audio-recorded during the classes observed, and also for 30 minutes before coming to the class and after leaving class. These 'border crossings' enabled us to audio-record the young people at home as well as in the schools. The young people's linguistic practices were recorded at home and as they crossed the border from home to school. Stakeholders in the schools were interviewed, including teachers and administrators, and the key participant children and their parents. We also collected key documentary evidence, and took photographs.

Heritage and Language as Capital

We asked the founder and administrator of one of the schools about the rationale for teaching Bengali to children in Birmingham:

ei bhaashar jonno 1952 te amaar theke dosh haath dure Barkat, Salam maara jaae < *because of this language in 1952 ten yards away from me Barkat and Salam were killed>* 1952 te *<in 1952>* I was also a student in year 10. From Sylhet to Dhaka was 230 miles we marched from Sylhet to Dhaka 230 miles with slogans. We want our mother language it is a raashtro bhasha *<state language>*. How I will forget about my mother language? My brothers gave their life for this language. I will never forget it while I'm alive. (Administrator interview)

For the school administrator the 'mother language' was a vital symbol of the founding of the Bangladeshi nation. More than 50 years earlier he had witnessed the incident in which the 'language martyrs' were killed while demonstrating against the imposition of Urdu as the national language by West Pakistan, and these events seemed to have informed his view that British-born children of Bangladeshi heritage should learn and maintain the Bengali language. The historic incident which marks the Bangladeshi calendar as '*Ekushey* February' continues to be celebrated as a key moment in the collective memory of the Bangladeshi nation, and in the Bangladeshi community in the UK (Gard'ner 2004). One of the senior teachers in the same school argued that learning Bengali was associated with maintaining knowledge of Bangladeshi 'roots': 'We may have become British Bangladeshi or British Indians but we don't have fair skin and we cannot mix with them. We have our own roots and to know about our roots we must know our language.' For both of these Bangladeshi-born men, teaching and learning Bengali was an important means of reproducing their 'heritage' in the next generation.

Many of the students' parents agreed. One mother typically told us that it was important that her children should be able to speak Bengali because:

Bengali is our mother land, where we come from; really we come from Bangladesh. Even if you are born in this country it doesn't matter, we need to know our mother language first. (Parent interview)

Asked why it was important to learn the language of the 'mother land', she said 'you need to know your side of the story, where your parents come from, you've got to know both from this country and the other one'. For her, learning the 'mother language' was closely associated with learning about the 'mother land', and both represented her 'side of the story'. We heard an explicit rationale from administrators, teachers and parents that a key aim of the school was for the children to learn Bengali because knowledge of the national language carried features of Bangladeshi/Bengali 'heritage'. For Bourdieu, 'heritage' is reproduced through 'class' and 'education', in the reproduction of 'distinction', 'an unacquired merit which justifies unmerited attainment, namely heritage' (Bourdieu and Darbel 1990b/1966: 110). Bourdieu (1993a/1980: 299) argues that in education there is an assumption of a community of values between pupil and teacher which occurs where the system 'is dealing with its own heirs to conceal its real function, namely, that of confirming and consequently legitimizing the right of the heirs to the cultural inheritance'. He further argues that '[o]nly when the heritage has taken over the inheritor can the inheritor take over the heritage' (Bourdieu 2000a/1997: 152). That is, young people must be invested in their heritage in order to inherit it. For the teachers, the process of teaching 'language', and teaching 'heritage', had the potential to invest their students with the aptitudes they required to inherit their heritage. The teachers, administrators and parents encountered in Birmingham had set up a grassroots movement to teach their children their heritage. The means by which they set out to do this was by teaching them the Bengali language. Recognizing that *habitus* may be confronted with market conditions of actualization different from those in which they were produced, they proposed to fill what they called the 'culture gap' with Bengali language teaching, and to shape dispositions which were 'characterized by a combination of constancy and variation' (Bourdieu 2000a/1997: 161).

Linguistic Practice and the Profit of Distinction

When we interviewed the administrators and teachers in the schools they spoke emphatically about the need for children to learn the standard variety of Bengali. This was frequently held to be oppositional to Sylheti. One of the school administrators was emphatic that Bengali was 'completely different' from Sylheti, and that Sylheti should not be allowed to 'contaminate' the standard form. He was concerned that Sylheti forms were beginning to appear in the spelling and grammar of Bengali newspapers in the UK, introducing 'thousands of spelling mistakes – Bengali newspapers I have seen in many places the spelling was wrong, sentence construction was wrong'. For the administrator non-standard resources were 'contaminating the language'. He made this point about the necessity for children to learn standard Bengali:

> I am always in favour of preserving languages and all these things. But it doesn't mean that this should contaminate other languages and give this more priority than the proper one. (School administrator interview)

This was a strongly articulated argument in the interviews. The administrator of the other school stated:

'Bhasha to bolle Bangla bhasha bolte hobe Sylheti kono bhasha naa'
<*When you talk about language it means Bengali, Sylheti is not a language*>
(School administrator interview)

For several respondents 'Bengali' constituted a more highly valued set of linguistic resources than 'Sylheti', and was regarded as the 'proper' language. It was clear that for them not all linguistic resources were equally valued, and while some sets of linguistic resources were considered to be 'a language', others were not. In this sense there was a constant reinvention of 'language' on the part of some participants.

Those who spoke 'Sylheti' were often criticized by 'more educated' people who spoke 'Bengali'. They were characterized by the administrator of one of the schools as members of the 'scheduled' or 'untouchable' caste – people without rights or resources in the Indian subcontinent:

Publicraa ki dibe amar aapne especially bujhben amader desher je shob lok aashche ora kon category lok aashchilo, mostly from scheduled caste, gorib, dukhi krishokra aashchilo. oder maa baba o lekha pora interested naa oder chele meye raa o pora lekha interested naa. Oraa baidhitamo-lok schoole jete hoe primary schoole sholo bochor porjonto jete hoe, ei jonne schoole jaai.
<*What will the public contribute? You* [the researcher, Shahela Hamid] *especially will understand what type of people came from our country. They belonged to the category of scheduled caste, they are the poor, the deprived, farmers. Their parents were not interested in education nor are the children interested. They go to school because it's compulsory>* School administrator interview)

Here the Sylheti speakers are referred to as the 'scheduled caste'. Regarded as the least educated group in society, with no resources of any kind, they are the lowest of the low (Borooah 2005, Borooah et al. 2007, Kijima 2006). Here linguistic features were viewed as reflecting and expressing broader social images of people. One of the teachers argued that children should learn Bengali for 'moral reasons'. Bourdieu and Darbel (1990b/1966: 112) argue that some more powerful groups provide 'an essentialist representation of the division of their society into barbarians and civilized people'. Bourdieu (1977c: 652) further suggested that 'a language is worth what those who speak it are worth'. Here the fact of speaking

'Sylheti', rather than 'Bengali', appeared to index the Sylheti group in particularly negative terms, despite the relative similarities between the 'Bengali' and 'Sylheti' sets of linguistic resources. In the multilingual marketplace some sets of linguistic resources were considered to have more value than others.

While some speakers in our study considered 'Sylheti' to be quite different from 'Bengali', others regarded the two sets of resources as indistinguishable. As we have seen, there were several instances of participants commenting on the differences between Sylheti and Bengali in terms of social status and value, but not everyone agreed about the extent to which these sets of linguistic resources were distinct. While the administrator of one of the schools argued that Bengali and Sylheti were 'completely different', a student's mother said they were 'thoraa different' <*a little differ-ent*>, while other parents also held this view, saying they were 'little bit different thaake <*only*>' and even 'the same'. Here there was clear disagreement about the nature and extent of the differences between the sets of linguistic resources used by the students' parents at home, and the literate version of the language taught in the complementary school classrooms. That is, there was disagreement about the permeability of the languages. These differences of perception were likely to be ideological. Those who argued that the 'languages' were completely different from each other were speakers of the prestige language, unwilling to allow the lower status language to contaminate their linguistic resources. Those who argued that the 'languages' were almost the same were speakers of Sylheti, which was held to index the lower status, less educated group. Here the use of particular sets of linguistic resources was indexically linked to, and indeed constituted, social distinction.

On many occasions the research participants interactionally evidenced their awareness of differences (perhaps mainly in status and value) between 'Sylheti' and 'Bengali'. There was also an awareness of Bengali as the higher-status language on the part of teachers ('I talk posh Bengali, and the children can't understand me'), students, administrators and parents. The following example was recorded at the dinner table in the family home of one of the students:

Mother: khitaa hoise? Tamim, khaibaani saatni? <*what is the matter? Tamim, would you like some relish?*>

Father: aaro khoto din thaakbo <*how many more days is that [voice recorder] going be with you?*>

Tamim: aaro four weeks <*four more weeks*>

Father: ( )
Student: no they said any. if you talk all English
Father: ginni, oh ginni [calling his wife using a highly sylized Bengali
            term of endearment]
Mother: ji, hain go daakso kheno <*yes, dear why are you calling me?*>
            tumaar baabaa shuddho bhasha bolen <your father is speaking
            the standard language>
Father: paan dibaa <*can I have some paan*> aapne aamaar biyaai
            kemne <*how are you my relation?*> (Home recording, Bengali
            case study)

Here the Sylheti-speaking parents play the roles of Bengali speakers, adopting the airs and graces which they see as characteristic of the Bengali-speaking group. The terms of endearment used here ('ginni', 'hain go') are forms of parody, exaggerations beyond common usage, as speakers of Bengali are mocked in neo-sophisticated discourse. This brief inter-action is situated in a whole hinterland of language ideological beliefs and practices, as the couple acknowledge differences between Bengali and Sylheti as sets of linguistic resources, and the conditions which differentially provide and constrain access to linguistic resources. Here Tamim's father is aware of what Bourdieu (1984a/1979) described as the construction of 'high' and 'low' culture, in which 'low' culture is vulgar, crude and clumsy, whereas 'high' culture is refined, pure and elegant (ibid.: 468). The parodic role play at one and the same time acknowledges these structures of power, while agentically engaging with them almost subversively.

In this section we have seen that for some of our participants, some sets of linguistic resources were very considerably privileged over other, similar sets of linguistic resources. While linguistic resources which were described as 'standard', or 'proper' or 'real' Bengali had come to represent the 'heritage' of the Bangladeshi nation, sets of resources described as 'Sylheti' had come to be associated with the uneducated poor, who were held to be disinterested in schooling, and unmotivated. However, we also saw that these distinctions were contested by others, who denied that clear differences existed, and at times made fun of the assumption that these differences were constitutive of differences in social status. That is, our participants represented disagreements about what constituted (a) language, and about the ideological links between speakers and the sets of linguistic resources which they called into play.

Transgressive Language in the Linguistic Market

In the extract below, the request to keep the languages separate is made explicit by the teacher in a Bengali school. However, this goes one step further when the teacher links the teaching of language/literacy to a national identity:

> T: Bangla-e maato etaa Bangla class <*speak in Bangla this is Bangla class*> khaali English maato to etaa Bangla class khene <*if you speak in English only then why is this the Bangla class?*>
> S: miss you can choose
> S: I know English
> S: why?
> T: because tumi Bangali <*because you are Bengali*>
> S: my aunty chose it. she speaks English all the time. (Classroom audio recording, Bengali school)

Here the teacher tells the students to use Bengali and connects the speaking of Bengali to *being* Bengali. Here only Bengali is the *legitimate language* (Bourdieu 1977c: 646) of the classroom. However, the students question this statement by the teacher and suggest that they have a choice about which languages they speak. The student's 'aunty', herself of Bangladeshi heritage, is offered as an example of someone who has resisted the notion of 'one-language-equals-one ethnicity/culture'. Two ideologies of bilingualism are in play here. On the one hand, the teacher insists on an idealized construction of bilingualism which argues that the languages must have separate functions, with Bengali accorded the status of classroom language. On the other hand, another ideology and practice of bilingualism comes into play, as language is used flexibly by the teacher ('because tumi Bangali') to interact with her pupils.

Migrants from different language backgrounds constitute a challenge for traditional nationalist discourses and ideologies in the institutions of multilingual democratic states, as multilingual reality faces monolingual ideology. Our audio recordings in the homes of the complementary school students revealed how they used a broad range of linguistic resources to create meanings. Characteristic of the linguistic interactions of the students we audio-recorded in and out of complementary school classrooms was a playfulness and creativity. Students engaged with and accessed a broad range of linguistic resources. Bangladeshi-heritage children watched Hindi films, and were familiar with Hindi songs. They sang along with the songs, and were able to express their preferences and dislikes. In the following example the two sisters Rumana and Aleha are watching a film just before going to Bengali class:

[Rumana sings with the music on TV]

Rumana: it's a funny movie that. this one, Hera Pheri. really funny, I like this song

Aleha: I like [to baby sister] (3) talk, talk, say amaar naam Durdana say amaar naam Durdana <*say my name is Durdana*>

Durdana: one khe <*who's there?*>

Rumana: [singing along in Hindi] rock your body, rock your body rock your body, rock your body, tumhare bina <*without you*> chaen na aaye <*there's no peace*> rock your body. (Home audio recording, Bengali case study)

Here singing along with the Hindi film music (rock your body etc.) seems to be a usual feature of the children's linguistic world, as they move in and out of English, Sylheti and Hindi while listening to, participating in and enjoying the Hindi film. At the same time they engage bilingually with their baby sister Durdana's attempts to speak into the digital recording device. On another occasion the same children were recorded listening to Hindi pop music before setting off for school:

[Hindi song playing in the background]

Rumana: [singing in Hindi] saatse aaja sa. this song's nice Asha Bhosle sings that Asha Bhosle amma, amma, amma, I hate him. what's his name?

Aleha: Amir Khan. wait, wait, I wanna see one. I wanna see one. I wanna see number one. is that number three or number two? is that number one? (Home audio recording, Bengali case study)

Here Rumana sings along in Hindi with the Indian pop music ('Saatse aaja sa'), and tells her sister that she likes the singer Asha Bhosle. At the same time she expresses a dislike for the well-known Bollywood actor, Amir Khan, who was also appearing on the show. Aleha is so enthusiastic about the Indian music that she is prepared to be late for class in order to find out which song is top of the pop charts.

Now Aleha and her sister are about to leave their house for school. Aleha says goodbye to her parents respectfully with the Arabic-derived 'salam alaikum':

Aleha: Rumana, come on. I'm going amma, salam alaikum
           <*mother, salam alaikum* >
           salam alaikum abba, zaairam aami
           <*salam alaikum father. I'm going*>

Notable here is the unmarked and quite usual multilingualism of the interaction: English, Sylheti and an Arabic-derived phrase enjoy a flexible and non-conflictual coexistence. We recorded many instances of flexible linguistic practice in the homes of students who attended the Bengali schools. In the following example, Tamim, a 10-year-old boy, is asking his mother whether he is allowed to go on the school camping trip:

amma aami camping-e zaaitaam. aafne last year here disoin aamaare disoinnaa. aami camping zaaitaam aafne aamaare disenna
   <*mother, I want to go camping you allowed him last year but not me. I want to go camping you didn't allow me last year*>

This is an unremarkable, quite usual example of flexible language practice in the students' family settings, of the sort we heard on each occasion that we audio-recorded the children and young people at home. Such multilingual practice at least partly constitutes the context for our investigation of multilingualism in the institutional setting of the complementary school. As we saw in Chapter 3, linguistic utterances should be understood as *dispositional*, based on individuals' linguistic competence and the 'linguistic climate' in which any they find themselves. This climate needs to be seen as the social conditions at any one time and place, which set the value of 'linguistic exchanges' (Bourdieu 1977c). At this moment, and others, these children are unconstrained by dominant structures which often insist that English is the only *legitimate language*, as they make meaning through the full range of their linguistic repertoires. In this domestic setting the linguistic climate is multilingual.

We were also fortunate to record some of the students who attended the Bengali schools reading the Qur'an, with their Qur'anic Arabic tutor. In the following example the tutor has come to the house of Tamim, Shazia and Kabir, and the children are reciting Arabic terms along with him:

Tutor:　　qaribun, qareebun, qareeb [reads along with Shazia, often repeating the same words] Re- yaa ze- yaa qaa ri- bun

Shazia:　　six times forsi <*I read it six times*>

Tutor:　　qaf zabar qaa, re zer ri, be pesh bu, nun, qareebun [spells the Arabic words. This is repeated many times] laam zabar laa

Tamim:　　Aami khaali ekhtaa mistake khorsi, ekhtaa mistake khorsi Sir <*I made only one mistake, only one mistake sir*> (Home audio recording, Bengali case study)

Here, the tutor is teaching the children to learn the words in Arabic by repeating them after him. Tamim uses Qur'anic Arabic, Sylheti and English side by side. None of the Arabic words are given a definition or meaning by the tutor. However, Tamim told us that although he was not able to understand as he was reading, the tutor would explain passages, and 'after I finish it, I am going to get an English version of the Qur'an so that I can understand every word of it'. Tamim read the verse fluently with little help from his tutor, and demonstrated (in Sylheti and English) his positive attitude to reading Arabic, saying proudly that he had made only one mistake in the passage he had been reading. Throughout our observations we saw that Qur'anic Arabic classes were privileged above Bengali classes, and indeed above other activity. Here, as in Bourdieu's early studies in Béarn (see 1977c, 2008b), the language of religion was accorded a legitimacy – indeed a sanctity – which eluded other languages. The language of the religious text is misrecognized as having a symbolic power, as if it were a consecrated text.

We recorded a 10-year-old student, Bodrul, who attended one of the Bengali schools, speaking to his father on the telephone. The father was in Bangladesh, and calling to speak to the family:

Bodrul:　　hello

Father:　　salam ditaa naa <*aren't you going to say salam to me*>

Bodrul:　　salam alaikum

Father:　　khontaa khoro <*what are you doing?*>

Bodrul:　　khontaa naa <*nothing*>

Father:　　how are you?

Bodrul:　　ji <*fine*>

Father:　　how are you?

Bodrul: fine
Father: good boy, good boy. amaar phute khi khore
<what is my [other] son doing?>
Bodrul: he khalaae *<he's playing>*
Father: Zakir khi khore *<what is Zakir doing?>*
Bodrul: he madrasath *<he's gone to the madrasah>*
Father: hain, madrasath *<yes the madrasah>*
Bodrul: jo oi *<yes>* Amma aai giyaa *<mother's coming>* (Home audio
           recording, Bengali case study)

Bodrul's father insists that his son uses the formal, Arabic-derived
greeting, 'salam alaikum', and moves between Sylheti and English in his
attempt to elicit responses from his son. Bodrul also appears to move easily
between Sylheti and English. In another, similar example, Bodrul's father
has returned from his visit to relatives in Bangladesh, and a visitor ('uncle')
has arrived at the house. The term 'uncle' here is one of respect within a
particular community, and does not necessarily indicate that the visitor
is a blood relation. In this interaction Bodrul has let 'uncle' into the house,
but is more concerned about a conversation with his sister Shazia, and
has not greeted the visitor in the expected way. Moments later 'uncle'
wants to know where Bodrul's father is, as he has not been shown in to
greet him:

Uncle: abbaae khoi *<where's your father?>*
Bodrul: I don't know. [to Shazia] I'm not going to play. I want my one
Shazia: I wanna watch this first
Bodrul: I'm prepared to do it as well. I'm prepared to do it as well take
           this man, please man
Father: oh fut, sasae dakhsenaani, sasae daakhsenani
<son, uncle is calling you, uncle is calling you>
Bodrul: aami zaaisi *<I'm going>*
Uncle: tumi khoiso khoite faartaam na *<you said you don't know>*
Bodrul: aami khoisina *<I didn't>*
Father: tumi sasare khoisoni khoite faartaam naa *<did you say to uncle
           I don't know?>*
Bodrul: naa *<no>*
Father: sasare salam khorso ni, khoiyya laao *<did you say salam to uncle,
           say it to him>*
Bodrul: [to 'uncle'] salam alaikum
Father: salam khorse sasare *<he's said salam to uncle>*

Uncle: waalaikum salam aami dui baar khoisi, teen baar khoisi <*I said salam twice, three times*>
Bodrul: [quietly] naam sasa, faagol beta <*he's called uncle he's crazy*>, fucking bitch, what's he on as?
Father: heh khitaa hoise? <*what's the matter?*>
Mother: furute name khomplain khorse aamaare furuter loghe khomplain aase <*he's complained about my son, he has complained about my son*> (Home audio recording, Bengali case study)

In this interaction once again there is an insistence on the formal, Arabic-derived greeting. Bodrul does not offer the greeting to the visitor until his father demands it of him. He appears to offend his 'uncle' with his brief and curt response ('I don't know'), which he then denies having made. Privately, or perhaps only to his sister, Bodrul uses the very opposite of formal language to refer to the visitor who landed him in trouble, saying (perhaps only to himself) in Sylheti that he's crazy, and in English referring to him as a 'fucking bitch'. Meanwhile, Bodrul's mother defends her son. Here the boy's private response is very different from the required formality of the Arabic-derived greeting, which itself becomes a site of symbolic contestation between the participants. There is insufficient space here to discuss the use of ritual language more fully, but we can acknowledge its role in the constitution of the linguistic market. Ritual here has a social function, a function of reproduction of the heritage of the group, and a function of setting limits which may be respected or transgressed (Bourdieu 2000a/1997: 117).

Many of the young people we spoke to and listened to articulated subject positions which were very little concerned with national or heritage identities. The following extract from an interview with two young (9- and 10-year-old) siblings was typical. The children had been asked what kind of music they like:

Tamim: I like Bhangra
R1:   really?
Tamim: I like Bhangra with rap
R2:   oh they have all kinds of crossover Bhangra music now don't they
Tamim: I like rap like Fifty Cent I mean
R2:   do you like Eminem?
Tamim: yes he's all right
R1:   so is that OK? I mean rap and all that is all right?
Shazia: erm yea

R: your dad doesn't?

Shazia: he doesn't really erm if it's in front of him he will shout but
             erm if we stopped it it's all right.

Tamim: RAP anyway I don't hear rap at home I might just hear it a bit
             cos I hear it from my friend's dad in his cars and everything
             because

R1:   is your friend Pakistani or Indian?

Tamim: English (. . .) I mean Bengali (Student interview, Bengali case
             study)

Here 10-year-old Tamim associates himself first with Bhangra, then 'Bhangra with rap' and finally 'rap like Fifty Cent'. This appears to represent a negotiation of an increasingly daring subject position. While listening to Bhangra music may be regarded as relatively mainstream and conservative, 'Bhangra with rap' moves towards an increasingly American pop culture position, and 'rap like Fifty Cent' is likely to represent a 'Gansta Rap' identity. Tamim is happy to be associated with 'my friend's dad', and the researcher assumes that his friend must be of Pakistani or Indian heritage, as it may be surprising for a good Bangladeshi to listen to this kind of music. In the final utterance in this excerpt, Tamim's pause between 'English' and 'I mean Bengali' may suggest that nationality, ethnicity and even language are not the salient categories for him at this moment – rather, he is more interested in positioning himself as a cool, streetwise consumer of contemporary, transnational music.

Conclusion

As we saw in Chapter 3, Bourdieu viewed language use as constituting a specific form of *field*, or market. His economic metaphor of the *linguistic market* described a system of relations which determines the price of linguistic products and thus helps fashion linguistic production. Key to understanding this metaphor is that the price of specific linguistic products can vary in different contexts. Furthermore, although one set of linguistic products may be the norm against which all others are valued, this is not to say that this is the 'dominant' language at all times and in all places. Rather, linguistic utterances can only be understood in relation to the linguistic climate in which speakers find themselves.

This climate is undoubtedly to some extent determined by family history. Migrants may reorient their dispositions towards the homeland and diaspora, as practices are features of a 'transnational *habitus*'. The second and subsequent generation may renegotiate and remake these practices, as local and global communities reshape transnational practice and 'multi-cultural *habitus*' contributes to performance of more diverse identities. These adaptations of Bourdieu's thinking tools appear to have some mileage. However, they also have the potential to be reductive, ironing out the complexity inherent in the messy stuff of ethnographic research. What Bourdieu offers ethnographic research with a language focus, and language research with an ethnographic focus, is a way of representing social and linguistic phenomena which specifically engages with dimensions of history, power and social structure. His metaphors enable us to situate interactions between people in the context of the relations of power that are obtained in the linguistic market. This is not a question of simple dichotomies, of 'this speaker has power while that speaker has none'. Instead, Bourdieu's metaphors offer linguistic ethnography a language with which to make visible, and make sense of, the messy stuff of linguistic interaction which is suffused with, and interpenetrates, complex relations of power in complex societies.

In the multilingual *linguistic market* ideologies and practices circulate in ways which can only be understood fully through investigations that focus on practice and situate that practice politically and historically. We have seen that different sets of linguistic resources function differentially as *linguistic capital* in this market, and accrue different values in different contexts. Underlying all the interviews and observations conducted in these communities in Birmingham was a powerful ideology which held English as the language with the highest value. Bourdieu argues that 'when one language dominates the market, it becomes the norm against which the prices of the other modes of expression, and with them the various competences, are defined' (1977c: 652). In relation to the dominance of English, other languages were 'rejected into indignity' (Bourdieu1998a/1994: 46). However, as Bourdieu demonstrated in his remarks about the distribution of *linguistic capital* in the Béarn (1977c: 657), this is not the whole story. The conditions within the multilingual marketplace are far from equal for languages other than English. We heard figures of authority argue that 'Bengali' has powerful associations with the making of the Bangladeshi nation, and 'Bengali' was profoundly associated with cultural heritage. We heard that 'Bengali' and 'Sylheti' should be kept separate, lest the purity of the standard variety be contaminated by contact with the non-standard form. We heard the view that speakers of 'Sylheti' were akin to the untouchable caste, the group with least economic capital of all. We saw that some linguistic rituals (e.g. formal greetings) were expected, and would precipitate retribution if neglected. We saw that Qur'anic Arabic played a specific role in the *linguistic market*, and constituted *linguistic capital* of a particular kind. We also heard the view that there were few, if any, differences between the sets of resources named 'Bengali' and 'Sylheti'. And when we listened to the way people spoke to each other in their homes and communities, it was clear that verbal repertoires were characterized by fluidity and diversity. Children and young people in particular used language flexibly, including in their verbal repertoires, resources which were not straightforwardly associated with their 'ethnic' group, or with a traditional view of bilingualism. They sang along with American pop music and popular Hindi songs; they listened to 'rap' and 'hip hop'; they mainly spoke English, and swore in that language; they spoke Sylheti to (some) family members; they learned to be literate in Bengali; they learned to read the Qur'an in formal Arabic; and they moved comfortably between what we have traditionally called 'languages'. We also saw a sophisticated metalinguistic sense of the social inequality of languages, as Sylheti-speaking adults spontaneously parodied speakers of the higher-status Bengali.

Bourdieu argued (1998a/1994: 92) that the same thinking tools can be used to analyse very different phenomena, from the actions of the Ford Foundation, to exchanges between generations within a family, to transactions in markets of cultural or religious goods. Indeed, the same can be said about investigations of matrimonial exchange (Bourdieu 2008b), the housing market (Bourdieu 2000b/2005) or social class and the judgement of taste (Bourdieu 1984a/1979). The analysis of language variation in Orléans, France, presented in Chapter 4, adopts a different method, and a different theoretical orientation, from the linguistic ethnography of a multilingual community conducted in Birmingham described here. However, both are informed by Bourdieu's metaphor of the linguistic economy of exchange. In both cases, as elsewhere, linguistic competence functions as *linguistic capital* in relationship with a particular market (Bourdieu 1977c: 651). What we saw in our investigations in these multilingual communities was that there can no more be an assumed consensus about what constitutes (a) language, that old boundaries and constraints are eroding and that certain sets of linguistic resources can no longer be held to straightforwardly represent particular 'nations', 'heritages' or 'cultures'. Individuals access sets of linguistic resources which draw from multiple sources: family, schooling, peer group and the virtual and polyphonic world of digital communication. They use these resources flexibly, in ways which enable them to negotiate cosmopolitan, multicultural identities characterized by mobility and dynamism. This notion of multiplicity, of resistance to the reification of identity, this globalization, is one side of the story. But, another side of the story we observed appeared to be in direct opposition to this. At the same time as traditional boundaries were becoming more permeable, and just as old markets were being broken apart, so we saw boundaries being shored up and constraints reinforced. At the same moment as new diversities were emerging, we saw moves to protect the purity of standard versions of languages which for some of those in these linguistic markets represented ways of being, and ways of belonging, which were not easily sacrificed or given up. What we saw were grassroots attempts to consecrate the standard language of the home territory and pass it on to the next generation, and in doing so to make Bengali again those who were in danger (according to this ideological position) of losing that way of being. In this process of making and remaking, the standard language must be kept separate and protected from contamination. In this ideology the language of the home territory comes to accrue associations beyond itself: of moral values, of respect, of heritage, of nation and of culture. And of course all of this was subject to the symbolic power of English. Just about everything we saw in these communities was in one way or another at the interstices of two ideological positions: one characterized by flexible linguistic production which indexed multicultural cosmopolitanism; the other rooted in linguistic affiliation to national and cultural heritage. These positions were not always oppositional, often coexisting in the crowded linguistic economy. In this economy linguistic resources evolved in practice as they came to accrue new values, affiliations and allegiances. Here language was up for grabs, traded, exchanged, bartered, wrangled over and negotiated, as language ideology and practice moved across time and space.

Chapter 7

Language Policy

Stephen May

Introduction

Debates over citizenship in modern nation states have often focused on the significance of language to both national identity and state citizenship. These debates have addressed, in particular, two key issues. First, whether speaking the state-mandated or national language(s) – that is, the majority or dominant language(s) of the state – is, or should be, a *requirement* of national citizenship and a demonstration of both political and social integration by its members (especially for those who speak other languages as a first language). Second, whether this requirement should be at the *expense* of, or in *addition* to, the maintenance of other languages – minority, or non-dominant languages, in effect – within the state. Or, to put it another way, whether public monolingualism in the state-mandated language(s) should be enforced upon an often-multilingual population or whether some degree of public as well as private multilingualism can be supported.

These two key issues are addressed directly by the field of language policy (see Ricento 2006 for a useful overview) and related debates about language rights (see May 2008). The former focuses on the mechanisms necessary for addressing and managing linguistic diversity at the level of the nation state, particularly in relation to the public recognition and promotion of state-mandated, or majority, languages. The latter explores how minority or non-dominant languages – those spoken by groups with less power, status or entitlement in a given society – might also gain entrance to the public arena, particularly in such core areas as education.

This chapter uses Bourdieu's general perspective on language – *habitus* and *linguistic markets* – as a background to a discussion involving a wide range of research texts on issues concerning language policy and language rights. These texts are used to exemplify a number of related issues. There are three particular points of focus in this chapter in relation to Bourdieu's work. The first of these, arising out of his wider critique of structural

linguistics, concerns his advocacy of a *diachronic* rather than a *presentist* study
of languages. A diachronic, or historicized, approach to language is necessary, Bourdieu argues, in order to highlight and explore how particular
languages come to accrue status and power over time in particular social
and political contexts, most often at the specific expense of other languages.
This situation is seen in the regular juxtaposition of 'majority' and 'minority' languages, already alluded to, where the former are viewed as languages
of power and wider communication, while the latter are seen as having little
wider social/political status, value or use. Bourdieu's core argument here is
that the language ideologies underpinning these processes of language
demarcation, and their related hierarchizing, are inevitably imbricated with
historical and contemporary processes of power and inequality, a core issue
that any study of language policy must take seriously.

A diachronic understanding of language also underpins the second key
aspect of Bourdieu's work relevant to this discussion: his exploration of the
emergence of modern nation states and the related construction of national
languages as their key linguistic marker. This involves, for Bourdieu, a critical
analysis of the role of the state, and its key institutions such as education,
in promoting national languages. Two key processes are crucial here: legitimation, or the official recognition of a language by the state, and institutionalization, its adoption in key/public language domains (Nelde et al.
1996). The role of nationalist discourse in linking these newly emergent
national languages *ineluctably* with modernization, progress and social
mobility, while simultaneously constructing competing languages as merely
local and, by extension, inherently antediluvian, also requires active critique. So too does the related emphasis on public linguistic homogeneity
(May 2008).

The third aspect of Bourdieu's work relates to the impact of the wider
socio-historical and socio-political processes, just described, on the public
and private language choices of individuals, particularly those who are
multilingual. Here Bourdieu's analysis allows us to explore critically how
individual speakers are influenced, and often constrained, by the multiple
linguistic markets in which they are situated. Take the phenomenon of
language shift, for example. Language shift/loss occurs when speakers of
a particular (invariably, minority) language 'shift' over time, usually within
two to three generations, to speaking another (invariably, majority) language. While this shift is often couched as a 'voluntary' one, or simply a
'rational choice', particularly by proponents of majority languages (see
Edwards 1985, 1994, see also below), it is rather the result of a complex
array of wider social forces which, over time, consistently valorize majority

languages and actively stigmatize minority languages, often also forcibly proscribing the latter from key domains such as education. Not surprisingly perhaps, speakers of these 'despised languages' (Grillo 1989) eventually internalize the associated negative attitudes towards these languages, a process Bourdieu describes as *méconnaissance* or misrecognition, which is a key contributor to eventual language shift. One only has to think of the historical treatment of indigenous languages in multiple colonial and postcolonial settler societies, and their current parlous linguistic state as a consequence (Grenoble and Whaley 1998), to see this demonstrated. While such language shift is most evident still in relation to national contexts, we are also, increasingly, beginning to see a similar pattern emerging at the supranational level with respect to globalization and the emergence of English as the current international language (Phillipson 2003). Contra to the 'voluntarist' explanation for such language shifts, a Bourdieusian analysis thus allows for a more critical, dialectical account of the relationship between language choice and constraint.

This chapter will illustrate how these three areas of Bourdieu's work can both usefully inform and extend current discussions of language policy, and unravel more fully the complex interstices of language and identity and the related issue of what language rights (if any) might be attributable to speakers of minority or non-dominant languages. Following from this, and again drawing on Bourdieu, the chapter will develop an argument for the extension of the public recognition of language(s) within nation states, via bilingual/multilingual language policies, and the related extension of the language rights attributable to individual speakers.

The Politics of Language

As outlined in Chapter 3, Bourdieu has written widely, though disparately, on language. Bourdieu's principal concern in these various accounts is to situate language in its proper socio-historical and socio-political context. As we have seen, he is particularly scathing of the preoccupation in modern linguistics with analysing language in isolation from the social conditions in which it is used. As he comments ironically of this process: 'bracketing out the social . . . allows language or any other symbolic object to be treated like an end in itself, [this] contributed considerably to the success of structural linguistics, for it endowed the "pure" exercises that characterise a purely internal and formal analysis with the charm of a game devoid of consequences' (1991c: 34). I shall not further rehearse Bourdieu's extensive

critique of this preoccupation with linguistic formalism at the expense of
a wider analysis of the social and political conditions in which language
comes to be used, since this has already been widely canvassed elsewhere
in the book. However, it is useful to point out briefly its contiguities with
allied critiques by both Vološinov (1973) and Mey (1985). Vološinov argued
cogently against the 'abstract objectivism' of structural linguistics, as represented by de Saussure (and, one could add, Chomsky), suggesting it
created a radical disjuncture between the idea of a language system and
actual language history. Mey observes 'that linguistic models, no matter
how innocent and theoretical they may seem to be, not only have distinct
economical, social and political presuppositions, but also consequences. . . .
Linguistic (and other) inequalities don't cease to exist simply because their
socio-economic causes are swept under the linguistic rug' (1985: 26).

Bourdieu describes the resulting orthodoxy, which posits a particular
set of linguistic practices as a normative model of 'correct' usage, as the
'illusion of linguistic communism that haunts all linguistic theory' (1991c:
43). By this, Bourdieu argues, the linguist is able to produce the illusion of
a common or standard language – and, as we shall see shortly, invariably
a *national* language – while ignoring the socio-historical conditions which
have established this particular set of linguistic practices as dominant and
legitimate. However, this dominant and *legitimate language* – this *victorious*
language, in effect – is simply taken for granted by linguists (Thompson
1991, see also Mühlhäusler 1996):

> To speak of *the* language, without further specification, as linguists do, is
> tacitly to accept the *official* definition of the *official* language of a political
> unit. This language is the one which, within the territorial limits of that
> unit, imposes itself on the whole population as the only legitimate lan-
> guage. . . . The official language is bound up with the state, both in its
> genesis and its social uses . . . this state language becomes the theoretical
> norm against which all linguistic practices are objectively measured.
> (1991c: 45; emphases in original)

This tendency towards a presentist approach to the study of language,
divorced from both the wider socio-historical and socio-political context,
and issues of language use, power and inequality, can clearly be seen in
the early years of the development of language policy as an academic
discipline – the 1960s and 1970s. During this period, language policy was
seen by its proponents as non-political, non-ideological, pragmatic, even
technicist (Ricento 2006). Its apparently simple and straightforward aim

was to solve the immediate language problems of newly emergent postcolonial states in Africa (e.g. Sudan, Tanzania), Asia (e.g. India, Pakistan), the Pacific (e.g. Indonesia, Malaysia) and the Middle East (e.g. Israel, Palestine). Status language concerns at this time – that is, those issues related to the recognition of particular languages in specific public and/or private language domains – thus focused in particular on establishing stable diglossic language contexts in which majority languages (usually, ex-colonial languages, and most often English and French) were promoted as public languages of wider communication. If promoted at all, 'local languages' – minority languages, in effect – were seen as being limited to private, familial language domains. While concern was often expressed for the ongoing maintenance of these minority languages, the principal emphasis of language policy at this time was on the establishment and promotion of 'unifying' national languages, along the lines of those in Western, developed contexts (see, for example, Fishman 1968a, 1968b, 1968c, Fox 1975, Rubin and Jernudd 1971).

What was not addressed by these early efforts at language policy were the wider historical, social and political issues attendant upon these processes, and the particular ideologies underpinning them. As Luke et al. observe, while maintaining a 'veneer of scientific objectivity' (something of great concern to early language planners),[1] language policy 'tended to avoid directly addressing social and political matters within which language change, use and development, and indeed language planning itself, are embedded' (1990: 26–7).

This omission was problematic for a number of reasons. First, it did not question or critique the very specific historical processes that had led to the hierarchizing of majority and minority languages in the first place. As we shall see in the next section, these processes were and are deeply imbricated with the politics of modern nationalism, and its emphasis on the establishment of national languages and public linguistic homogeneity as central, even essential, tenets of both modernization and westernization. Consequently, the normative ascendancy of national languages – Bourdieu's 'victorious language' – was simply assumed, even championed, by early advocates of language policy and all other languages were compared in relation to them. This is highlighted by the various language typologies developed at the time, such as Kloss (1968), which attempted to rank languages in relation to their relative 'suitability' for national development.

Second, the notion of linguistic complementarity, so central to early language planning attempts at establishing 'stable diglossia', was itself highly problematic. Linguistic complementarity, as understood by early language planners, implied at least some degree of mutuality and reciprocity, along with a certain demarcation and boundedness between the majority and minority languages involved. Situations of so-called stable diglossia, however, are precisely *not* complementary in these respects. Rather, the normative ascendancy of national languages – and by extension, international languages such as English – specifically *militates* against the ongoing use, and even existence, of minority languages. As Dua observes of the influence of English in India, for example, 'the complementarity of English with indigenous languages tends to go up in favour of English partly because it is dynamic and cumulative in nature and scope, partly because it is sustained by socio-economic and market forces and partly because the educational system reproduces and legitimatizes the relations of power and knowledge implicated with English' (1994: 132). In other words, if majority languages are consistently constructed as languages of 'wider communication' while minority languages are viewed as local(ized) languages, useful only as carriers of 'tradition' or 'historical identity', it is not hard to see what might become of the latter. Minority languages will inevitably come to be viewed as delimited, perhaps even actively unhelpful languages – not only by others, but also often by the speakers of minority languages themselves. This helps to explain why speakers of minority languages have increasingly dispensed with their first language(s) in favour of speaking a majority language – as reflected in increasing patterns of language shift and loss in the world today (see also below).

For Bourdieu, such synchronic, ahistorical approach to language policy in these early years simply ignored the wider issues of power and inequality that led to the hierarchizing of languages vis-à-vis each other. A synchronic analysis to language policy takes no account of human agency, political intervention, power and authority in the formation of particular language ideologies that privilege so-called majority (often national) languages over minority (often local) languages. Nor, by definition, is it able to identify the establishment and maintenance of majority languages as a specific 'form of practice, historically contingent and socially embedded' (Blommaert 1999: 7). Bourdieu's analysis is thus a significant corrective to the problem of presentism exemplified in much early work in language policy.

Language and Nationalism

When one recognizes the social and political embeddedness of languages in a Bourdieusian way, their status and their use, a different, more critical view of language policy immediately becomes possible. Such a view also requires an understanding of the central role of nationalism, and the related construction of modern nation states, another key concern of Bourdieu's. This concern emerges from his broader analysis of the processes of language hierarchization, previously discussed, via his notion of the single linguistic community:

In order for one mode of expression among others (a particular language in the case of bilingualism, a particular use of language in the case of a society divided into classes) to *impose* itself as the only legitimate one, the linguistic market has to be *unified* and the different dialects (of class, region or ethnic group) have to be measured practically against the legitimate language or usage. Integration into a single 'linguistic community', which is the product of the political domination that is endlessly reproduced by institutions capable of imposing universal recognition of the dominant language, is the condition for the establishment of relations of linguistic domination. (1991c: 46–7; my emphases)

The single 'linguistic community', or the 'unified' *linguistic market*, to which Bourdieu refers is most clearly represented by the modern nation state. Specifically, modern nation states require their citizens to all speak a state-mandated language in the public, or civic, realm as a prerequisite for full participation in the wider society. This construction of a culturally and linguistically homogeneous civic realm is actually a relatively recent historical phenomenon, deriving from the rise of political nationalism in Europe from the middle of the last millennium onwards (see Edwards 1985; Fishman 1989a, 1989b, May 2008, Wright 2000, for further discussion). Previous forms of political organization had not required this degree of linguistic uniformity. For example, empires were quite happy for the most part to leave unmolested the plethora of cultures and languages subsumed within them – as long as taxes were paid, all was well. The Greek and Roman Empires are obvious examples here, while 'New World' examples include the Aztec and Inca Empires of Central and South America respectively. More recent historical examples include the Austro-Hungarian Empire's overtly multilingual policy. But perhaps the clearest example is that of the Ottoman Empire, which actually established a formal system of 'millets' (nations) in order to accommodate the cultural and linguistic diversity of peoples within its borders (see Dorian 1998).

But, in the politics of European nationalism – which, of course, was also to spread subsequently throughout the world – the idea of a single, common 'national' language (sometimes, albeit rarely, a number of national languages) quickly became the leitmotif of modern social and political organization. How was this accomplished? Principally via the political machinery of these newly emergent European states, with mass education often playing a central role. As Gellner (1983) has outlined, the nationalist principle of 'one state, one culture, one language' saw the state, via its education system, increasingly identified with a specific language and culture – invariably, that of the majority ethnic group. The process of selecting and establishing a common national language as part of this wider process usually involved two key aspects: *legitimation* and *institutionalization* (May 2008, Nelde et al. 1996). Legitimation is understood to mean here the formal recognition accorded to the language by the nation state – usually, by the constitutional and/or legislative benediction of official status. Accordingly, 'la langue officielle a partie liée avec l'État' (see Bourdieu 1982a: 27) – the legitimate (or standard) language becomes an arm of the state. Institutionalization, perhaps the more important dimension, refers to the process by which the language comes to be accepted, or 'taken for granted', in a wide range of social, cultural and linguistic domains or contexts, both formal and informal.

Both elements, in combination, achieved not only the central requirement of nation states – cultural and linguistic homogeneity – but also the allied and, seemingly, necessary banishment of so-called minority languages and dialects to the private domain (see also below). These latter language varieties were, in effect, *positioned* by these newly formed states as languages of lesser political worth and value. Consequently, national languages came to be associated with modernity and progress, while their less fortunate counterparts were associated (conveniently) with tradition and obsolescence. More often than not, the latter were also specifically constructed as *obstacles* to the political project of nation-building – as threats to the 'unity' of the state. The inevitable consequence of this political imperative is the establishment of an ethnically exclusive and culturally and linguistically homogeneous nation state – the ultimate source of Bourdieusian *linguistic norm* – a realm from which minority languages and cultures are effectively banished. Indeed, this is the 'ideal' model to which most nation states (and nationalist movements) still aspire – albeit in the face of a far more complex and contested multi-ethnic and multilingual reality (see May 2008, McGroarty 2002, 2006). As Dorian summarizes it, 'it is the concept of the nation state coupled with its official standard language . . . that has in modern times posed the keenest threat to both the identities and the languages of small [minority] communities' (1998: 18). Coulmas observes, even more succinctly, that 'the nation state as it has evolved since the French Revolution is the natural enemy of minorities' (1998: 67). In short, these processes ensured that both national and minority languages were literally 'created' out of the politics of European state-making and not, as we often assume, the other way around (Billig 1995).

The mention of France here is important, as it is often regarded as the first and/or archetypal modern nation state. Indeed, the triumph of official languages and the suppression of their potential rivals within the context of modern nation states are starkly illustrated by the rise of French as the 'national' language of post-revolutionary France. Certainly, Bourdieu was much interested in tracing this history of language domination within his own national context (see, for example, Bourdieu 1975), so let us look at this more closely as a useful illustrative example.

Prior to the French Revolution of 1789, three broad language groups were present in the territory we now know as France. The *Langue d'Oïl*, comprising a wide range of dialects, was spoken in the North. Of these, the *Francien* dialect, spoken in and around Paris, was the actual antecedent of modern French. The *Langue d'Oc* (Occitan), also comprising a wide range of dialects, was spoken in the South. And in central and eastern France, Franco-Provençal was spoken. But, not only that, Basque was spoken in the south-west, as was Breton in Brittany, Flemish around Lille, German in Alsace-Lorraine, Catalan in Perpignan and Corsican (a dialect of Italian and Napoleon's first language) in Corsica (Ager 1999). In addition, Latin was the administrative language, at least until the sixteenth century, although it was as such largely confined to the church, the university and the royal administration (Johnson 1993). Pre-modern 'France', like so many other administrations prior to the rise of political nationalism, was thus resolutely multilingual.

The French Revolution was to change all that, although it is an interesting irony that it was only during the early stages of the Revolution that the linguistic diversity of France was fully apprehended. A linguistic survey carried out by the abbé Henri Grégoire in 1790 revealed that over 30 'patois' were spoken in France (for political reasons, he was reluctant to accord them the status of languages; see below). More pertinently perhaps, he concluded that as few as three million people – not more than a tenth of the actual population – could actually speak French with any degree of fluency (Johnson 1993).

The initial response to this linguistic diversity was cautious magnanimity. For example, the new Assembly agreed on 14 January 1790 a policy of translating decrees into various 'idioms' and 'dialects' in order to better disseminate Republican ideas among the majority non-French-speaking population (Grillo 1989). But this was soon to change. In short, it quickly became apparent to the Jacobins that the ideal of the Revolution lay in uniformity and the extinction of particularisms. For the Revolutionaries, regional languages were increasingly regarded as parochial vestiges of the *ancien régime*, the sooner forgotten, the better. This was reflected in their pejorative labelling as 'patois' rather than as languages. As Bourdieu observes of this process, 'measured de facto against the single standard of the "common" language, they are found wanting and cast into the outer darkness of *regionalisms*'. As a result, 'a system of *sociologically pertinent* linguistic oppositions tends to be constituted which has nothing in common with the system of *linguistically pertinent* linguistic oppositions' (1991c: 54; emphases in original).

In contrast, French was seen as the embodiment of civilization and progress. Consequently, the adoption of French as the single national language, representing and reflecting the interests of the new revolutionary order, was increasingly regarded as an essential foundation for the new Republic and its advocacy of *égalité*. As the Jacobins came to insist, 'The unity of the Republic demands the unity of speech. . . . Speech must be one, like the Republic' (cited in Weber 1976: 72). Bourdieu comments that this perceived imperative 'was not only a question of communication but of gaining recognition for a new *language of authority*, with its new political vocabulary, its terms of address and reference, its metaphors, its euphemisms and the representation of the social world which it conveys' (1991c: 48; my emphasis).

The obvious corollary to this also came to be accepted and actively promoted – that the ongoing maintenance of other languages was specifically opposed to the aims of the Revolution. Indeed, Barère, in his report of 1794, went so far as to assert:

> La fédéralisme et la superstition parlent bas-breton; l'émigration et la haine de la République parlent allemand; la contre-révolution parle l'italien, et le fanatisme parle le basque. Cassons ces instruments de dommage et d'erreur. [Federalism and superstition speak Breton; emigration and hatred of the Republic speak German; counter-revolution speaks Italian, and fanaticism speaks Basque. Let us destroy these instruments of damage and error.] (Cited in de Certeau et al. 1975: 299)

These sentiments were also reflected, albeit somewhat less iconoclastically, in the final report of the abbé Grégoire on the linguistic state of the new republic. This report was eventually published in 1794, 4 years after the survey had been commissioned, and concerned itself principally with corpus issues – on 'perfecting' the French language. However, its overall position on other languages in France is clearly indicated by its subtitle 'Sur la nécessité et les moyens d'anéantir les patois et d'universaliser l'usage de la langue française' ['On the need and ways to annihilate dialects and universalize the use of French']. It should come as no surprise then that Grégoire went on to conclude:

> Unity of language is an integral part of the Revolution. If we are ever to banish superstition and bring men closer to the truth, to develop talent and encourage virtue, to mould all citizens into a national whole, to simplify the mechanism of the political machine and make it function more smoothly, we must have a common language. (Cited in Grillo 1989: 24)

The Grégoire Report proved a watershed. Earlier attempts at translation were quickly dispensed with in order to expedite this vision of a brave new world, represented (only) in and through French. More importantly, the legitimation and institutionalization of French came to be inextricably intertwined in the minds of the Jacobins with the active destruction of all other languages. But there was still a problem. Such was the linguistic diversity highlighted by Grégoire that it could not be easily or quickly displaced. Even as late as 1863, official figures indicated that a quarter of the country's population, including half the children who would reach adulthood in the last quarter of the nineteenth century, still spoke no French (Weber 1976). What to do? The answer lay in a combination of legal enforcement of the language, via a series of court decisions requiring the use of French in all legal documents (see Grau 1992) and, more significantly, a central role for education.

The use of education as a key, perhaps *the* key agency of linguistic standardization (some might call it linguistic genocide), began as early as 1793. At that time, French schools were established in the German-speaking Alsace region, as a kind of form of doxic *linguistic capital*, while the ongoing use of German was banned (Grillo 1989). This was to provide the template for the use of French education throughout the nineteenth (and twentieth) century. A central goal of the *hussards noirs*, the Republic's teachers, was to eradicate all regional languages, which were by then regarded as worthless, barbarous, corrupt and devoid of interest (see Bourdieu 1982a). Given the ongoing linguistic diversity, this process took some time. It was not until the establishment of a fully secularized, compulsory and free primary system in the 1880s that education really began to have its full effect, principally through the formal proscription of all other languages from the school. But, even prior to that time it had not been for want of trying. A poignant illustration of this is provided by a prefect in the Department of Finistère in Brittany who, in 1845, formally exhorted teachers: 'Above all remember, gentleman, that your sole function is to kill the Breton language' (cited in Quiniou-Tempereau 1988: 31–2).

This state-led 'ideology of contempt' (Grillo 1989) towards minority languages has resulted in their inexorable decline in France over the last two centuries to the point where less than 2 per cent of the French population now speak these as a first language (see Héran 1993, Nelde et al. 1996). It has also at the same time entrenched deep into the French national psyche a view that the promotion, and even simply the maintenance, of minority languages (and cultures) are fundamentally at odds with the principles and objectives of the French state (Ager 1999).

The example of France illustrates clearly the plight of minority – or more accurately, *minoritized* – languages in modern nation states. Their effective banishment from the public or civic realm has significant implications for a more critical approach to language policy. First, it highlights that the distinctions that are regularly made between languages and dialects (or patois, in the case of France) are inherently political rather than linguistic – indeed, it is almost impossible to distinguish between languages and dialects on a linguistic basis. Second, it illustrates clearly how and why minority languages have come to be so marginalized and pathologized as languages 'not fit' for the modern world – as have, more often than not, their speakers as well. And yet, this juxtaposition of majority languages as ineluctably linked to modernization and minority languages as antediluvian is simply a product of nationalism. Third, if linguistic homogeneity is recognized as a specific product of the politics of nationalism, it is, by extension, neither inevitable nor inviolate. Other more inclusive and multilingual conceptions of the nation state are clearly possible, albeit only when there is sufficient political will to implement them. For this to occur, however, language policies would have to recognize the rights of minority language speakers within national contexts. They would also need to address directly the issue of language shift and loss by explicitly *re*valuing minority languages in the public or civic realm. This is beginning to occur in some national contexts. For example, after centuries of the proscription of Catalan in Catalonia and Welsh in Wales, these languages have, in the last 20 years, re-emerged as civic languages, alongside the majority state languages of Spanish and English respectively (see May 2000, 2002, 2004 for further discussion). But even here, the challenge is still immense. Specifically, how can language policies effectively address/ameliorate ongoing language shift and loss among minority language speakers – the result of historical state-led 'ideologies of contempt', coupled with Bourdieu's notion of *méconnaissance* – in favour of majority national languages and/or international languages such as English?

These arguments about the historical and geopolitical situatedness of national languages also clearly apply at the supranational level. In particular, a number of prominent sociolinguistic commentators have argued that the burgeoning reach and influence of English as the current world language, or lingua mundi, is the result of an equally constructed historical process (see Holborow 1999, Maurais and Morris 2003, Pennycook 1994, 1998a, 2000, Phillipson 1992, 1998, 2003). First, there was the initial pre-eminence of Britain and the British Empire in establishing English as a key language of trade across the globe. Second, there has been the subsequent socio-political and socio-economic dominance of the USA, along with its current pre-eminent position in the areas of science, technology, media and academia (see Ammon 1998, 2000). And third, there have been recent geopolitical events such as the collapse of the former Soviet Union, and much of communist Central and Eastern Europe along with it, which have further bolstered the reach and influence of English.

As with the construction of national languages then, the current ascendancy of English is also invariably linked with modernity and modernization, and the associated benefits that accrue to those who speak it. The result is to position other languages as having less 'value' and 'use', and by extension, and more problematically, to delimit and delegitimize the social, cultural and linguistic capital ascribed to 'non-English speakers' – the phrase itself reflecting the normative ascendancy of English. The usual corollary to this position is that the social mobility of the minority language speaker will be further enhanced if they *dispense* with any other (minority) languages – the language replacement model of nationalism extended, in effect, to the global(ized) level. Addressing these issues directly at both national and supranational levels is the focus of the final section.

Language, Habitus and Pluralism

Because of the social and political processes just outlined, the promotion of national languages and/or English is almost always couched in terms of 'language replacement' – that one should/must learn these majority languages *at the expense of* one's first language. Consequently, the promotion of cultural and linguistic homogeneity at the collective/public level has come to be associated with, and expressed by, individual monolingualism. This amounts to a form of linguistic social Darwinism and also helps to explain why language shift and loss have become so prominent, particularly among minority language speakers.

Central to these language replacement arguments is the idea that the individual social mobility of minority language speakers will be enhanced as a result. Relatedly, those who choose to continue to speak a minority language are consistently constructed in wider public discourses as deliberately confining themselves to a language that does not have a wider use, thus actively constraining their social mobility. This is illustrated, for example, by the English Only movement in the USA, as well as by a range of academic and social commentators, who regularly dismiss Spanish as simply a language of the ghetto (see, for example, Barry 2000, Edwards 1994, Huntingdon 2005, Schlesinger 1992). Little wonder, such critics observe, that many others within the linguistic minority itself choose to 'exit' the linguistic group by learning another (invariably, more dominant) language. It is one thing, after all, to proclaim the merits of retaining a particular language for identity purposes, quite another to have to live a life delimited by it – foreclosing the opportunity for mobility in the process. We can broadly summarize the logic of this argument as follows:

- Majority languages are lauded for their 'instrumental' value, while minority languages are accorded 'sentimental' value, but are broadly constructed as obstacles to social mobility and progress.
- Learning a majority language will thus provide individuals with greater economic and social mobility.
- Learning a minority language, while (possibly) important for reasons of cultural continuity, delimits an individual's mobility; in its strongest terms, this might amount to actual 'ghettoization'.
- If minority language speakers are 'sensible' they will opt for mobility and modernity via the majority language.
- Whatever decision is made, the choice between opting for a majority or minority language is constructed as oppositional, even mutually exclusive.

These arguments appear to be highly persuasive. However, the presumptions and assumptions that equate linguistic mobility *solely* with majority languages are themselves extremely problematic. For a start, this position separates the instrumental and identity aspects of language. On this view, minority languages may be important for habitus/identity but have no instrumental value, while majority languages are construed as primarily instrumental with little or no identity value. We see this in the allied notions, evident in early language policy attempts, of majority languages as 'vehicles' of modernity, and minority languages as (merely) 'carriers' of identity (see above). However, it is clear that *all* language(s) embody and accomplish both identity and instrumental functions for those who speak them. Where particular languages – especially majority/minority languages – differ is in the *degree* to which they can accomplish each of these functions, and this in turn is dependent on the social and political (not linguistic) constraints in which they operate (Carens 2000, May 2003). Thus, in the case of minority languages, their instrumental value is often constrained by wider social and political processes that have resulted, as we have already seen, in the privileging of other language varieties in the public realm. Meanwhile, for majority languages, the habitus characteristics of the language *are* clearly important for their speakers as part of identity, but often become subsumed within, and normalized by, the instrumental functions that these languages fulfil. Moreover, this process operates largely independently of particular languages, being determined primarily by social and political context. How else can we explain, for example, how Spanish in one context (the USA) is constructed as a minority language, while in many other contexts (South America, Spain), it is clearly a majority language?

On this basis, the perceived limited instrumentality of particular minority languages at any given time need not always remain so. Indeed, if the minority position of a language is the specific product of wider historical and contemporary social and political relationships, changing these wider relationships positively with respect to a minority language should bring about both enhanced instrumentality for the language in question, and increased mobility for its speakers. This is what is happening currently, for example, in Wales and Catalonia (see above). Likewise, when majority language speakers are made to realize that their own languages fulfil important identity functions for them, both as individuals and as a group, they may be slightly more reluctant to require minority language speakers to dispense with theirs.

Or to put it another way, if majority languages do provide their speakers with particular and often significant individual and collective forms of linguistic habitus, as they clearly do, it seems unjust to deny these same benefits, out of court, to minority language speakers. This does not preclude cultural and linguistic change and adaptation – all languages and cultures are subject to such processes. But, what it does immediately bring into question is the necessity/validity of the unidirectional movement of cultural and linguistic adaptation and change *from* a minority language/ culture *to* a majority one.

Dismantling the identity-instrumental opposition between minority and majority languages thus immediately brings into question the idea of incommensurate linguistic identities, or *habitus*, on which it is based. In other words, the distinctions often made with respect to majority and minority languages are themselves predicated on a singular, exclusive and oppositional notion of linguistic identity – we must have one linguistic identity/ habitus *or* the other, we cannot have both. In contrast, a more nuanced sociological understanding of the complex links between language and identity can, in turn, allow for the possibility or potential for holding multiple, complementary cultural and linguistic identities at both individual and collective levels. On this view, maintaining a minority language – or a dominant language, for that matter – avoids 'freezing' the development of particular languages in the roles they have historically occupied, or perhaps still currently occupy. Equally importantly, it questions and discards the requirement of a singular and/or replacement approach to the issue of other linguistic identities. *Linguistic habitus* – and social and cultural identities more broadly – need not be constructed as irredeemably oppositional. Narrower identities do not necessarily need to be traded in for broader ones. One can clearly remain, for example, both Spanish-speaking and American, Catalan-speaking and Spanish, or Welsh-speaking and British. The same process applies to national and international language identities, where these differ.

Bourdieu's work is therefore directly pertinent to unpacking further the complex relationship between the identity and instrumental functions of language, discussed previously, particularly in relation to *habitus*. *Habitus* allows us to understand the historical relationship of particular languages to particular groups, while at the same time allowing for the fact that such historical relationships, expressed across *fields* and with the *linguistic market*, can be ruptured or severed – hence, language shift and loss – by the wider political processes discussed throughout this chapter. Furthermore, *habitus* enables us to explore the ongoing *significance* of languages to particular groups, while avoiding an essentialist understanding of language and identity that delimits or defines such groups solely by these languages. In particular, the four key dimensions of *habitus* highlighted in Bourdieu's work – *embodiment, agency, the interplay between past and present* and *the interrelationship between collective and individual trajectories* – provide us with a useful means of examining both the continuing purchase *and* malleability of identity, and the particular languages associated with them, at any given time and place (see May 2008 for an extended discussion). I now want to reconsider some key aspects of Bourdieu's concept of *habitus* in order to draw out its significance for language policy.

For Bourdieu, *habitus* is not simply about ideology, attitude or perception; it is a set of *embodied* dispositions – or ways of viewing, and living in the world. This set of dispositions – what Bourdieu would call *bodily hexis* – operates most often at the level of the unconscious and the mundane and, in the case of group identity, often involves language use. Indeed, *linguistic habitus*, in Bourdieu's terms, is a subset of the *dispositions* towards language use which comprise the *habitus*: it is that set of *dispositions* acquired in the course of learning to speak in particular social and cultural *field* contexts. The key point for Bourdieu is that group attitudes and practices, including language use, are usually lived out implicitly as a result of historical and customary practice. As such, they may provide the parameters of social action for many. However, they are also never limited to those parameters, and may change over time, both internally, as a result of their ongoing use, and externally in relation to wider economic, social and political influences. This helps to explain why languages that have been traditionally associated with a particular group can continue to hold such importance for their collective identity. However, it can also explain why such languages can equally come to be replaced over time with other languages, via the wider social and political processes highlighted in this chapter.

This ongoing tension between continuity and change is further explained via Bourdieu's other key dimensions of *habitus*. For example, in relation to the complex interaction between agency and structure, Bourdieu argues that *habitus* does not *determine* individual behaviour. A range of choices, or strategic practices, is presented to individuals within the internalized framework of the *habitus*. Moreover, these practices, based on the intuitions of the practical sense, *orient* rather than strictly determine action. Choice is thus at the heart of *habitus*. However, not all choices are possible. As Bourdieu observes, 'habitus, like every "art of inventing" . . . makes it possible to produce an infinite number of practices that are relatively unpredictable (like the corresponding situations) but [which are] also limited in their diversity' (1990c: 55). These limits are set by the historically and socially situated conditions of the *habitus*' production; what Bourdieu terms both 'a conditioned and conditional freedom' (1990c: 55). In short, improbable practices, or practices viewed as antithetical to the mores of a particular group, are rejected as unthinkable. Concomitantly, only a particular range of possible practices is considered, although this range of possibilities may evolve and change over time in relation to changing circumstances. Thus, Bourdieu posits that individuals and groups operate strategically *within the constraints* of a particular *habitus*, but also that they react to changing external conditions: economic, technological and political (Harker 1984, 1990, Harker and May 1993).

This recursive position allows Bourdieu to argue that the *habitus*, including our *linguistic habitus*, is both a product of our early socialization, yet is also continually modified by individuals' experience of the outside world (see Di Maggio 1979). Within this complex interplay of past and present experience – the third key dimension of Bourdieu's work highlighted here – *habitus* can be said to reflect the social, cultural and linguistic position in which it was constructed, while also allowing for its transformation in current circumstances. However, the possibilities of action in most instances will tend to reproduce rather than transform the limits of possibility delineated by the social group. This is because *habitus*, as a product of history, ensures the active presence of past experiences, which tend also to normalize particular cultural and linguistic practices, and their constancy over time (Harker and May 1993). Nonetheless, this tendency towards reproduction of group mores and practices does not detract from the *potential* for transformation and change, as evidenced in the linguistic context by language shift.

The fourth element of *habitus* – the interrelationship between individual action and group mores – also reflects this tension. In many instances, individual practices, including language practices, will conform to those of the group since, as Bourdieu argues, 'the practices of the members of the same group . . . are always more and better harmonized than the agents know or wish' (1990c: 59). Yet Bourdieu also recognizes the potential for divergence between individual and collective trajectories. In effect, *habitus* within, as well as between, social groups differs to the extent that the details of individuals' social trajectories diverge from one another. Again, the differing language choices that group members might make in relation to either maintaining or dispensing with a particular language reflect this tension.

In combination, this fourfold Bourdieusian understanding of *habitus* in relation to language and identity also complexifies the simplistic notion, regularly propounded by advocates of majority languages, that individual language choices are a wholly voluntarist process, as demonstrated in the increasingly widespread processes of language shift and loss discussed earlier (see, for example, Brutt-Griffler 2002, Edwards 1994). As I have argued elsewhere (2003), this is a reductionist form of *rational choice theory* that simply does not do justice to the complex interaction between choice and constraint in most hierarchized language contexts or linguistic markets, shaped as we have already seen by power and inequality and internalized via *mécconnaissance*. Instead, one can legitimately assert that so-called individual choice – particularly, for speakers of minority languages – is neither as unconstrained nor as neutral as proponents of language shift suggest. It is at best a 'forced choice', propelled by wider forces of social, political, economic and *linguistic* inequality and discrimination (see also below).

The question one might then begin to explore from a more critical, pluralistic conception of language policy – and one that the work of Bourdieu directly illuminates – concerns the extent to which individuals should be allowed to benefit from the currency of a dominant language while also, at the same time, being allowed to 'stay put' with respect to their own minority language(s). In other words, we can legitimately ask to what extent the 'language replacement' ideology underlying the nationalist principle of cultural and linguistic homogeneity is necessary or justified. After all, as the political theorist, Kymlicka has argued, 'leaving one's culture [and language], while possible, is best seen as renouncing something to which one is reasonably entitled' (1995: 90).

With this key question in mind, let me turn finally to the wider social and political consequences of adopting this more nuanced, Bourdieusian, perspective on language and habitus/identity for the *field* of language policy. What might a more critical view of language policy, based on Bourdieu's theoretical understandings, potentially look like?

Directions for a Critical Approach to Language Policy – à la Bourdieu

It is, I hope by now, clear that the imperative of linguistic uniformity at the level of the nation state, the equation of majority languages with modernity and the related ideology of language replacement are all specific products of the (recent) history of nationalism. Comparable arguments about the pre-eminent role of English as the current international language, more often than not, simply extend these ideological principles to the global stage (cf. Phillipson 2003). And yet, it is also increasingly clear that, despite ongoing pressures to dispense with so-called minority languages (of whatever ilk), they remain important nonetheless for many of their speakers. It is these ongoing, often multilayered and hybrid language and identity connections that a more critical approach to language policy must first recognize and address, particularly in those multilingual contexts in which they are most evident (see, for example, Makoni and Pennycook 2007, Pavlenko and Blackledge 2004). Thus, Blommaert (2005), in his discussion of Tanzanian language policy and use, observes that 'the social environment of almost any individual would by definition be *polycentric*, with a wide range of overlapping and criss-crossing centres to which orientations need to be made, and evidently with multiple 'belongings' for individuals (often understood as 'mixed' or 'hybrid' identities')' (p. 394). Likewise, Canagarajah (2005), in discussing language use in Jaffna, Sri Lanka, comments: 'Not only are local identities hybrid (shaped by a mixture of English and Tamil) . . . they can also be fluid, shifting, and strategically renegotiated according to changing social contexts. Tamil identity has been defined differently through history' (p. 438).

However, the recognition of linguistic hybridity is only a necessary starting point, since a critical language policy approach must also acknowledge that historically associated languages continue often to hold considerable purchase for members of particular cultural or ethnic groups in their identity claims. Canagarajah again observes: 'Hybridity of identity doesn't change the fact that ethnicity and mother tongue have always been a potent force in community relations. . . . Change doesn't mean irrelevance or irreverence. Attachments to ethnicity and mother tongue are resilient, despite their limited value in pragmatic and material terms' (p. 439).

To say that language is not an inevitable feature of identity is thus *not* the same as saying it is unimportant. In other words, just because language is merely a contingent factor of identity does not mean it cannot (ever) be a *significant* or *constitutive* factor of identity. Bourdieu's conceptual understandings, discussed above – particularly, the embodied nature of linguistic *habitus*, and the relationship between language choice and constraint – clearly help us to address directly, rather than simply ignore, this dialectical tension. Holding onto this tension also helps to explain an apparent ongoing conundrum in the wider politics of language policy: the heightened saliency of language issues in many historical and contemporary political conflicts, particularly at the intrastate level (see Blommaert 1996, 1999, May 2008, Weinstein 1983, 1990). In these conflicts, particular languages clearly *are* for many people an important and constitutive factor of their individual and, at times, collective identities. This is so, *even* when holding onto such languages has specific negative social and political consequences for their speakers, most often via active discrimination and/or oppression.

Franco's Spain, or the ongoing plight of the Kurds in Turkey, are but two examples – there are numerous others.

The *will* to maintain historically associated languages in often highly oppressive contexts also problematizes in turn the notion of 'rational choice', discussed earlier. The assertion that speakers only make decisions on purely instrumentalist grounds, or at least that instrumental reasons are the only valid or rational choice available to minority language speakers, is at best one-sided, and at worst simply wrong. Specific groups may hold on tenaciously to a particular language precisely because greater functionality in another language is not, in itself, enough. Or if it is, the price for achieving it via that dominant (legitimate) language – given that it is usually at the specific *expense* of the other language – may be regarded as simply too high.

And this brings me to the final imperative of a critical language policy based on a Bourdieusian perspective: adopting a more pluralistic, inclusive approach to the public recognition and use of languages is actually crucial for *enhancing* social and political stability, rather than undermining it, as the political rhetoric of nationalism would have it. Indeed, as Fernand de Varennes argues, 'any policy favouring a single language to the exclusion of all others can be extremely risky . . . because it is then a factor promoting division rather than unification. Instead of integration, an ill-advised and inappropriate state language policy may have the opposite effect and cause a *levée de bouclier*' (de Varennes 1996: 91).

This, in turn, poses a central challenge for language policy in this current century – how to rethink nation states, and the identities therein, in more linguistically plural and inclusive ways in order to better represent the various and varied cultural and linguistic communities situated within them (cf. Parekh 2000). On this basis, one can argue that changing the language preferences of the state and civil society, or at least broadening them, would better reflect the diverse and legitimate linguistic interests of *all* those within them. Not only this, it could significantly improve the life chances of those minority individuals and groups who are presently disadvantaged in their access to, and participation in, public services, employment and education as a result of restrictive, majoritarian language policies (May 2008). Specific examples of critical language policy based on these premises, drawing explicitly on Bourdieu, include Ó Riagáin's (1997) analysis of Irish and Norton's (2000) exploration of the language choices of immigrant women in North America. And yet what is equally clear is the basic unwillingness evident in many national language policies to countenance this possibility – to continue to view the historical and ongoing minoritization of languages as, in Bourdieu's words, a 'game devoid of consequences'. This is unfortunate, not least because such a position simply reproduces, rather than contests, the static, closed and essentialist view of the nation state, as forever culturally and linguistically homogeneous, that is the product of nationalism. In the process, no account is taken of the historical contingency, arbitrariness and recency of this particular form of social and political organization – the diachronic view of language, espoused by Bourdieu, with which this chapter began.

Conclusion

But there is also cautious room for optimism. Research in language policy is increasingly exploring and unmasking its own ideological influences, along with its often deleterious consequences for minority language speakers (see Blommaert 1999, May 2008, Phillipson 2003, Ricento 2006, Schiffman 1996, Schmid 2001, Woolard 1998). There is also growing recognition of the need to explore language policy in relation not only to macro policy and rights' principles – a key concern of language rights' proponents – but also in direct relation to complex, mixed and fluid micro-linguistic contexts, that is, the need to engage with the complexities of everyday multilingualism. This is important because, as Canagarajah (2005) observes, '[p]eople negotiate language policies in their favour in their everyday life in micro-social domains' (p. 427). Following from this, Patrick (2005) has asserted that there is a need to develop 'a sociolinguistic framework that serves to link macro-level rights, legal and political discourse, and socio-cultural and economic processes to actual patterns of language use' (p. 371). This is increasingly beginning to occur. Addressing this potential disjuncture between macro sociolinguistic policies and microlinguistic contexts of use is a prominent feature of recent work in language policy. Such studies include the work of those already cited, such as Pavlenko and Blackledge (2004), Blommaert (2005), Canagarajah (2005), Patrick (2005) and Makoni and Pennycook (2007), as well as other important contributions, such as Freeland and Patrick (2004) and Blackledge (2005).

A key arena that has emerged here is the exploration of language use among and across domains – particularly, what might be said to comprise formal and informal language economies (cf. Heller 1999, Rampton 1995), and their implications for language policy. Ethnographic accounts of language policy are also increasingly to the fore (see McCarty 2010).

If such research continues and, more importantly, begins to influence actual language policy development, we may finally be able to address directly, and remediate, the linguistic and wider social harm that the politics of nationalism have inflicted on minority language groups. Certainly, Bourdieu's central insights discussed in this chapter provide us with the necessary conceptual tools to do so, – but, one might add, his wider academic, social and political activities as well. This is most evident in the last decade of his life, when he became increasingly committed in his role of public intellectual in engaging with, and shaping, public policy in more socially just ways, particularly in relation to ameliorating the negative effects on the poor and marginalized of an increasingly rampant globalization and capitalist global economy (Bourdieu 1998b, 2008a). While this later work extends far beyond language and linguistics, it continues to provide an exemplary illustration of just what can be achieved when the academic and policy fields (or markets) are specifically combined. Critical language policy scholars are increasingly recognizing the importance of this connection. As McGroarty observes, for example, 'advocates for positive language and education policies must constantly articulate the value of bilingualism [and multilingualism], and to be able to do so in varied terms that respond to a protean environment of public discussion' (2006: 5–6). Bourdieu's life and work shows us how.

Note

[1] Language planning and language policy are used interchangeably throughout this chapter.

Chapter 8

Language and Education

Cheryl Hardy

Introduction

This chapter builds on the theoretical discussion of Chapter 3 which considered Bourdieu's own approach to language and linguistic study. It focuses on how this approach can usefully inform the study of language and pedagogy. Here, Bourdieu's thinking tools – *habitus*, *capital* and *field* – are used to examine a number of distinct practical pedagogical settings in English classrooms and the language implications of each. Particular examples of classroom discourse are offered.

Part 1: Conventional Approaches to the Study of Classroom Language

In the first part of the chapter, conventional approaches to the study of classroom language such as those of Stubbs (1976), Mercer and Edwards (1981), Mercer (1995), Barnes (1976), Britton (1970) and Alexander (2001) are reconsidered from a Bourdieusian perspective. Differences between these approaches to language and pedagogy and Bourdieu's epistemological approach are highlighted and, in particular, the relational nature of Bourdieu's theoretical concepts.

   In any classroom, language is both the medium and the subject of students' learning. Consequently, the study of classroom language is fraught with issues concerning what constitutes pedagogic competence for students and their teachers; what it is that is recognized and valued at particular times and in particular classrooms as literary and linguistic competence. During the last 30 years, studies have demonstrated a wide variety of perspectives on classroom language: from the identification of different genres of classroom discourse, through a focus on teachers' use of language, to the analysis of the power relationships in classrooms between students, teachers and other agents (see among others, Flanders 1965, Heath 1983, Hicks 1995, Wenger 1999). Writing in the 1970s, Stubbs says of language learning that 'Pupils are judged bright or dim according to whether they interact appropriately, and as adults expect, in particular in sociolinguistic situations' (Stubbs 1976: 129). In other words, pupils' language competence is defined and recognized by the adults they meet at particular times and places. Some years later, but in a similar vein, Gee claimed that 'being literate' is 'a matter of using the "right" language in the "right" ways within particular discursive settings' (Gee 1996: 67). For Bourdieu, like both Gee and Stubbs, competence in language is to be understood as relational, dependent on both the linguistic dispositions of an individual (*linguistic habitus*) and the social and linguistic settings (*fields*) within which they function.

At about the time that Bourdieu was writing *Reproduction* (Bourdieu 1977a/1970), other authors (Barnes 1976, Britton 1970 for example) were examining classroom language interactions in some detail in relation to individual pupils and exhorting their readers to 'forget about teaching altogether' and 'to take time off to think about learning' (Barnes et al. 1969: 91). Here, the focus was almost exclusively on individual personal experience and linguistic use. While a pupil's socio-economic origin – their class – was open to discussion, the roles of significant individuals beyond the classroom, of particular institutions or of state policy were overlooked by these authors. In *Reproduction*, Bourdieu reinstated both institutions and the State, demonstrating their roles in structuring the *field* of education through the acquired dispositions (*habitus*) of dominant individuals including teachers. Other, more recent, studies have explored how students' classroom language is embedded within broader socio-cultural language use, particularly across social groups differentiated and often marginalized by language, culture or geography. Other contemporary researchers have been interested in how teachers' varying cultural backgrounds, 'preferred' interactional practices and ideological dispositions intersect and influence their teaching practices and their resulting structuring of classroom talk within a given school (for example, Grenfell 1998, 2004).

As Chapter 3 indicates, in *Reproduction* Bourdieu argued that any classroom is a site of inculcation into what is valued both linguistically and more generally in society: a site where the teacher's role is to show pupils how to use language in ways that are recognized by others and by institutions (Bourdieu 1977a/1970). In this book, he highlights the dual dependency of every definition of *linguistic capital* on other *field* participants, particularly the most powerful, and on legitimated *field* institutions. Since membership of the most dominant groups and the most powerful institutions varies over time, what acts as *field capital* – here linguistic – is specific to the time and place in which it is acquired. Pupils acquire *cultural capital*, which in this context is called linguistic competence, through the legitimation of their language practices by the adults they encounter – their teachers and family. Where the linguistic practices of the family match the language use promoted in school, children acquire *linguistic capital* which matches that of the most dominant in society – those who occupy positions in the *field* of power. Hence, the child from an educated family will be 'at home' with the school's view of language and will therefore be more easily educated or 'brighter'. Bourdieu sums this up when he writes that 'the informative efficiency of pedagogic communication is always a function of the receivers' linguistic competence' (Bourdieu 1977a/1970: 115). However, the language practices of the family do not always match the language practices endorsed by the school on behalf of the State. This is the case, for example, for the children of immigrant families or for children of poor and disadvantaged families. Bourdieu writes that, for many children from less educated families, 'The world of the classroom, where "polished" language is used, contrasts with the world of the family' (Bourdieu et al. 1994/1965: 9). These children, faced with conflicting linguistic practices at home and in school, have the double task of acquiring language appropriate for two markedly different field contexts. Contradictions like these early in life – contradictions which Bourdieu himself experienced – lead to what Bourdieu called a 'cleft habitus' (Bourdieu 2007/2004: 100), where the dispositions which a child develops as a result of early experiences in the home are at odds with the attitudes learnt through other experiences, most often at school. Since these early dispositions, in this case linguistic, are the most durable constituents of *habitus* (see Bourdieu 1977b/1972: 77), they continue to have an effect on an individual's behaviour, attitudes and social trajectory long after that individual has moved beyond the *field* setting which gave rise to the dispositions themselves. So does this differentiation occur in classrooms?

Mercer (1995) writes about three levels of analysis which he sees as necessary to describe and evaluate the talk which goes on in classrooms. These are:

- the linguistic – the talk as spoken text;
- the psychological – the talk as thought and action;
- the cultural – the nature of educational discourse and the kinds of reasoning which are valued by educational institutions (pp. 105–6)

Mercer's third level, the cultural, is very close to the Bourdieusian notion of pedagogical language – a form of *cultural capital* legitimated by educational institutions. However, Mercer's approach to classroom language pays little heed to the temporal, geographical or cultural contexts of classroom talk, and entirely omits reference beyond the field of education to a wider society which conditions values in the classroom. In contrast, Bourdieu avoids any consideration of the psychological in favour of the functional by asking what interests are served by using language in a particular way in a classroom setting, what is being recognized, what ignored and in what way this affects how students learn to reproduce the most valuable language forms.

In a contrasting approach, Alexander focused on a broad international context when he carried out a major survey of how primary age children are educated in different countries (see Alexander 2001). He discusses the practice of teaching in each country, placing his classroom observations and analysis of lesson interactions within an explicit cultural context. In this regard, his approach is much like Bourdieu's own – relational. Classroom language is here considered within its cultural setting, so that Alexander's work is in line with Bourdieu's edict that the 'sociologist always pays particular attention to individuals and to the concrete environment in which they are inserted' (Bourdieu 1999/1963: 13). Where Alexander's approach differs from Bourdieu's is in the absence of any consideration of the local and national institutions implicated in education in each country. In a similar vein, Alexander (2004) acknowledges the role of the learner's environment on their acquisition of linguistic competence, and in particular, discusses the effect of their social origins on children's early language development. He claims that 'children's access to opportunities for talk outside the classroom varies considerably, as does the quality and potency of the talk they encounter' (p. 18). In fact, he notes that, typically, middle-class children are encouraged by the adults they encounter, whereas children from less affluent homes are discouraged. Further, Alexander quotes an American study which found that, by the age of 4, a child from a professional background 'may have had nearly twice as many words addressed to it than a working class child, and over four times as many as the child on welfare' (see Hart and Risley 1996). Much earlier, and in the context of English schooling, Mercer wrote about the differential relationships between classroom language and the success of the advantaged and disadvantaged child (Mercer and Edwards 1981: 31). He offers the example of research (Tough 1977) into 'those uses of language which were thought to reflect complex thinking' and more significantly the finding that 'children's inadequate language is taken to reflect inadequate thinking' (p. 159). Thus, Bourdieu was not alone in realizing that a student's success in the classroom is conditioned by his or her linguistic competence, which in turn is shaped by early experiences at home and therefore by parents' and grandparents' own academic and linguistic skills. Early learning conditions how a child is able to learn in classrooms. However, Bourdieu goes further still and claims that 'educationally profitable *linguistic capital* constitutes one of the best hidden mediations through which the relationship (grasped by our tests) between social origin and scholastic achievement is set up' (Bourdieu 1977a/1970: 116). In other words, through an apparently objective process like testing, linguistic advantage, endowed on their children by educated parents, is transmuted into 'ability' or 'talent', and misrecognized as such within the school system. A recent study of pupils' attainment in England (DCSF 2009) shows that at age 16, the odds against students from the most deprived areas of the country achieving national standards are 6.4 times greater than their peers (p. 31). Similarly, students from poor families – eligible for Free School Meals at age 11 – are three times less likely to enter higher education than their peers (p. 25). These effects of social deprivation on scholastic achievement are not therefore historical phenomena, but of practical and political significance to individuals and the wider society. Since language is the medium of this social differentiation, I shall now turn to examine how this misrecognition actually happens in classrooms.

Part 2: Language Use in Educational Settings

The second part of the chapter focuses on actual empirical examples of language use in educational settings and will develop further the practical analyses of classroom interactions undertaken by Grenfell (see Grenfell and James 1998, Grenfell 2004b) through the application of a three-level method of analysis, used previously in socio-cultural settings (see Grenfell and Hardy 2003, 2006, 2007, Hardy 2009). Discussion highlights how this method was adapted to study pedagogical language in classroom settings in England in terms of individuals, institutions and the broader *field* contexts of language and education.

Bourdieu's approach to researching an object of study, be it language, cultural consumption, photography or poverty, is always relational in nature. It is an investigation of the *patterns* in how things occur *together* rather than a search for causal factors for events, including language episodes. Bourdieu's logic of practice serves to connect the history of the context with the thing studied and with the participating institutions and people. The approach is essentially an empirical one – the drawing of conclusions from correlative data analyses (see LeRoux and Rouanet 2004 among others) rather than a testing of a pre-existing theory. Based on his large-scale statistical invest-igations, Bourdieu describes *three levels of analysis* (Bourdieu and Wacquant 1992b). So what are they?

The first considers the relationships between the most dominant, influ-ential and richest groups in society (the *field* of power) and different and distinct *fields* of activity such as education, art, commerce, politics, religion, etc.

The second level analyses the interrelationships between significant individuals in the *field* studied and the institutions with which they are associated.

The third level looks at particularly significant individuals and their socio-economic characteristics and inherited dispositions – that is, their *habitus.*

A Bourdieusian analysis is, therefore, seeking to reach a representation of the functioning of any social phenomenon as it encompasses both the objective – *field* structures and power relations between the most domin-ant and the dominated and the more personal – and subjective individual characteristics and dispositions of those within a social space. Both per-spectives, and the relationships between them, are necessary to gain as rich and realistic a picture of the object of study and its functioning as is possible.

So what does this look like for language and education?

In what follows, pedagogical language is considered as it occurs in practice through a number of extracts of classroom dialogues and associ-ated data about teachers and their context. What is sought is a picture of what constitutes specific *field capital* in classroom settings and how language functions to achieve what we call teaching and learning. The case examples discussed here were chosen to show how this approach might be applied to different *field* contexts and to explore the usefulness of these thinking tools in relation to educational and linguistic activities at specific times and places, and perhaps to find from these particular cases some invariant features. As Bourdieu writes, 'a particular case that is well constructed ceases to be particular' (Bourdieu and Wacquant 1992b: 77).

The first example reconsiders a short extract of classroom dialogue previously published (see Grenfell and James 1998: 85) and focuses on how language was used to support students' learning mathematics. The second case example considers younger children who are learning to read. Here, language is both the subject and the medium for students' learning. The third case example focuses on a class of 9- and 10-year-olds who are develop-ing their writing skills.

Case Example 1: A Maths Classroom Revisited

The first case example is based on an extract of the classroom interactions in a mathematics lesson (Edwards 1994). It was published over a decade ago and was discussed from a Bourdieusian viewpoint in Grenfell and James (1998: 85f). Here, the dialogue is revisited to demonstrate how to undertake a Bourdieusian analysis where the *field* context, *field* institutions *and field* participants are viewed in relation to one another – that is, a three-level analysis.[1]

The lesson took place in a secondary school and was a practical session for 12–13-year-olds investigating the volume of a cuboid. The lesson was one of a series of lessons on area and volume undertaken over a period of 2 weeks. This extract took place near the beginning of a lesson in the second week.

1	Teacher:	*What I want to know is . . . and what you are going to calculate*
2		*. . . while I'm bringing round the Sellotape is . . . how big your box is.*
3	Pupils:	*Area . . . It's the area.*
4	Teacher:	*How big (emphasizes) . . . (writes on board)*
5	Pupil 1:	*It's the area.*
6	Teacher:	*Not the area.*
7	Pupil 2:	*It's the perimeter.*
8	Teacher:	*Not the perimeter . . . The Volume.*
9	Pupil 3:	*How much it contains.*
10	Teacher:	*How much it contains, exactly that.*
11		*The volume .*
12	Teacher:	*Right.*
13		*What I want to know is*
14		*'how many small cubes you could put in here' . . . right*
15		*. . . so the answer to 'how big?' . . . is . . .*
16		*. . . how many small cubes . . . can you get in here?*
17		*If you want the proper name for them,*
18		*they are called cubic centimetres, aren't they?* (Edwards 1994)

Grenfell's discussion of this extract centred on the relationship between the teacher and students, and was situated within the dominant pedagogy of that time, a pedagogy associated with Vygotsky – in particular, scaffolding. The teacher was setting up a problem-solving task by asking questions, for example *how big? how many small cubes?*, rather than by giving instructions.

However, the nature and quality of the linguistic exchanges demonstrate the structures of the pedagogical situation, where the teacher alone has the power of legitimation: see, for example, Line 6 where the teacher asserts 'No, not the area' or Line 12 where she affirms a pupil's response with 'Right'. Here are structures which necessarily imply *symbolic violence* as students are being 'taught' to reproduce established meanings – mathematical *doxa*. This discussion highlighted the curious linguistic structure of the extract where it is the 'pupils who are first to present the *legitimate language*, the authorized vocabulary of the field' (ibid). Grenfell also noted how the teacher was knowingly 'out of line' with the pedagogic practice in this school. Study of the whole lesson transcript shows the students' engagement with the practical task they were set, and strongly suggests that despite its 'deviance' this would have been judged to be a good lesson at that time.

A re-examination of this extract in terms of Bourdieu's three levels outlined above requires analysis of individuals' *habitus* (level 3), their relationships to *field* institutions (level 2) and a broader perspective of the inter-relationships of *fields* and the *field* of power (level 1). The epistemological return from this analytical method is the possibility of understanding, at a particular time and place, how the objective and systemic structures of the educational *field* gave rise to one individual's subjective classroom practice: that is, the possibility of a more complete understanding of the pedagogic and linguistic significance of the classroom interactions.

The **first level** of Bourdieusian analysis therefore addresses the question: How does the *field* of education relate to the *field* of power? In 1994, when this lesson took place, the *field* of education in the UK was undergoing a process of change with increasing national regulation through state bodies such as National Curriculum Council, Standards and Assessment Agency and Department of Education and Employment. The regular inspection of schools had recently been moved from Her Majesty's Inspectorate (HMI) to inspectors trained and accredited by the Office for Standards in Teaching and Education (OfSTED). These structures were significantly mediated by local regulation through local education authorities that were funded to support curriculum and pedagogic initiatives in schools, develop assessment processes and provide in-service training for teachers and senior managers in schools. Increasingly often, local authority advisers trained as OfSTED inspectors and undertook inspections. In 1992, the Department of Education Circular, 9/92 (DfES 1992), introduced national regulations for the length, format and organization of all initial teacher training courses including those taught in previously autonomous university departments of education. In other words, the form and exchange rates of *capital* within the *field* of education were increasingly determined by the state and local authority rather than by the headteacher and governors of an individual school.

For teachers in the school discussed here, a local authority subject adviser was an agent for legitimation, and a source of both *economic capital* through funding for classroom projects and of *cultural capital* which could lead to promotion. Why is this relevant to the case example here? The teacher featured in this dialogue was previously employed by the local authority in an advisory capacity, working with teachers in this school. She would be seen to occupy a dominant *field* position.

The **second level** of Bourdieusian analysis addresses the question: What are the important relationships between institutions and individuals that are active in the *field* studied? For this case example, three institutions, the secondary school, the local university and the government Department for Education and Employment (DFEE), are central to an understanding of the functioning of the *field* at this particular time and place. Each institution has significant relationships with different *field* participants and to varying degrees. The school was a long established and successful comprehensive school for girls aged 11–16 years. The school was also set in a respectable lower-middle class area of a large dockland town. As the only non-denominational girls' school in the town, the school was the preferred choice for many Pakistani families. In other words, the school was a key institution for its pupils, particularly those in the lesson studied. There was a large university within a few miles of the school and strong links between the two institutions. A secure teacher-training partnership had been developed between the school and the university's Faculty of Education. Many of the school staff had studied at the university as trainee teachers or as Master's students. University tutors were regular visitors to the school and knew the head teacher, deputies and many of the teaching staff. The school was often included in small-scale research projects undertaken by university tutors. It was therefore an appropriate host for university tutors returning to the classroom for a term's recent and relevant teaching experience. Here, a highly legitimate institution had a strong relationship with the school's staff as a source of consecrated *cultural capital*, for example, qualifications and an even stronger relationship with the teacher of the lesson studied, since as a university lecturer she was known to school staff as an individual with the 'power' of consecration.

As already indicated, the third key institution in this example was the local authority: a large and successful one, which was able to fund school-based innovations and provide an extensive professional training programme for teachers and school managers. This local education authority deployed teams of its advisers to inspect its schools. Staff associated with the local education authority, including the teacher in this dialogue, were to be treated with circumspection. In other words, the teacher was strongly linked to a legitimate and legitimating institution – the local education authority.

It was *cultural capital* from the teacher's clear association with legitimated institutions – the local university and the local authority – which gave her relatively easy access to the school and allowed her to 'deviate' from the established practice within the mathematics department without incurring negative sanctions. Consequently, an important element of understanding how this interaction came about is an understanding of both the relationship of the teacher with the school as an institution and her stronger relationship with more legitimated institutions, recognized by the school as such: a university and a local authority.

The **third level** of Bourdieusian analysis asks: What can be said about the individuals involved in this lesson? What was their **habitus**? The 32 students in this class were 13-year-olds: all girls; almost all hard working and well motivated; about a third of whom spoke English as a second language; many of whom were of Pakistani origin. They were in a middle set for mathematics – in other words, they were of 'average' achievement. In the school context, therefore, this group of girls were not particularly well endowed with *capital* based on their mathematical achievement. More significantly, the dual language competence of many of the Asian girls was not recognized by the school as *linguistic capital* but was seen as an obstacle to learning – as the absence of *pedagogic capital*. Language and English technical language in particular were constantly at stake in their lessons because the distinctive character of *habitus* of these students was such that language competence was crucial to how pedagogic competence was constructed in this school context.

The class teacher was a qualified and experienced mathematics teacher who had previously worked as a Local Authority Advisory teacher (strong legitimate *pedagogical capital*). She was, in fact, a university lecturer in mathematics education who was spending 3 months teaching in a school which was used for initial teacher-training students. She was collecting data for a research project about lesson planning and initial teacher training. She therefore had a large volume of *highly consecrated cultural capital* from her association with a university and a lower volume of less valuable capital overall through a much weaker association with the school – a less legitimate institution.

Through this detailed consideration of the three levels of analysis and their interrelationships, Grenfell's analysis (op. cit.) of this lesson extract is extended by setting it within the broader *field* context of the particular place and time, and in relation to the *field* participants and associated institutions. From this short lesson transcript, it can be seen that the *pedagogical capital* of the teacher herself is reflected in her use of language, while the students' more problematic *linguistic capital* has shaped the interest of both teacher and students in using subject specialist terms appropriately. See, for example, Lines 4–11 of the extract where the meaning of 'volume' is negotiated between teacher and pupils. Further, the maverick character of this part of the lesson is permissible because the volume and consecration of the *capital* configuration of the teacher's *habitus* supports a dominant *field* position. In this way, a detailed Bourdieusian analysis offers a more complete understanding of the functioning of language in this particular classroom. In the next section, a more recent case example is analysed and discussed from a Bourdieusian perspective.

Case Example 2: Classroom Language in a Primary School Literacy Lesson

The second example is based on the pedagogical interactions of a group of six pupils and their teacher recorded in the summer of 2006. The pupils are between 8 and 9 years old, in Year 4 of a primary school in the south-west of England. The lesson was observed and recorded by a researcher who later discussed the lesson with the teacher. This analysis therefore uses an extract from the transcript of teacher/pupil interactions together with material from the follow-up interview between teacher and researcher (Fisher 2007). My own later discussion with the researcher and the researcher's evaluative notes about the teaching also inform the analyses.

An extract from an episode of guided reading.

Three girls and three boys chosen by the teacher as more able readers are sitting in a row on a bench facing an interactive whiteboard. The group are discussing a novel about a fantasy world: an activity identified by the National Literacy Strategy (NLS) (DfES 1998) as appropriate for the spring term of Year 4. The extract presented here takes place about quarter of an hour into an hour-long lesson, the length of a lesson recommended by the NLS (ibid.).

Line 1   Teacher: Let's look at the next question.
2   *What clues are there that Orin is not an ordinary boy?*

3		*What clues are there that Orin is not an ordinary boy?*
		Angela?
4	*Angela:*	*That he began to walk down the wall?*
5	*Teacher:*	*Yes. At the beginning there, he's walking down the wall.*
6		*That doesn't normally happen. John, d'you think*
7		*. . . something else that he's not an ordinary boy?*
8	*John:*	*Six inches shorter?*
9	*Teacher:*	*OK, yes, so he's short, isn't he?*
10		*So that's a bit . . . is it six inches shorter, so he isn't an ordinary*
11		*boy; is that the only bit of information? Does that tell us that he*
12		*isn't ordinary?*
13		*'Cos we've got different heights in our class, some shorter than*
14		*others and they're perfectly ordinary. So . . .*
15		*we've got walking down the wall, the fact that he's shorter . . .*
16		*Other things? Steven?*
17	*Steven:*	*Erm, he doesn't know what 'a break' means?*
18	*Teacher:*	*He doesn't know what 'a break' means.*
19		*Can we find out more than that?*
20	*Martin:*	*He thinks a 'holiday' is a room?*
21	*Teacher:*	*He thinks a 'holiday' might be a room.*
22		*OK. So Orin isn't an ordinary boy. He's something strange.*

(Teacher shows pupils a photocopied page with an illustration).

23		*Now interesting . . . by looking at that you could tell me that*
24		*Orin isn't an ordinary boy.*
25		*Now I'm going to show you, and you're going to . . .*
26		*how do you know Orin isn't an ordinary boy?*
27	*Angela:*	*Because of the way he looks in the picture.*
28	*Teacher:*	*OK, because of the way he looks in the picture.*
29		*Now we . . . the text we looked at this morning . . .*
30		*somebody said 'Oh I can tell it's Africa because the people are*
31		*black.'*
32		*But we said that's not true. We can't use pictures to tell us*
33		*what the story says.*
34		*We are beyond that now. We can't rely on the picture.*

35	*We're too clever for that. The pictures illustrate the story,*
36	*but the pictures aren't what the story is saying.*
37	*No, we need to pick out, like we did, that he is walking down*
38	*the wall, he was six inches shorter, ok,*
39	*that he doesn't know what a 'hobby' is,*
40	*he doesn't know what 'a break' is.*
41	*You have to pick things out of the text to make sure you know*
42	*what . . . that you understand what the text is about.*

(Extracted from Fisher 2007)

The lesson shows the teacher asking open questions (Lines 2, 11, 19) to his students, who are struggling to find answers that the teacher judges to have value – that is, that contribute to understanding the text. He asks 'What clues are there that Orin is not an ordinary boy?' (Lines 2, 31). Angela, in particular, gives two answers (Lines 4, 27), which the teacher then takes up, for example, towards the end of the extract (Lines 34–40) where he explains why Angela's suggestion that the picture gives information is an over-generalization. He uses this question to emphasize that it is linguistic information which is valued here (Line 41). This extract can be interpreted as an example of a teacher inculcating into pupils the ways of interpreting text which are accepted in the broader social *field*. He is 'helping' his pupils to develop dispositions which contribute positively to their success in the classroom. As constituents of *habitus*, these dispositions are also likely to enhance future position-taking in the *field* of education and more broadly. It is the teacher's imposition of a particular way of understanding the classroom which both constitutes *symbolic violence* for Bourdieu and also provides students with *linguistic capital* with value in the *field*.

Although the questions in this extract are open, for example, 'Can we find out more about that?', the researcher felt that closed questions, which were content-based, predominated in the lesson as a whole and that pupils simply focused on identifying correct answers. She indicates that this 'guided reading' session did not conform to NLS recommendations where teaching during guided reading 'should focus increasingly on guided silent reading with questions to direct or check up on reading to meet text level objectives' (DfES 1998: 12). The researcher writes that 'There was very little which the National Curriculum or NLS would value in the lesson' (Fisher 2007). Thus, behind the initial analysis of this example lies an apparent contradiction: the researcher who observed the lesson described it as 'awful', but, at the same time, she confirms that the teacher is well thought of in the school. How can this be?

Further light is thrown on these interactions by an extract from the discussion between the teacher and the observer:

Line 1	Observer:	Do you see any particular value in guided reading?
2	Teacher:	*Well. Yes. It's a good opportunity to push the children to*
3		*understand inferences in the text.*
4		*That's not always possible with the whole class when some of*
5		*them are still reading for coding.*
6	Observer:	*How have you been able to develop your work on inference?*
7	Teacher:	*I went on an excellent course. It really made me think about my*
8		*questioning. If you don't ask higher-order questions, those*
9		*about inference, they can't see it in the text. I'm not saying*
10		*SATs (Standardized Assessment Tests) are everything, but they*
11		*do need to understand what the question's asking for.*
12		*I try to, I try to make sure I teach them strategies for*
13		*understanding what the question means.*
14	Observer:	*I noticed you aren't afraid to say 'no'*
15		*when the answer is wrong.*
16		*Do you feel, erm, do you think that is important?*
17	Teacher:	*Yes. Because you aren't doing them any favours if you don't.*
18		*Of course, with the less able readers, it's important to find*
19		*other ways of saying they're wrong. I mean, you don't want to*
20		*de-motivate them or undermine their confidence.* (Extracted from Fisher 2007)

This discussion indicates that the teacher was intending to develop 'reading for inference' (Line 2) with these 'better readers' – a skill he sees as crucial to success in the national standardized tests taken at age 11. When he states that 'I try to make sure I teach them strategies for understanding what the question means' (Lines 12/13), he confirms that he is indeed intending to work within national pedagogical regulations – a prudent position for a young teacher with little *symbolic capital* and a dominated *field* position. The National Curriculum for English (DfES 1999) identifies 'beginning to use inference and deduction' as a target for reading which is appropriate for all pupils at age 11. The teacher has therefore chosen a very challenging target for his 9-year-old able readers. He claims to differentiate the approach he takes with 'more able readers' like these pupils – a direct and challenging one – from more supportive responses he feels are needed with 'less able readers' (Lines 4/5, 18–20). Despite the researcher reservations, the teacher is indeed trying to match his approach to the learning needs of his students – a stance advocated by NLS (DCSF 2007c).

What would a Bourdieusian analysis of this scenario offer? And, might this throw further light on the contrasting views of these classroom interactions? As indicated in the earlier example, there are three steps to such an analysis: first, the relationships between the *field* in question and the *field* of power are examined; second, the relationships between these participants and the *field* institutions are considered; and third, the people involved are analysed in relation to their *dispositions* and histories – their *habitus*.

The **first** question to be addressed is then: How can the *field* of education be seen to relate to the *field* of power in this example?

The process of increasing regulation in the *field* of education which began in the earlier 1990s (as noted in the above example) had continued in the intervening period so that, by 2006, curriculum and classroom practice were largely controlled by central government. New government agencies had been established, for example, the Training and Development Agency (TDA) and Qualifications and Curriculum Agency (QCA). OfSTED now had a dominant role in determining practice through inspection in schools, in higher education teacher training and in local authorities. Commercial institutions, such as The National Strategies/Capita, had bid successfully for training contracts and acted on behalf of the Department of Education in providing guidance, training and national evaluation of practice in primary schools in England. Consequently, the role of local authorities in the curriculum was greatly decreased so that they were often becoming simply conduits for funding to schools. Primary school practice in language teaching was shaped by the work of National Strategy consultants, and by detailed guidance from the NLS for a standard lesson structure, generic lesson plans and detailed progression guidance through national assessment criteria. The term 'guided reading' was one component of the recommended lesson structure for literacy. This changed *field* structure now gave rise to differently constituted *field* structures where *capital* derived from local authorities was much less valuable, but *capital* derived from the new national organizations, for example NLS, supported newly created and dominant *field* positions.

As in the first example, the **second level** of a Bourdieusian analysis addresses the question: What are the important relationships between institutions and individuals that are active in the field studied?

As before, the *field* participants here – the teacher, the researcher and the students – are related to several different institutions:

A primary school in the south-west of England where the teacher was employed and which considered him to be a successful teacher (*cultural capital* derived locally from the school) and which the researcher visited.

A local teacher training college in the south-west of England where the teacher had trained (institutionally based *cultural capital*) and where the researcher was employed (*cultural capital* derived from a consecrated institution).

The NLS, which set the national parameters for teaching literacy, in this case for reading, for the school and for the teacher. NLS occupied a dominant *field* position at this time, a position highly consecrated by its association with the national State, but nonetheless, essentially commercially based. The observer here had a particularly strong relationship with the NLS since she had previously been employed as a local NLS consultant (nationally consecrated *cultural capital*). At the time of the lesson considered here, she was engaged in NLS funded initiatives within the college (locally and nationally consecrated *cultural capital*). In the above discussion extract, the teacher makes reference to a 'course' – training provided by a local NLS consultant.

To a lesser extent, national bodies such as QCA and OfSTED are also influential in this example because of their regulatory role on both the primary school (the teacher) and the training college (the researcher): QCA as responsible for the national Standardised Assessment Tests (SATs); OfSTED as arbiters of the quality of teaching, curriculum and partnership for schools and initial teacher training.

The **third** perspective of the Bourdieusian analysis again is provided by addressing the question: Who are the participants and what can be said about their histories and dispositions (*habitus*)? In this example, this information is offered in tabular form.

Table 8.1 shows that 'geography' is significant to the *capital* configurations (*habitus*) of the *field* participants in this example. When it is derived from highly legitimate institutions in the national *field*, the *capital* accrued by the participants is relatively valuable to participants in their struggles for desirable *field* positions. When *capital* is derived from local, less legitimate institutions it is of most value in the local sub-field.[2] The researcher, a college tutor, has accumulated a large part of her *capital* from NLS,

Table 8.1 Habitus constituents of participants

Habitus	Students	Teacher	Observer
Age	8–9 years old	20+	50+
Location	Live in town in the south-west of England	Lives and works in the south-west of England	Lives and works in the south-west of England
Highest qualification	KS1 SATs exams	Undergraduate degree in Education Qualified teacher status	Undergraduate degree in Education Qualified teacher status Master's degree in Education Studying for doctorate at Exeter
Employment		Employed as Year 4 class teacher in Junior school	Employed as Senior Lecturer in Higher Education Institution
Previous experiences		Studied at higher education institution where observer works	Employed locally as National Strategy Literacy consultant
Other marks of distinction	Identified by teacher as able readers	Seen as good teacher by school	Involved in Early Reading project funded by National Strategies
Summary	Dominated field positions Cultural capital as able readers In process of accruing cultural capital from successful SATs exams	Dominant field position in school, but dominated position nationally - Locally based cultural capital from school - Institutional CC from college (national qualifications)	Dominant field position derived from national and local capital - Institutional CC from qualifications - Nationally based CC from association with highly legitimated institution: NLS - Locally based CC from association with legitimate institution: college

a highly legitimated national institution. Her qualifications, particularly her study for a doctorate, provided her with institutional *cultural capital* associated with a nationally legitimated educational institution. Her present employment as a tutor in a local college provides additional *cultural capital* – legitimated within the local sub-field, but of less value in the national *field*. The teacher, on the other hand, has *habitus* which is highly dependent on locally based *capital*, either from within school (his head teacher's approval) or from a local training college (qualifications). The students here are also accumulating locally based *capital* from their teacher's recognition that they are able readers – *linguistic capital*. Since they are working towards SATs examinations when they are 11, success with this will bring their first nationally recognized *cultural capital*.

The apparent contradiction between the evidence of the lesson extract and the researcher's view in judging the 'worth' of this lesson is explained in part by the differing strength of relationship of the teacher and the researcher with the national *field* and the more local sub-field: the researcher's *habitus* is high in nationally based *capital* while the teacher's *habitus* is based firmly in the local *field* – his school and local college. It is in his *interest* (see Grenfell 2008) to accrue local *capital* through his head teacher's approval when his pupils succeed rather than seek nationally based *capital* through strict adherence to the latest national guidance, for example NLS guidance on guided reading. In contrast, the researcher has achieved a dominant position in the local sub-field by conforming to and promoting NLS approaches.

Case Example 3: Guided Writing with 9- and 10-Year-Olds

The next case example is of a literacy lesson[3] focusing on improving the writing of a class of 9- and 10-year-olds (Year 5). There are 23 boys and 12 girls in the class, working with a teacher and a teaching assistant. The extract is taken from near to the beginning of an hour-long lesson. The students sit at tables and face their teacher in the front of the room where an interactive whiteboard displays the text of an e-mail from a friend who is visiting another country.

Line 1	Teacher:	Because today we are going to be writing an email,
2		*I thought it would be really nice for you to read one first. (Reads out e-mail)*
3	*Teacher:*	*'Mrs Harrison has told me so much about you that I thought I'd*
4		*say hello from China. I am just in my fourth and last week here*
5		*and I've been extremely busy all the time . . .*
6		*There are so many other difference but I haven't got the time to*
7		*tell you them all as I have got to go now or I'll miss my train.*
8		*Take care and be good for Mrs. Harrison. Love Elisa.'*

9	Teacher:	*With your partner I would like you to come up with three things*
10		*that you have noticed about this email. Off you go.* (*Pupils talk in pairs*)
11		*Tell me what you noticed about this email because it's kind of a*
12		*letter and we've done lots of letters this term*
13		*but it's very different to the ones we wrote.*
14		*What did you notice Student 3?*
15	Student 3:	*It's got brackets.*
16	Teacher:	*It's got brackets, so it's got lots of . . . ?*
17	Student 3	*Punctuation*
18	Teacher:	*Well done, good. Anything else though? Student 4?*
19	Student 4:	*She's used everyday language not 'Yours sincerely, Elisa'.*
20		*She's like just used 'Love Elisa'.*
21	Teacher:	*It's a bit more familiar, isn't it?*
22		*So she's informal rather than that formal language that we*
23		*used when we were writing our persuasive letter. Good point.*
24		*Student 5, what have you noticed?*
25	Student 5:	*They are quite short.*
26	Teacher:	*That's the point.*
27		*They are quite short, they get straight to the point. Well done.* (DCSF 2007b)[1]

This short extract has some characteristics in common with the previous extract: the teacher's questions are open ones, for example, 'What did you notice . . . ?' (Line 14), 'Anything else?' (Line 18), while the students' answers are short and factual, for example, 'Punctuation' (Line 17). The teacher then confirms the correctness of each response by repeating the response or directly by saying 'Well done' (Lines 18, 27). The teacher is clearly in control of the dialogue and what is to be valued. She is in the dominant position and, by legitimizing her student's answers (or not), she teaches her pupils how to 'accrue symbolic capital' through their responses.

What does this extract look like when analysed using a Bourdieusian method? Since this lesson took place in 2006/2007, an analysis of the relationship of the *field* of education to the *field* of power, **level 1**, will parallel that given above for case example 2. At this time, central government and its institutions, particularly the Department of Education and the National Strategies determined both curricular content and teaching methods recommended to schools and teachers. In fact, the lesson considered here is presented on the web site of the Department of Children, Schools and Families (DCSF) as part of training materials for teachers which exemplify how to improve writing (DCSF 2007b).

So what can be said of the key relationships between *field* institutions and *field* participants in this example (**level 2**)?

As before, the school is one of the significant institutions, since it is the prime site for both students and teacher. The school is described as

a one-form entry voluntary aided, mixed primary school situated in a suburban area drawing mainly on the local parish and some neighbouring parishes. During the past two years the school has actively reviewed its teaching and learning using the Primary Framework, developing units of work that incorporate the effective use of speaking and listening, drama, ICT, success criteria and peer review. (DCSF 2007a: 31)

This description reveals the nature of the *field capital* in this context – peer review, using the Primary Framework (DCSF 2007a) as active review of teaching and learning – but it also points clearly to other undisclosed participants who have made these judgements. It is these agents, most probably Local Authority consultants and National Strategy regional advisers, who hold the power of consecration for the school and the teacher. These advisers, who are empowered to recognize and claim as legitimate the practice which is recorded in this extract and in the video clips which accompany it, are associated with the same State institutions that played a part in structuring the *field* in earlier examples. The age and degree of legitimation of each institution determine the value of *capital* derived from association with it. Thus, the agents and institutions in this example form a clear hierarchy which reflects the overall structure of the *field* of education at that time: National Strategy advisers are able to legitimate the judgements and practice of local authority consultants who are able to judge the value of the practice of teachers who, in turn, make judgements about the achievements of their students. This hierarchy is reflected in the transcript itself where students' speech is recorded only when they are spoken to and the teacher breaks from the lesson narrative to tell us – her audience – about what she is trying to do. A narrator, representing a slightly sinister absent authority, interposes evaluative comments to ensure that the teachers for whom this video and its transcript are intended recognize what they are to value. An example is:

> *Narrator: Writing for a real audience is important. The teacher here makes use of an email sent to the class by a friend who is visiting another country.* (op. cit.)

What can be said about the participants' experiences and their dispositions (**level 3**)? In this example, relatively little is known about the school, teacher and pupils who are presented anonymously on the DCSF web site. However, the video reveals a young, energetic and confident teacher who talks with an educated but regional accent. Her teaching assistant is slightly older and a bit less confident, as befits a 'junior colleague'. The students are wearing school uniform and are articulate. In other words, the participants reflect their socio-cultural context – a small, oversubscribed suburban primary school. However, it is the 'hidden' participants, in this example, who chose this classroom and this lesson to represent good practice, who occupy the most dominant *field* positions through their close association with national educational institutions. The meaning and value of this lesson are thus clearly determined by representatives of a government agency, The National Strategy, through their choices and their decisions about how to present the video.

Further, it is policy makers and politicians – from the *field* of power rather than the *field* of education – who provide structure to the *field* of education itself by establishing and supporting policies and institutions to support it. Just as politicians and policies and educational institutions change, so do the values of linguistic and pedagogical *capital*. Here, the temporal nature of *capital* is revealed. At the present time, the demise of the National Strategies has been announced, a consequence of the credit crunch. Changes are inevitable, first to the structure of the *field* of education and its major institutions, and later, to what is valued in the classroom itself.

It is only by examining at particular times and places the linguistic and pedagogical interactions of individual teachers and their students within this complex network of their interrelationships with local and national institutions, and the position of the *field* of education itself in relation to the *field* of power, that we will understand as fully as possible how classroom dialogue functions as it does. As these three case examples show, Bourdieu's theory of practice and in particular a three-level method of analysis yield rich insights into how pupils, teachers and associated advisers and researchers talk to and with each other as they do. The final section of this chapter offers a brief summary of the theoretical and practical implications of adopting a Bourdieusian methodology to studying language and pedagogy in classroom contexts, and suggests ways in which this approach might be developed further.

Part 3: Concluding Thoughts

As shown in these examples, a Bourdieusian analysis requires a wider range of data than a purely linguistic one, but the dividends for the researcher are that richer and more complex representations of the pedagogical and linguistic functioning of classroom interactions in relation to their settings can be achieved. As described in Chapter 2, Bourdieu's theory of practice is a dynamic one, and so is well suited to the *field* of education where change is not only frequent but endemic. The broader socio-political *field* itself is open to continual change, and structures and restructures the *field* of education, so that any Bourdieusian analyses are, of course, specific to particular times and places, as is the case with my examples. Educational institutions do change over time since their continued existence and degree of consecration in relation to one another must vary in step with State policy.

The relational nature of Bourdieu's approach ensures that the personal experiences and histories of individuals, whatever their ages, are seen in the light of the socio-cultural context at that time. These two are not connected directly but are mediated through their relationships with institutions key to the functioning of the *field* of education. Thus, a study of *field* institutions is both a crucial and distinguishing feature of any Bourdieusian analysis, in particular of the functioning of language in education.

I have argued that linguistic competence in the context of classroom is an amalgam of *pedagogical capital* and *linguistic capital*: both are always at stake in classrooms. In the case examples here, and in every Bourdieusian analysis, the form this *capital* takes is specific to the *field* at a particular time and place. For the participants in these examples, it was their associations with particular institutions – schools, colleges, local authorities and the National Strategies – which gave rise to the variously legitimated *capital* that were powerful constituents of their *habitus*. The institutions, which are the sources of these *capitals*, structure and are in turn structured by the experiences of the *field* participants. In the first example, the teacher/researcher had accrued the legitimated *capital* from dominant institutions – local authority and university – which allowed her to be a 'maverick'. In the second example, the researcher had accrued a high proportion of her *capital* from a government agency – the NLS – and this structured her reading of the lesson she observed. In the third example, the direct intervention of anonymous participants from the NLS had chosen the teacher to show to others what 'pedagogical capital' would look like in a classroom. Among the hidden participants in these examples is, of course, the author herself whose own position with the field[5] will condition the analyses offered. See Chapter 9 where *participant objectivation* is discussed in further detail. As I have found in cultural settings, an investigation of the key *field* institutions at play, this time in classroom language contexts within the *field* of education, is perhaps the best starting point for any and every Bourdieusian analysis, since institutions provide the linkage between individuals and the field of power.

Bourdieu's approach is an empirical one – based on data from particular times and places and on identified individuals and institutions. This three-level method is iterative so that each level is explored successively and may be revisited a number of times (see Hardy 2009 for further discussion). As a better understanding of a situation begins to emerge from the data, it is always tempting to over-interpret what can be said about a particular case. Generalization from such small-scale studies as have been offered here would not be defensible, but speculation is appropriate provided it is recognized as such. What such analyses always offer is a fertile source of further questions about how language functions in classrooms at different times and places.

What remains to be done is twofold: first, to continue this investigation of Bourdieu's logic of practice in relationship to classrooms in order to refine how best to use this approach in these language contexts; and second, to amass a variety of studies of classroom language analysed from a Bourdieusian perspective so as to understand more fully the nature of the insights which this analytical approach can offer, and how it can best be deployed to expand our understanding of how and why classroom language works as it does.

Notes

[1] The lesson transcript has been supplemented by additional data which were collected at the time the lesson was taught. This includes information about the class, the school and curriculum policy at that time. National policy documents used in the analysis are referenced in the text.

[2] A primary school in the south-west of England is at some considerable distance from London and from the centre of the national field of education. It is not

unusual for practices to be particularly slow to change in relatively rural areas like this.

3 Video extracts from the lesson are available at http://nationalstrategies.standards. dcsf.gov.uk/node/85981

4 Viewing the video shows that the text as presented in this extract has been tidied up to remove hesitations, repetitions, etc.

5 Over several decades, I have been employed in schools as a teacher, in higher education as a lecturer and in local authorities as an adviser – the very institutions which are discussed in my analyses.

Part III

Towards a Science of Language and Linguistic Study

Part III includes just one chapter entitled 'Towards a Science of Language and Linguistic Study'. It begins by revisiting the ways in which language features across Bourdieu's work, both as an object of study itself, and as his own language use in the theory of practice he developed. This discussion leads to questions of methodology. It is constructed around three principal sections, each of which might be seen as being an essential part of approaching a Bourdieusian study of language. The first of these is referred to as **Language: the Construction of an Object of Research**. In it, we address the various ways that language itself is conceived across the academic disciplines, and the importance of scrutinizing such conceptualizations at the outset when approaching any linguistic study. Bourdieu's take on language is contrasted with others. This section also includes an extended discussion of the critique that the linguist Ruqaiya Hasan has made of Bourdieu's position in order to highlight a number of conceptual issues, as well as their methodological implications. The second section then explores what the study of language might mean in terms of a *Field* **Analysis**, in particular through three distinct levels – relations between *fields*, within *fields* and the *habitus* of those involved with them. This section is exemplified with reference to the practical chapters in Part II by way of considering the empirical aspects of language study from a Bourdieusian perspective. The discussion makes extensive use of Bourdieu's concepts – *habitus, field, capital* – to illustrate the dynamics of language within particular social contexts, and raises issues concerning the insights such an approach provides. The chapter then leads towards a consideration of what a Bourdieusian science of language and linguistic study might look like. The third section of this emerging methodology is therefore entitled **Participant Objectivation**. Here, aspects of reflexivity, and the way they feature in a Bourdieusian approach are highlighted. I use the example of 'linguistic ethnography' to illustrate the issues that such a reflexive perspective might give rise to and the implications they might have for the research conduct of those working within this discipline. The chapter concludes with a summary of the key features of a Bourdieusian 'science of language'. The whole is envisaged as offering methodological principles to guide practice for those considering working in this way.

Chapter 9

Towards a Science of Language and Linguistic Study

Michael Grenfell

Introduction

In the introduction to this book, I drew attention to the ways in which language featured in Bourdieu's work. To begin with, there are his own doubts about language as it presents itself in the world of the everyday, and the common-sense understandings that implies. For Bourdieu, language is implicated in the very construction of the world – the way we speak about it structures the way we see it and vice versa. For him, such an empirical approach to language cannot be context- or value-free. It follows that any notion of language as a simple purveyor of meaning, or as a neutral medium for communication in some Lockean sense, simply overlooks the way that language, both in form and content, comes saturated with values. These values are arbitrary, since they can take a range of representations, but they are never relative, in the sense that just any value will do. Rather, such values have provenance in the structures of social space. In other words, and to employ a further Bourdieusian term, language always carries with it *interest*; that of individuals and of the social groupings they represent. We have seen how – in opposition to such writers as Comte (further implied by modern linguistics) – Bourdieu argued against the notion of 'linguistic communism', the idea that we can all share in language as a common resource and that, by implication, there is the potential for 'linguistic equality'. For Bourdieu, linguistic form cannot speak for itself. The extreme versions of the latter point include not only any study of linguistic differences as merely a matter of variation but also all those 'internal linguistic' analyses which take language as an object of study *in itself*. So, Bourdieu not only has his own view of language – as an object of study – but that view itself implies a radical critique of conventional approaches to linguistic analysis. Consequently, the second way that language features in Bourdieu's work is in terms of his attack on professional linguists and the models of language they hold. For Bourdieu, such models imply a certain 'reading' of language, one which separates it from its provenance and function in the *social space*. The very way that linguists conceptualize language somewhat 'misrepresents' it, for Bourdieu. There are then dangers from the repercussions that inevitably follow, which have real practical consequences in terms of the claims that are made for and on behalf of language in areas like linguistic policy, education and training: for example, when one takes language form as a study in itself without seeing how it is locally and nationally constituted (to account for both the subjective and objective aspects of language). Part of Bourdieu's concern is, therefore, to establish a truer representation of language and its functions with a view to establishing more meaningful practice as a result.

The third way in which language is important in Bourdieu's work is in the very terminology which he develops to talk about his social version of reality (including language itself). In fact, we might sum up Bourdieu's project on language as the development of a language to discuss language as a critique of those who are studying language – that is, the language linguists use when speaking about language and the methodological practice implied by Bourdieu's own approach. Chapters 2 and 3 described the provenance of Bourdieu's conceptual terms – *habitus, field, capital*, etc. – and the epistemological view they sought to represent, as well as their linguistic equivalents. Of course, Bourdieu was not only interested in language, but rather language was intimately connected with his understanding of social systems – the way they operated and changed. Therefore, as indicated in Chapter 3, we can understand how and why language featured in a range of other social arenas – culture, education, politics, etc. Language is crucially important not only in terms of its own systems of representation and operations, but also in the way it pervades everything we take to have sense and meaning in society. It is almost as if language is invisible and, by being invisible – like air – is everywhere.

We have seen examples of the way any Bourdieusian approach to the study of social phenomena proceed primarily though a *field analysis* of a *social space* as structured (and structuring); however, language itself is not a *field*, but a symbolic representation of one. This is why Bourdieu adopted the notion of 'linguistic market' in order to conceptualize language as something that was both structured and valued across *fields*. Behind this distinction lies an essential paradox of language which might be summed up most succinctly as the dichotomy between *language-as-form* and *language-as-meaning*. Not all language has meaning; not all meaning has language. Moreover, behind the fairly neutral definitions of words found in dictionaries, there is a multitude of nuanced sense and meanings constructed in situ, including systems of expression and gesture adapted to particular contexts. It is possible to consider this dichotomy from perspectives other than the purely linguistic; indeed, the whole case against the science of linguistics might be that it has not done precisely this 're-visioning' of language in its analyses. For example, from a social perspective, language has a moral as well as functionally mechanical aspect in that meaning always implies power, authority and ultimately the rule of the totality (the state) over the individual. This moral aspect calls for a social and philosophical interpretation. In a very real sense, the 'problem of language' conjures up the fundamental division of Western philosophy, that between fact and value. We can know things (language) as entities, but there is always a moral dimension to understanding since it implies differentiation and thus structuration (in all the terms outlined previously). At its most basic level, this dichotomy can be seen in the 'product–process' dilemma of modern-day linguistic study, in that we can only surmise linguistic processes – and by implication, the social systems which involve them – by reference to their product. This is the 'black box' syndrome: the space within the human mind which seems impenetrable to the would-be analyst. Behind the difference of fact and value therefore lie further oppositions: essence and existence, structure and meaning, knowledge and understanding. However, before further exploring these divisions, I want to return to questions of methodology.

One can ask whether it was possible to construct a 'science of existential analytics' (see Dreyfus and Rabinow 1993). This question is useful in describing what a Bourdieusian approach is attempting to do: namely, to have a method and results which are at one and the same time 'scientific' and 'analytic' without betraying the existential authenticity of the phenomena under study. This, in a nutshell, is what we have attempted to construct and what constitutes a Bourdieusian approach. But, how do we do it? The *field* of language and linguistics is large and multivariate. Each discipline within the *field* seems to have a different model of language from which to work. I therefore want to begin this discussion of a 'Bourdieusian science of language and linguistic study' by addressing this issue of the 'construction of language'. In short: How should we view language and model it?

Language: Construction of an Object of Research

The previous section has, in fact, already alluded to different ways of conceptualizing language: language in its empirical and/or scientific sense.

However, beneath this dichotomy lie finer distinctions in the way that particular views of language are constructed in distinct academic disciplines, which themselves need to be regarded as distinct *social spaces*: for example, language in its phenomenological sense; language in its cognitive sense; language in its social and cultural sense; language as a form of constructivism; language as an autonomous structure; and language as dependent on its particular context. How linguists construct language is fundamental to both the way they undertake the practical activity of studying it and, by necessity, the resulting outcomes. Such outcomes must consequently include all the limits and potentialities of that original construction. Bourdieu begins Part II of 'The Craft of Sociology' with a chapter headed 'The Social Fact is Constructed, the Forms of Empiricist Surrender'. Here, he quotes Saussure to the effect that 'the point of view creates the object' (1991/1968: 33). He then further cites Marx to the effect that any 'totality of thought is a product of the thinking head which appropriates the world in the only way it can'. Each appropriation – artistic, religious, practical – has a different way of constructing the world. Of course, the same applies to the 'scientific world'. Bourdieu underlines what he calls 'the same epistemological principle' for 'breaking with naïve realism' in the work of Max Weber: 'it is not the "actual" interconnections of "things" but the *conceptual* interconnections of *problems* which define the scope of various sciences' (ibid.). These quotes highlight the importance that Bourdieu gives to making a distinction between the empiricist and scientific world view, and the importance he consequently gives to understanding that a certain view of the world – in this case language – *creates* that world for interpretation. Little surprise, therefore, that Bourdieu puts such an emphasis on researchers' (in this case, linguists') actual 'construction of the research object', not only in terms of the way it is perceived in an everyday, naive sense, but in the very construction made of the research object within scientific *fields*.

> The *summum* of the art, in social science, is, in my eyes, to be capable of engaging very high 'theoretical stakes' by means of very precise and often mundane empirical objects. We tend too easily to assume that the social or political importance of an object suffices in itself to grant importance to the discourse that deals with it. What counts, in reality, is the rigor of the *construction* of the object. I think that the power of a mode of thinking never manifests itself more clearly than in its capacity to constitute socially insignificant objects into scientific objects. (Bourdieu 1989c: 51)

There are three key points here. First, that we cannot represent the actual constituents of the world, but we can represent the interconnections between them. Second, that the epistemological bases of that representation are critical, and, in this sense, Bourdieu clearly would argue for his own epistemological toolkit. And, third, that often the most mundane and everyday items and phenomena have the greatest significance in the construction of scientific accounts of social phenomena, including language. For example, Bourdieu draws attention to his own work, which took in something as apparently trivial as certificates of illness, validity and schooling in order to show the effects of the monopoly of the state over the means of symbolic power in imposing its policy. And, to emphasize, a further central key point, it is that in the construction of the research object – here language – that existing orthodoxies of representation are most deeply embedded. There is a kind of 'double historicization': first, a social phenomenon – such as language – is represented in a manner which characterizes a certain way of thinking at a particular historical point in time, and then that historicized version is subject to a further historicization as it develops and enfolds over time. Ironically, the double historicization ends up being 'dehistoricized'; in other words, the socio-historical genesis of phenomena is made transparent, and therefore rendered unseen or misrecognized. In this process, views of language themselves become institutionalized in ways which define what can and cannot be thought about language, or what can be uttered in formal discourses in its name without reference to the original socio-historic construction, and thus represented in a historic constructions. The 'construction of the research object' is consequently possibly the most difficult to undertake. Unless that construction is represented in conventional ways of thinking (acceptable as orthodox in the relevant consecrated academic *fields*, or *sub-field*), it will challenge the status quo, with all that implies in terms of defining what is consecrated and legitimate; in short, it will confront the power structures which lie behind academic *capital*.

Bourdieu is therefore encouraging researchers to approach a major significant object like language in an unexpected manner. *Thinking relationally* is central to this 'reconstruction', including the topography of the object of research: this is as true in making the everyday 'strange', and thus breaking from the pre-constructed, as it is in objectifying the field of research which is targeting it, with all the presuppositions it possesses. Here, Bourdieu is in fact following Cassirer's fundamental distinction between *substantialist* and *relational* thinking. The former, he argues, 'is inclined to treat the activities and preferences specific to certain individuals or groups in a society at a certain moment as if they were substantial properties, inscribed once and for all in a sort of biological or cultural *essence*' (Bourdieu 1998a/1994: 4, emphasis in original). In contrast, a *relational* way of thinking accepts that such activities and preferences as our research uncovers are understandable in terms of social spaces, positions and relationships pertaining to a particular time and place. Here, Bourdieu's own illustration echoes the quote from Weber above: '[W]hat is commonly called distinction, that is, a certain quality of bearing and manners, most often considered innate (one speaks of *distinction naturelle*, "natural refinement"), is nothing other than *difference*, a gap, a distinctive feature, in short, a *relational* property existing only in and through its relation with other properties' (1998a/1994: 6, emphasis in original). *Thinking relationally* in language studies necessitates seeing linguistic events in terms of the relationships between distinct people, organizations, time and place – Who? When? Where? – in other words, with respect to specific *field* sites or context. For example, in the case of 'language in education' in Chapter 8, rather than taking at face value the validity or utility of specific individual or institutional definitions of language learning, we might seek to understand them in terms of their location among a series of possible socially positioned definitions in use.

The 'object of research' often remains taken for granted in a positivist approach, when it could usefully be seen as socially produced and interrogated in terms of its own principles of construction. Bourdieu gives several examples of the way a signified object of research becomes literally 'more real' than the thing it is meant to represent. For example, the word 'profession' (1992b: 241ff), when taken as an instrument rather than an object of research, leads to all sorts of assumptions grounded in the preconstructed, and thus socially sanctioned – even by researchers. Indeed, language – words – acts as a kind of epistemological and semantic Trojan horse, clandestinely importing all sorts of logical attitudes and values into the research exercise which are powerful precisely because of the way they are *misrecognized* for what they are, and are thus seen as taken-for-granted instruments of knowledge rather than interest-laden objects of construction. In the case of profession, as Bourdieu remarks on more than one occasion, the would-be researcher ends up with a conceptual construction that has been analysed in terms of the logic of its own construction, rather than the thing itself.

This issue of the 'construction of language' as an object of research lies at the heart of one of the few sustained critiques of Bourdieu's views on language, that of Ruqaiya Hasan (1999). The next section explores the two sides of this critique.

Bourdieu and Hasan

At the core of the argument lie two apparent fundamentally opposed constructions of language: one internalist and one externalist. Bourdieu mounts his critique of professional linguistics in terms of its 'idealization' of language, with all that entails in terms of its consequent internalist and interactionist readings which overlook the *praxis* of language. Hasan (1999) comes to the defence of linguistics and sees dire consequences, in terms of the potential for change, if we adopt Bourdieu's version of language. Her own critique of Bourdieu is constructed initially in terms of his readings of the founding fathers of linguistics and his apparent misrepresentations of them, and an overly formalist view of language on the part of Bourdieu, which she seeks to replace with her own functional–semantic one.

Hasan begins her attack really from Bourdieu's own *point de départ*, namely this distinction between an 'internalist' and an 'externalist' reading of language. She takes Bourdieu to task for 'totalizing' the linguist as a homogeneous species, and for not acknowledging all those language researchers who precisely have sought to develop methodologies which do take account of the social aspects of language (for example, Gumperz, Halliday, Hymes, Weinreich, Volosinov). To talk of 'the linguist', as Bourdieu does, is for her to commit the same essentializing error which Bourdieu himself so consistently criticizes. In a similar vein, she attacks Bourdieu for too quickly adopting a conventional version of Saussure, one which simplifies key components of his thesis. Saussure, she argues, has been 'synchronized' and 'postmodernized'. Now she claims that in Bourdieu's work, he is simply being misrepresented, although she does admit that, even among linguists (herself excluded), the sophistication of Saussure's theory is yet to be recognized. In fact, she does not draw attention to the nuanced discussion of Saussure in Bourdieu's work (for example, the references in *The Craft of the Sociologist* referred to above). The argument here hangs on the distinction between *langue* and *parole*. She criticizes Bourdieu for adopting the synchronized version of Saussure which asserts a clear distinction between the two, thereafter focusing on the former as the proper business of linguistics. For Hasan, this is a 'problematic reading' of the *Course in General Linguistics*. In fact, she argues that the project Saussure was engaged in was not so far from Bourdieu's own, some 80 years later, namely to grasp the 'invariant' structure behind variation – in this case language (p. 31). She admonishes Bourdieu for equating Saussurian *langue* with Chomkyan *competence*, noting among other points that the former does not have the biological foundations claimed for the latter. In essence, Hasan seems to be holding Bourdieu to account for too readily accepting what linguists have subsequently made of Saussure and Chomsky rather than the original work itself. Indeed, and despite his direct attacks on Chomsky, at some points Bourdieu seemingly refers to him approvingly, and we can see that the idea of a finite generating structure (be it linguistic or socio-cultural), on the basis of which an infinite number of utterances can be made, is analogous to Bourdieu's own understanding of the co-terminus nature of *habitus* and *field*. In the case of language, Bourdieu's *legitimate language* might similarly be seen as being akin to *langue*, in that it exists in a codified form which has been recorded in dictionaries and grammar books. It is not the case, as Hasan claims, that Bourdieu is arguing that 'the linguist' is only ever interested in these orthodox forms. Rather, he is criticizing the general thrust of contemporary linguistics and the way its practitioners focus on the structural forms of language rather than on the mechanisms of its social construction in situ at any one particular time and in relation to the overall mechanisms of the *fields* in which it is operated, which themselves involve an interplay with the *linguistic market*. In brief, the points that Hasan makes about Bourdieu's treatment of Saussure and Chomsky hardly undermine his main critique of the direction of linguistic studies, with their predisposition for 'internalist' readings, since so many academic sub-disciplines to linguistics essentially look into words and (universal) grammar for the meaning of their (various) processes rather than to the conditions of meaning making in the construction of language. An essential point to note is that Bourdieu is not adopting this position simply as a counter to a particular tradition in the social sciences, but because it is symptomatic of an entire 'objectivist mode of thinking' which he finds to be both pervasive and pernicious. As noted earlier, Bourdieu's entire theory of practice is mounted in terms of a series of 'breaks' from existing knowledge: from empirical, everyday knowledge; from the subjective and phenomenological; and from objective and structuralist knowledge. The problem with linguistics, for Bourdieu, is that as in many social science disciplines, its practitioners too easily slide from 'a model of reality to the reality of the model' (1990d: 39) – a phrase which Hasan also quotes. By implication, the task is to stay with and produce a better and more authentic 'model of reality'.

In one sense, the problem itself is an intellectualist one, in that it poses a kind of linguistic dichotomy of models of language: one is essentially absolutionist; the other is essentially relativist. The tension between form and context, internal and external, code and practice, is summed up by Hasan in her discussion of the relationship between official language and 'non-official' variation. She makes the point that if official language has no specific properties in itself – in other words, conforming to the Saussurian notion of the arbitrary relationship between signifier and signified (which itself becomes a socially prescribed arbitrary) – then we are left with a puzzle: namely, 'what is it on the basis of which the speakers recognise whatever it is they do not recognise' (p. 43). Hasan uses the question, accompanied by a carefully chosen selection of texts from Bourdieu, to highlight the 'non-language' aspects of *habitus*: factors of which 'are transmitted without passing through language' (Bourdieu 1992b: 51 quoted by Hasan, p. 43) but which involve 'the whole body'. Hasan mocks Bourdieu's presumption that implying 'the linguist' is useless in capturing this level of comportment, a task only (his) sociology can undertake. But, this puzzle itself is once again based on differences of 'intellectualist' perspective. Really, Hasan's question is less of a puzzle if we put it under a different – non-linguistic – spotlight. As noted earlier, phenomenology is an essential component of Bourdieu's theory of practice. 'Embodiment' of knowledge (about phenomena) is central to phenomenology, indeed was a key component of Merleau-Ponty's version of this philosophy. It is not therefore surprising to find that the notion of *Hexis* (embodiment) features in Bourdieu's own work. However, again as I noted above, phenomenology is not just a philosophy, it is also a psychology. In describing the primary cognitive act between the participant and the world – and the language used to express it – as one of structural relation, we are again led to an essentially structuralist, internalist, langue-based view of language, if we do not also accept that consequent meaning also has sense, and that sense is value-laden in terms of the *interests* (initial and ongoing) which saturate language, and which constitute a particular world view, but a world view in terms of not just its meaning but also the values around which it is based. Certainly, values, no less than symbolic value, are not the normal arena of enquiry for linguists, and it is further debatable to what extent Bourdieu himself succeeded in capturing their provenance and actualization. However, one will remain in the linguists' trap personified in Hasan's puzzle if the possibility of this knowledge and way of knowing is not taken on board.

The same tension between form and value emerges in what Hasan sees as Bourdieu's overly formalist approach to language. She highlights Bourdieu's argument that language – words – is a way of naming things, and that power is incarnate in the process of naming. Furthermore, she draws attention to Bourdieu's preoccupation with the relationship between grammar, official language and the state – that the latter prescribes the former – in establishing linguistic norms. By state, of course, what is implied is the whole structure of society. Indeed Bourdieu does want to see language – in both its formal and symbolic forms – in terms of social structures within the *fields*, groupings and markets. However, this is a long way from claiming, as Hasan does, that in fact Bourdieu sees language ('if we have read him carefully!') as 'simply an epiphenomenon' (p. 46) and, as such, himself buys into a formalist view of language at the same time as castigating it. It is surely only possible to make this argument by ignoring the whole dialectic between language and *social space* which Bourdieu advocates so consistently in terms of structuring and structured structures in the basic epistemological treatise he sets out in *Outline of a Theory of Practice*. Essentially, the question seems to be 'whether we begin with what is structured and search for the structuring operations that gave rise to it', or 'whether we develop an understanding of the structuring principles in operation and look for structured evidence of their work'. If we are committed to exploring the relationship between *social space* and its symbolic systems, the answer to these question must surely be that we must do both. The practical chapters in Part II suggest this is indeed possible in practical terms.

Hasan makes a great deal of depicting Bourdieu as an 'externalist' – presumably as opposed to the 'internalist' – linguist. She quotes him saying that 'authority comes to language from outside' (1991c: 109) in order to underline his formalist tendencies, and his declaration that 'it is clear that not anyone can assert anything, or else does so at its peril' (p. 72). Such acts of subversion are necessary and dangerous. However, for Hasan, it is the fact that language enables such utterances in functional terms that is the key to understanding what *is* language rather than the *field* context of its realization. Again, she is able to concede that context is significant. At the very least, the systemic functionalist linguist (of which she is one) can ask how the privileged and privileging meanings of dominant groups are characterized by the 'semo-logic' of the language, but the stress is on the language itself rather than the *field* operations which shape it. In fact, Systemic Functional Linguistics are sensitive to social contexts, and the way these may be 'semiologically' actualized and represented. However, Hasan's argument still turns on an intellectualist one and there is in it no sense of the social constructive nature of language as a phenomenological, socio-cognitive act which is predisposed by an existing world of salient structural information. The broader sense of Bourdieu's 'authority comes from outside' is simply that language is never uttered in a vacuum and, as I have argued, exists saturated with *interests* which reflect ongoing social groupings expressed through language. There are language choices, and these are set by the limits of linguistic forms themselves – Hasan's semo-logic – but there are dispositions to speak and how to speak which are both environmentally acquired and individually incarnate (Hymes' 'rules of use without which the rules of grammar would be useless' (1972)), and which mean that any utterance can be both unique and at the same time conforming to an invariant logic of language and the part it plays in social processes as a whole. It is difficult to see the part that the 'moral' dimension of language could play in Hasan's position, while it is difficult to appreciate Bourdieu's position without it. Indeed, it is that social life is based on distinction through which value enters into all processes – both social and cognitive – as an expression of difference. This is the base of authority which sanctions one and censures another. It is not simply an epiphenomenon to the nature of language.

This section has looked at some of the very real issues in the way we construct language from a theoretical point of view. In Bourdieu's approach, we might regard any interrogation of the research object, and how it is constructed, as constituting a kind of pre-reflexive reflexivity – the objectivation of the research which is the object of the knowing subject – except, of course, it is not 'pre-' but everywhere present in the research process. Ultimately, of course, within a Bourdieusian-orientated study, this process of 'objectifying the construction of the research object' is carried out through the use of such 'conceptual tools' as *habitus*, *field*, *capital*, etc. Bourdieusian language is used here as an antidote to the acceptance of everyday classifications and categories, or as a means of breaking from orthodox language. It must be stressed that Bourdieu saw the necessity of a break not only in terms of common everyday sense and language, but in the actual language of science as well. Methodologically, it is as well to begin at this 'pre-reflexive' stage before embarking on any practical study of language. Chapter 8 begins with just such a reconceptualization, one which draws out the distinction between a Bourdieusian approach to language in education and conventional approaches. It also shows the consequences of 'thinking language' in this different way and the insights it provides. After the 'reconstruction' of the research object in this way, a key methodological procedure is to study language in terms of a *field analysis*. The next section considers how this might be undertaken.

Field Analysis

Bourdieu fully acknowledges the methodological difficulties at stake. He argues that while you remain within the realms of the socially constructed, the orthodox view, there is no difficulty, and we have to recognize that linguistics is now a highly developed academic *field*: a social space with numerous subspecies, all vying for dominance. Each of these has their own *interest* in particular orthodox methodologies, shared in the *interests* of the group. There is much at stake in terms of academic *capital* for the researcher. No wonder that the model becomes more important than reality. Bourdieu:

> [A]s soon as you undertake to work on a genuine object, everything becomes difficult: 'theoretical' progress generates added methodological difficulties. 'Methodologists', for their part, will have no difficulty finding plenty to nit pick about in the operations that have to be carried out in order to grasp the constructed as best one can. (ibid.)

But how to proceed? Clearly, from the above discussion, we can see that there are a lot of epistemological and methodological issues to be taken into account. However, at a basic practical level, Bourdieu advocates undertaking any study in terms of three distinct levels.

1. Analyse the position of the field vis-à-vis the field of power

Here, it is necessary to look at a *field* in relationship to other *fields* in particular the recognized source *field* of power. Ultimately, this is political power and government, although there are a number of mediating institutions and *fields*: royalty, international business, etc.

2. Map out the objective structure of relations between the positions occupied by agents who compete for the legitimate forms of specific authority of which the field is a site

In level two, the structural topography of the *field* itself is considered: all those within it and the positions they hold. This positioning is expressed in terms of *capital* and its configurations. We previously described *capital* in terms of three forms: economic, social and cultural. *Economic* refers to monetary wealth; *Social* to useful or prestigious network relations; and *Cultural* to symbolically powerful cultural attributes derived from education, family background and possessions. They are all *capital* because they act to 'buy' positioning within the *field*. *Capital* therefore has value derived from the *field* as the recognized, acknowledged and attributed currency of exchange for the *field* so that it is able to organize itself and position those within it according to its defining principles. The generating principles of a *field* have a *logic of practice*, a common currency expressed through the medium of its *capital*. It defines what is and is not thinkable and what is do-able within the *field* by systems of recognizing, or not, which give differential value according to principles of scarcity and rarity. In other words, that which is most valued is most rare and thus sought after and valuable; that which is most common is of least value.

3. Analyse the habitus of agents: the systems of dispositions they have acquired by internalizing a deterministic type of social and economic condition

In level three, the actual individual agent within the *field* is analysed: their background, trajectory and positioning. This level is expressed in terms of specific features of the characteristics of individuals, but only in so far as they relate to the *field*, past and present. In other words, we are interested in particular attributes which are social in as much as they only have value in terms of the *field* as a whole. We are not concerned with individual idiosyncrasies. *Habitus* then directs and positions individuals in the *field* in terms of the capital configuration they possess and how this resonates, or not, with the ruling principles of the logic of the *field*. We can then compare individuals, groups and the way structures intersect and resonate in the homologies set up in the course of the operations of this *field* with other *fields*. (Chapter 8 attempts such a 3-level approach.)

What this three-level approach amounts to in effect is a methodological application of a 'theory of situatedness' or the 'existential analytics' referred to earlier. Of course, Bourdieu anticipated criticism: 'The questioning of objectivism is liable to be understood at first as a rehabilitation of subjectivism and to be merged with the critique that naïve humanism levels at scientific objectification in the name of "lived experience" and the rights of "subjectivity"' (1977b/1972: 4). However, it is absolutely essential if we are to free ourselves of the mistakes of the past and 'to escape from the ritual either/or choice between objectivism and subjectivism' (ibid.). Bourdieu's way of doing this was expressed by visualizing these three levels as representing the various strata of interaction between *habitus* and *field*, together with a 'playing back and forth' between them. But how might this be applied to the study of language and linguistics?

It is possible to read each of the practical chapters in terms of these three levels. Clearly, it is not necessary that the same amount of detail be given to all three. For any one particular study, the accent is more likely to be on one level more than on another. For example, the study on individual linguistic variation in Chapter 4 focused on the *linguistic capital* of language users. However, this topic could not be approached through studying their language in a vacuum. It is only through interaction that *linguistic capital* can be seen to be expressed as a function of *habitus* and *field* conditions in situ. Various methodological issues follow. We saw how linguistic variation manifested itself at a particular point in time. That there was linguistic variation is not a surprise. It is the nature and processes behind that variation which are crucial to understanding the issue at stake. Thus, we saw apparent contradictions between *linguistic capital* and *habitus*, the latter expressed in terms of education and occupation, where actual linguistic variation was only understandable with reference to external factors: this was also true for the beliefs and attitudes held by the participants in question. To this extent, the *linguistic habitus* market operated across *fields* – education, home and occupation – to shape both use and understanding of language. However, it is as well to remember that not only was the linguistic corpus at the empirical basis of this work collected at a particular point in time but, most pertinently, each interview formed part of an exchange between two particular individuals. Bourdieu has written a great deal about the need for interviews to be set up in a certain way so that the difference between the interlocutors is minimized. In an ideal world, the questioner and the interviewee come from a similar habitus background (this was taken to its logical conclusion in *The Weight of the World* where many interviews were carried out with people known to, or associated with, the researcher (1999a/1993)). Ultimately, the interviewer would be aware of ALL the possible positions and utterances which could be employed by the interviewee before they actually make them (see Bourdieu 1991g). In the examples in Chapter 4, the level of analysis focuses on level three but makes reference to level two (*field* contexts) and level one (national language policy and norms – *legitimate language*).

Chapter 8 on classroom language similarly showed how the *habitus*-based dispositions of both teachers and students interacted in a site context in the *field* of education. It is often assumed that education can somehow take place in an ideal world where there is little clash between cultures of teaching and learning, and where, if there is a difference between the dispositional cognition of the learners and the pedagogical principles enshrined in national curricula documents, all that needs to happen is for pupils and learners to be ''talked back' online through various *scaffolding* techniques. But, this assumes the natural rightness of the super-ordinate – legitimate and consecrated – ways of doing things: an assumption itself which positions teachers and learners in respective power positions in the pedagogic *field*. This chapter considers *field* institutions as sources of *capital* to exemplify the differences and structural relations of the *field* of language in education. Critical here are the roles that the various state institutions play in the construction of pedagogic orthodoxies and how these are actualized in the classroom. Especially important in the UK context is the role of 'National Strategies' to direct how teachers behave in the classroom. The earlier discussion of Hasan's critique of Bourdieu is pertinent here. The opposing views on language that Hasan and Bourdieu represent may have very real repercussions for what is claimed in its name. So, for Hasan, because Bourdieu gives undue weight to independent structures and constantly uses them as a way of expressing both power relations as they evolve and are expressed autonomously in language, he ends up with a version of language which is blanched of its representational meaning, acting simply as a carrier of class characteristics. The consequence of Bourdieu's argument for Hasan is that language cannot exist in its own right, but can only ever express (class-based) power positions: hence, the 'disempowerment game' (the title of her article), where, for example, in pedagogical situations, language is a slave to *interest* rather than a means of emancipation. It follows that, in this scenario, knowledge about language processes can hardly be brought to the awareness of a teacher, since it is beyond what they can know, and, even if it is, the underlying logic of linguistic practice will subvert any attempt to not use language, or to exemplify language, to change the inevitable course of social reproduction. The scope for 'resistance' to the pernicious effects of language is, therefore, limited, about which more later. Methodologically, a Bourdieusian approach to the study of language and education would still imply greater attention being given to such aspects of an analysis as the links between actual individual cognition and the principles of pedagogy enshrined in official documents and ultimately expressed in classroom interactions.

The chapters on language and ideology (Chapter 5) and language policy (Chapter 7) locate themselves primarily within level 1 of the above framework. Both studies, and others, make it clear that language policy can be both overt and covert and, in defining language, a certain valuation is realized in practice, which can be seen as the operation of the linguistic market at a national level, one which will filter through a number of *fields* – education, media, politics, culture and commerce, for example. Consequently, language policy discussion often takes place between and across several *fields*, and therefore lacks practical exemplification. There is a need then to link issues of language policy with examples of how these play out in practice and according to individual linguistic groupings (and linguistic *habitus*), not simply in general terms but in individual exchanges in *field* contexts with the resultant presumed repercussions for those involved. However, as shown in Chapter 4 on linguistic variation, such repercussions are always likely to be realized in ways which are almost idiosyncratic corresponding to different *habitus* profiles – diverse in themselves in ways which mask the process of variation underlying it.

Chapter 6 on linguistic ethnography showed how linguistic groups can express and use language in ways which demonstrate their own internal social dynamics. However, such studies need other micro and macro levels of analysis. This demands that greater attention be given to such aspects as biography, trajectory (life and professional) and site practice – each with their respective *logics of field practice* as expressed in language. The structure of *fields*, their defining logic, derivation and the way such logics are actualized in practice are equally important, especially those dependent on official discourses. Finally, the links between individuals (*habitus*), *field* structures and their positioning both within and between *fields* form a conceptual framework suited to rigorous linguistic ethnographic study.

At the core of the discussion of this *field analysis* is a concern with the links between the three levels as set out – the subjective and objective, the particular and whole, the singular and general. There is a need (on the subjective/internalist side) in any Bourdieusian approach to connect linguistic detail to its determining conditions, both at the level of an immediate *field* site and in the national contexts, and to tease out the precise variations in the exchanges and relationships. However (on the objective/externalist side), there is an equal need, on the part of those who would, for example, discuss language policy – in whatever context (multilingual, bilingual, plurilingual) – to seek linguistic exemplification of the principles of practice which are highlighted in their discussions. Each of these positions, as well as the variants in between, necessitates a degree of awareness on the part of researchers about what they are doing and why. Such a reflexive element of methodology is a further critical component to Bourdieu's approach. This is the subject of the next section.

Participant Objectivation

We have seen how Bourdieu's theory of practice looks at the social world in terms of *habitus* and *field* as a way of developing an approach to research

practice through a sort of epistemological complementarity between objective structures and cognitive structures. Any account of the world, by the
specialist or non-specialist, involves a symbolic assertion of truth in the
struggle for *legitimation*, that is for recognition of authenticity. Different
points of view imply a struggle for a true representation of the world. As
noted previously, if Bourdieu is wishing to break from everyday, empirical,
naive accounts of the life world, he is also seeking to go beyond conventional scientific paradigms. This dual project does raise the question of the
status of the resultant knowledge. Chapter 2 of this book set out this theory
of practice in terms of 'breaks' from objectivist and subjectivist approaches
in the social sciences. The current chapter has considered what such breaks
amount to in terms of the essential components of methodological practice: the *construction of the research object, field analyses* conducted according
to three levels and the deployment of instruments of analysis such as *field,
capital, habitus.* In various methodological statements, Bourdieu argues that
this approach is necessary in order to include what has been omitted by
conventional approaches, namely, the subjective aspect of objective experience, and the 'invariant nature' of objective relations found at the core of
subjective practice. In brief, Bourdieu saw this as restoring what had been
overlooked by such approaches as structuralism and phenomenology in
their own construction of scientific knowledge. Bourdieu seeks to maintain
what has been gained by these approaches, all while transcending them
with a new form of science.

It is worth pausing on the word 'science'. Of course, the founding father
of contemporary scientific theory was Karl Popper, with his famous claim
that falsification was the key measure of scientific objectivity (see, for example,
Popper 1968). Briefly, a hypothesis was considered true until it had been
disproven. Indeed, the extent to which any statement was able to be disproven
became a measure of the strength of objectivity and science themselves.
From a Bourdieusian perspective, there are three points to make. First, it is
doubtful whether or not any human science can attain this test of objectivity since so much of it is dependent on social context. Second, 'theoretical
statements' have themselves to be articulated *in language*, which raises the
question of the ability of language to be sufficiently 'objective' to deliver
statements which can be subjected to such a falsification test; at base, this
is again the issue behind the sign/signified dichotomy and the doubtful
possibility of objective representation through language. Third, objective
knowledge without a 'knowing subject', World 3 in Popper's terminology,
would be anathema to Bourdieu. All we know and can know is a product
of social construction, and thus liable to be conditioned by its formative

environment and the 'knowing subject' within it. Bourdieu's alternative is variously known as 'praxeological knowledge' or 'reflexive objectivity'. Indeed, at this point, the nature of objectivity returns as a key issue of the Bourdieusian approach. He argues that it is not enough simply to pay attention to the construction of the research object, employ the key conceptual terms and proceed through *field* analysis. These stages are only the means to the end of this new form of scientific knowledge. To realize it, a fourth crucial component is needed: reflexivity. Of course, reflexivity is a ubiquitous term in the social sciences, and the 'reflective practitioner' (see Schön 1983) a guiding metaphor in contemporary 'epistemologies of practice'. What Bourdieu intends by the word, however, is more than the common practice among researchers to declare themselves 'self-aware'. For Bourdieu, this latter position was little more than an illusion: the belief that thought could somehow be transcended by thought itself (see 2000a/ 1997: 10). Rather, for him, it is necessary to go beyond conventional scientific knowledge itself in order to produce (a better, truer or more authentic) *scientific* knowledge, one characterized by this 'reflexive objectivity'. We have seen how any knowledge for Bourdieu was both ontological and political, since it represented a certain world view, and thus the *interests* at stake there. This was no less the case for researchers themselves. Indeed, for Bourdieu, they are guilty of three 'presuppositions' or biases (ibid.). First is the view of the world from their own position in the *social space* and their particular trajectory. Gender is also an issue here, since the elective affinity that exists between social structures and cognitive structures can orientate entire ways of thinking (for example, in selecting which objects to study). Second is the orthodox ways of thinking as set by the conventions of various academic *fields* (religious, artistic, philosophical, sociological, linguistic, etc.). And third, perhaps most importantly, is the bias endemic in the relationship that researchers hold with regard to their object of study as a result of the relative position of *skholè*, or leisure, inherent with the scholastic – detached – view. A 'non-practical' (non-empirical) relationship to any social phenomenon presupposes a lack of immanent necessity to live it in an empirical manner. The researchers' regard, itself akin to the Kantian notion of the aesthetic 'pure gaze', with its sense of detached involvement and transcendent knowledge, presupposes a certain freedom from the world, that is, a distant position inherent in the nature of observation. This remark has many ramifications. An extreme form of the scholastic gaze can be found in the tendencies of postmodernists to act as if the (arbitrary) world can somehow pass us by. Less obvious versions are also recognizable in the work of a number of philosophers and researchers of a neo-Kantian persuasion, who regard thought as somehow omnipotent. For Bourdieu, these positions – and indeed any other non-reflexive academic stance (themselves characteristic of particular positions in the academic space) – are seen as a kind of *scholastic fallacy* or an act of ultimate intellectual *mauvaise foi*. In brief, such researchers do not know, and do not want to know, the limits of their thought, or to acknowledge the social conditions of its construction. The only way to check this tendency is to adopt what Bourdieu calls *Participant Objectivation* (see Bourdieu 2003b) as an essential feature of the research process. At its simplest, the very same tools of analysis – in Bourdieu's case, *habitus, field, capital* – are here turned back on the researchers themselves as a way of purging what they produce from their own constituent *interests*. Bourdieu made explicit attempts to undertake such a process on various occasions: for example, in *Homo* academicus (Bourdieu 1988a/1984) and *Sketch for a Self-analysis* (Bourdieu 2007/2004), although, of course, 'reflexivity' equally pervades Bourdieu's entire work. He argued that this is the only way of partially escaping from the social, economic, political and philosophical determinisms that are necessarily at work in a knowledge *field*, and therefore limit science.

That being said, very few researchers, even those dedicated to a 'Bourdieusian approach', have seemingly undertaken such a process of reflexivity in any developed or explicit way – a fact that is equally true of linguists. In what follows, therefore, I want to use a particular case example – that of linguistic ethnography – to draw out some important features of this constituency in terms of a sub-field of the knowledge *field* of linguistics, and consider the various socio-historical forces at play in its constitution and operations. If this type of exercise were undertaken by those active in the *field*, it would perhaps develop reflexive aspects of their work in shaping the knowledge that is formed there by opening out what is to be done and how. The particular case of linguistic ethnography was selected simply because it is represented in one of the practical chapters in Part II, and because its socio-genesis is more easily traced as a result of its relatively recent emergence in the *field* of linguistic studies.

The Case of Linguistic Ethnography

Although I have chosen to use the example of Linguistic Ethnography in order to exemplify issues of reflexivity and participant objectivity, a similar exercise could be undertaken by any other sub-field of applied linguistics. What is at stake is the scientific necessity and integrity of this approach to the study of language in terms of its modus operandi. In other words, what does this approach offer that others do not? What are the extent and limits of its 'science'?

In a seminal article, Rampton (2007) sets out what we are to understand by this 'new' academic field of 'linguistic ethnography'. He refers to it as 'the development of an arena for the analysis of language in society' (p. 1). It is not, he argues, a 'school' or a 'definitive synthesis' but 'a site of encounter' where existing lines of research 'interact', are 'pushed' together as they are by circumstance. Linguistic Ethnography can be understood as a hybrid of ethnography, as a form of anthropological study, and linguistics, the technical study of language. Of course, neither ethnography nor linguistics exists in isolation from one another, nor from other approaches to the study of language. The article also refers to some of the other qualitative shifts that have taken place in linguistics, including Conversation Analysis, New Literacy Studies and Critical Discourse Analysis. From a Bourdieusian perspective, there would be value in examining the way socio-cultural issues have been approached in the various forms of ethnography – ethnology, anthropology and sociology – raising just the sort of questions about culture and structure considered in Chapters 2 and 3. The main virtue of Linguistic Ethnography, Rampton argues, is that 'ethnography opens linguistics up' and 'linguistics ties ethnography down' (p. 8). By 'opening up', they clearly mean developing cultural sensitivity, reflexivity and contextual understanding; by 'tying down', they intend technical descriptions, systematic analysis and delimitable processes. In a way, this argument is similar to the internalist/externalist debate referred to earlier, and raises a similar range of issues. Therefore, one might ask whether linguistic ethnography is a necessary approach, one that offers what other disciplines cannot. Does it go far enough in addressing the above issues? Does it resolve them?

Linguistic Ethnography is a 'young' academic sub-field. It is therefore not possible to comment on the realization of this agenda: a special addition of the *Journal of Sociolinguistics* in 2007 was preoccupied almost entirely with issues of definition, with virtually no empirical exemplification. However, in Bourdieusian terms, we can see such processes of definition as involving attempts at establishing *legitimation* in the academic space (to be 'recognized' in the field of linguistics) and consecration (to be acknowledged). What I want to do in this context is draw further on Rampton's article, to reflect on this sub-field as it is constituted, and thus make a contribution to the construction of Linguistic Ethnography as a research object itself.

In an informal survey of institutional affiliations of members of the UK-based Linguistic Ethnography Forum in 2006, 54 were aligned with education, 53 with language, 17 with culture and area studies, 6 with anthropology and 10 with disciplines such as computing, psychology, medicine and geography. This statistic highlights the disciplinary dispositions of those within the Linguistic Ethnographic grouping: predominantly language and education. The latter are characterized by their multidisciplinary nature. Their position within the academic *field* is therefore often ambiguous, as is the *cultural capital* that mediates their functions: for example, the enormous tension between education and language practitioners and theory/research. There are also issues here of its national and international constitution and status. In terms of its hybrid form, Rampton points out that the institutional links between linguistics and anthropology have traditionally been weaker in the United Kingdom than in the USA, which might indeed be the reason for the emergence of Linguistic Ethnography as a UK-based discipline. UK researchers in education and linguistics have also tended to be older, as entrance into these disciplines generally occurs after individuals have undertaken some years work as a teacher or language specialist – therapist, for example. They consequently emphasize the practical in contrast to the focus on scholarship in the USA. They also have a more personal investment in the research; their own experience is then a central motivation for research. This has methodological implications: moving from 'inside outwards', in trying to get analytical distance on what is close by. So, traditionally, language specialists and teachers begin research by examining their own practical and immediate context in this way. Rampton argues (op. cit.: 5) that this characteristic implies a totally different relation to the object of research when compared to 'professional researchers' (in the USA) who, by moving 'outside inwards', are attempting to become familiar with the strange. In the academic *field*, knowledge helps the researcher feel empowered as a professional. The quickest way to acquire it may, therefore, be to address immediate practical interests. Here, there are again issues of theory and practice and the traditional tension between scholarship and practical relevance, which are also at the core of 'linguistic ethnography' and Bourdieu's own 'theory of practice'. These aspects of Linguistic Ethnography demonstrate the importance of the *habitus* of researchers in shaping their methodological approach and preoccupations, as well as the significance of the social conditions that surround them: in this case, the structure of the academic space, its logic of practice and the *capital* that is valued there.

Personal dispositions are therefore tied up with the nature of the academic *field* itself. Rampton further points out that academia is generally more fragmented in the UK than in North America. 'Cross-disciplinary' dialogues are therefore easier to establish and maintain in the UK than in the USA. This issue involves the strength, or permeability, of discipline boundaries within and between the two countries; it might simply be easier 'to hybridize' in the UK than USA. US linguistic anthropologists are also younger, and are therefore less likely to have practical experiences in their respective fields compared to their UK counterparts. Consequently, they are more motivated by theoretical interests than personal experience. Orientations are also distinct: American anthropologists, for example, tend to see cultural differences in classrooms while the British sociologists of education come from a tradition that sees class-based social structures in pedagogic systems. These issues go to the heart of the way an individual academic researcher might sense their whole being within the *social space* – as certainty or uncertainty – and the resultant confidence it gives them in terms of how to act and what to think. It follows that Linguistic Ethnography might be seen as a haven for researchers who sense themselves least secure in the academic space, where disciplinary purity is often an asset in terms of *cultural capital*. In a way, it is a support and a protection, but it also declares – by its very existence – an inherent disciplinary insecurity, that is, by implicitly declaring that it is for those with interests who do not 'fit' in elsewhere. The key point here is that if those involved in Linguistic Ethnography undertook a process of reflexivity – as part of a process of participant objectivation – some of these issues may emerge in a way which might bring to light issues of contingency about their practice: a contingency with epistemological and methodological implications.

However, academic *habitus* is not simply constituted by personal background and institutional space. Academic sub-fields are also framed by professional associations. For example, the relationship between the Linguistic Ethnography Forum (LEF) – the main British body for Linguistic Ethnography – and other academic associations is a significant one. Two associations have played important roles in developing LEF: The Sociolinguistics Symposia (SS) and the British Association of Applied Linguistics (BAAL) in the UK. Each has a distinct formative influence. While BAAL is a learned society with larger financial resources – Cambridge University Press (CUP) co-sponsors 3–4 specialist seminars each year – the SS take place only every 2 years and are free-standing events, unsupported by the type of ongoing administrative infrastructure provided by BAAL. These relationships themselves need to be understood in Bourdieusian terms as the relations between the commercial world of publishing (CUP) and the academic world of scholarship (SS). Such relationships will have an impact on the form and direction of scientific knowledge that Linguistic Ethnography takes, for example, in terms of what is deemed as marketable and saleable within an (academic) international market. This may be one reason why, as Rampton argues, the academic constitution of Linguistic Ethnography in the UK itself does not provide ideal conditions for the processes of cumulative generalization, and why there is a lack of unified theory in Linguistic Ethnographic research, although a certain amount of conceptual theoretical language has emerged at a micro-linguistic level: performance, indexicality, entextualization, metadiscursive framing, etc. It is hard not to see this partly as an outcome of the state of the academic *field* itself.

Applied linguistics is a larger and broader constituency under which a number of other traditions have grouped, each of which has adopted particular models of language and linguistics, together with the relevant and methodological procedures. Are these traditions compatible and consistent with respect to the issues of theory and practice raised by Bourdieu's approach? In fact, it is impossible not to see these traditions as in some ways competing with each other for what Bourdieu called a 'monopoly of truth', that is, struggling for dominant *field* positions. We are reminded of Bourdieu's view of the *field* of artistic production as a series of generational shifts (1996b/1992: 159) in which 'to impose a new producer, a new product or a new system at any given moment on the market, is to relegate to the past a whole group of producers, products and systems of taste (*or academic perspective*), all hierarchised in relation to their own degree of legitimacy' (ibid. my words in italics). In this respect, the academic *field* behaves just like any other knowledge *field* with generations of activists both displacing and being displaced in a general dynamic for consecration – *connaissance* and *reconnaissance* – within the *field*; all this is played out in terms of the relative logic of practice and *capital* configurations at stake there, and with the resultant rewards and penalties (see Grenfell 1999). Participant Objectivation is intended to raise such issues.

As noted, it is common for researchers to claim 'awareness' of what they are doing and why. However, reflexivity for Bourdieu – Participant Objectivation – is more than this, because it involves an 'objectification of objectification' itself through an 'Objectivation of the Knowing Subject'. As stated, to bring this about, such 'objectivation' requires the application of terms such as *habitus, field* and *capital* – and the epistemology underlying them – to both the particular *field* of academic discourse and those involved within it, researcher and researched. However, it is both an individual and (essentially) a collective undertaking. The products of any language and linguistic analyses need to be understood in terms of their characteristic position within a particular academic space, itself understood in terms of the socio-historical structure of the academic *field* at a particular time. This awareness permeates Bourdieu's work and makes up the 'realist third way' (2001c: 200) which he is advocating.

Towards a Science of Language and Linguistic Study

This section sums up the main features of a Bourdieusian approach to the study of language and linguistics. Its title implies that there is the possibility of re-founding, or at least re-grounding, our scientific approach to language study: that there might be a new linguistic 'science'. Such a suggestion might seem odd in a *field* already awash with language and approaches to language. In the special edition of *Journal of Sociolinguistics* (2007) on Linguistic Ethnography, both this particular approach and a number of other associated disciplines are referred to: Critical Discourse Analysis; Linguistic Anthropology; Conversation Analysis; New Literacy Studies; Interactional Sociolinguistics; Objectivity Linguistics; Interpretative Applied Linguistics; the Ethnography of Communication; and Discourse Psychology. How many of us can put our hand on our heart and say exactly what each of these means? However, presumably many of us would subscribe to one or more of these titles in defining our own work. The point is that there is a proliferation of sciences of language, and almost a surfeit of language about language. Even in Hasan's account of 'literacy in society', in a volume appearing under the same title (see Hasan 1996), she identifies a number of forms of literacy: as simply *making sense*, as *language-based semiosis*, *learning literacy*, *teaching literacy*, *recognition literacy*, *action literacy*; and *reflection literacy*. Can all these be literacy? Although literacy is indeed a multifaceted phenomenon, there comes a point where one wonders about the usefulness of a term – at least from a scientific, analytic point of view – which can be connected to so many other aspects of language and education. And yet, lacunae remain. For example, this same volume on 'literacy in society' makes no mention of New Literacy Studies (NLS) despite seminal work by writers such as Street (1984) to distinguish 'autonomous' approaches to literacy (literacy as an independent skill) from a more critical, socio-cultural perspective (literacy in terms of its context and ideological content). We might surmise that 'literacy' is a hazardous *field* to enter, one where it may be difficult to define and position oneself. Moreover, such lack of clarity and definition will lead to uncertainty over what *capital* to accumulate, how, and the best academic trajectory to build it. This may seem to be a personal problem rather than a scientific one. However, real issues are at stake concerning the science of language and the impact it will have on education, learning and policy, as well as the consequent practical usefulness of what results in terms of pedagogy and curricula.

Rampton (op. cit) quotes Bernstein approvingly on the distinction between 'singulars' and 'regions' in the organization of academic knowledge: 'singulars' are structures that give their creators a unique name in the *field*, with their own intellectual texts etc. and strong bounded hierarchies protected by professional interests; 'regions', on the other hand, are 'recontextualized singulars' who have appropriated a space between intellectual (internal) and practical (external) *fields*. So, while physics, chemistry and history are singulars, engineering, medicine and architecture are regions. However, there are further distinctions to be made, since, for example, it is not just that the 'applied sciences' are regions. Contemporary examples include such multidisciplinary subjects as cognitive science, management, business studies, communications and the media. In this sense, Linguistic Ethnography discussed earlier is clearly a 'region'. However, as suggested in the previous section, one surely must ask if, in these terms, regions are not simply aspiring to be 'singulars' by assuming their virtues. In other words, are particular disciplines logically, practically and theoretically necessitated by the object of research, or are they rather an epiphenomenon of the interests of those pursuing its study. In a postmodern age (some might claim post-postmodern), fragmentation and hybridization are, of course, common characteristics to many social processes. The reconceptualizations of old into new occurs, for example, in the way that the study of 'Interlanguage' gets re-presented as ELF (English as Lingua Franca), with all the accompanying features (journals, conferences, edited volumes, association). I am not wishing to launch a cull of academic disciplines. However, while they proliferate, issues of basic definition, methodology remain, as well as key questions about the nature of language. Such questions are not necessarily answered by developing further discipline areas. What Bourdieu's logic of practice can offer to this academic area is a means of understanding the structure of the linguistic field in terms of its participants, its institutions and its relationship to the state.

If Bourdieu's approach has a key feature, it is that it is both simple and complex: simple in terms of its modus operandi; complex in terms of what it attempts to synthesize. This is why the 'construction of the research object' is of primary importance to Bourdieu, as it is here that the underlying epistemology of practice is foregrounded in terms of language as a social, cognitive, phenomenological and physical event. Rather than the simple opposition between an externalist and an internalist model,

Bourdieu sees language as a dialectic between social and cognitive structures, and one which is in a constant state of flux with any particular context of the social environment: and here, positioning and the subsequent patterns of *interest* are all important. It is as well to recall that Bourdieu always insisted that he began his work with a practical problem, and that it was in the relations that he found in it that he was able to develop his conceptual framework. Such a framework, of course, includes his full conceptual lexicon: *habitus, field, capital, hexis, interest*, etc. However, these terms are only as powerful as their philosophical bases. In other words, without understanding them as epistemological matrices, as concepts which emerged from practical, empirical contexts in a dynamic manner, they become little more than metaphors used to embroider commentary. Whenever a particular term is used, the theory of practice which underpins it must constantly be kept in mind. We might say that any one term only arises as a result of empirical (not theoretical) necessity, and from the relationships observed in data.

The point is that in matters of research engagement, there is a need for practical focus and exemplification. But, equally, the approach needs to be a principled one, with a clear epistemological rationale. I have suggested that, besides 'the construction of the research object', such an approach to linguistic study needs to be undertaken through a three-level *field* analysis in order to connect a particular context within a network of *field* relations with the individual subjectivities to be found there. For language and linguistics, it is clear that what is needed is not further data collection and techniques of analysis, since from the phonetic, structural, discursive and paralinguistic levels of language, the technical arsenal of instruments is already quite formidable. There are, however, issues about how these techniques are deployed and the ways they are embedded in a general strategic view of the research project. It is clearly necessary to look more into the biographical elements, *habitus*, of language users, the way they interact with local site features, *fields*, how that local site is configured and the way it links with broader social structures, including the social, political and economic. As has been repeatedly argued, it is not enough to search for social meaning in the words themselves. At the same time, linguistic data from ethnographic and biographical studies are too often taken as ends in themselves in their richness as a source of generating local grounded theories. What is needed is a clear focus on the logics of practice of individual language use and its surrounding networks, especially in the way *fields* interconnect and re-express particular dominant forms. For example, it is not possible to study 'inclusion' in British education today without understanding it as

Inclusion, that is, as the governmental strategies which drive policy and practice, and how that intersects with individual dispositions. Not to do so is to impose a certain view of language use on language users. Under a Bourdieusian approach, inclusion takes on a different quality: a reconnection with issues of social mobility; questions of social provenance (*habitus*); the impact of local communities; the language (*linguistic capital*) of those included and excluded; institutional versions of inclusion and the *doxa* inherent in them; the *misrecognized* forms of exclusion; the *interests* of the advocates of inclusion; the structural relations (*fields*) between the governmental agents of inclusion and the *habitus*-based dispositions of those involved; the *cultural capital* of inclusion; and the outcomes of such policies for 'the included'.

There is then the need to explore further the links between the social and the cognitive in actual practice. Bourdieu's approach is avowedly constructivist; as noted, he often refers to it as 'structural constructivism'. In practice, there is no reason why the sort of cognitive language models developed in such frameworks as Anderson's ACT model could not be applied to the social as well as the psychological constructs of language use. In this case, dichotomies between cognition and metacognition, and declarative and procedural knowledge, may furnish us with tools which can bridge the social/psychological divide. *Dispositional* behaviour – for example, language and thought itself – can be understood in terms of *elective affinities* and goal-orientated action. Such action itself involves both 'knowledge of' (declarative) and 'knowledge how to do' (procedural) things. Here, action is also *interest*-laden, and takes place in environmental (*field*) conditions which may, in practice, promote or hinder ultimate success. Indeed, calculation of the likelihood of success or failure is part of the strategic action, or *field* struggles, that individuals undertake in the contexts in which they find themselves. In other words, and in contrast to Habermas, Bourdieu does not see language as being simply employed to the end of 'communicative action' (see Habermas 1984): to understand and be understood. Rather, language is always employed according to *field* positioning. The objective of linguistic enquiry is then to show up this dynamic in a multitude of settings. As Chapters 4–8 have demonstrated, Bourdieu's analytical tools are a means to do that. However, we should add a note of caution. The terms themselves should be seen more as a 'final vocabulary' than an end in themselves. This term of Richard Rorty can be employed to stress the fact that these concepts are only the 'best we can do' at a particular point in time (see Rorty 1979). Such a vocabulary is both contingent and robust, not relative or tentative. It is not enough simply to offer a narrative gloss on data in Bourdieusian terms; this is to become ensnared by them. Such terms as *habitus*, *field* and *capital* are to be seen as temporary and ongoing – necessitated by the need to represent relationships observed in data sources – not as substantive entities in themselves. Scientific theory for Bourdieu is always

> a temporary construct which takes shape for and by empirical work. Consequently, it has more to gain by confronting new objects than by engaging in theoretical polemics that do little more than fuel a perpetual, self-sustaining and too often vacuous metadiscourse around concepts treated as intellectual totems. (Bourdieu 1989c: 50)

Finally, there is the dimension of 'reflexivity' in Bourdieu's science. I have argued that what Bourdieu advocates is more than the simple self-awareness often claimed by researchers in pursuit of their research. He demands more than a declaration of position, background and self-perceived biases. Bourdieu describes 'participant objectivation' as the process whereby the researchers turn back the tools of analysis on themselves. However, this element itself is neither a one-off enterprise nor a bolt-on action to bolster one's claims. Rather, it is an ongoing aspect of the entire research undertaking and, just as with the basic conceptual terms themselves, it must be open to constant probing and exploration. Bourdieu writes about how it took him years (2000d) to understand the distinction between the way an Algerian peasant might see the world in terms of the choices he had to make about economic activity and the marriage of his children, and his own French intellectual view. To see the world from another's point of view is indeed a major step for any would-be researcher, and this statement by Bourdieu is one that is both very personal and profound. In one interview (1995a), Bourdieu talked about how, with age, and in this way, the 'scientific *habitus*' (the scientific Bourdieu) could in fact impact on and influence the 'empirical *habitus*' (the empirical Bourdieu). This description is, in one sense, a kind of liberation from seeing the world solely in terms of one's own *interests*. This type of reflexivity was present for Bourdieu throughout his work and was most explicitly expressed in *Sketch for a Self-analysis* (2007/2004) at the end of his life. Finally, what Bourdieu advocates is a similar process, but this time as a collective act: in this case, within an academic space and, by extrapolation within our present *field* of linguistics (a collective *habitus*). What would applied linguistics look like in a 'post-reflexive' world? What is at stake is a new way of seeing language and the world, a *metanoia* – a new kind of science. The possible result is a 'better' kind of knowledge, a more practically useful knowledge: one based on 'reflective objectivity', one possibly purged of individuals' *interests* and the perspectives of a science *field* which, by reflecting their own positionings, limits what can and cannot be thought there.

Chapter 10

Conclusion

The principal aim in creating this book was to give a special focus to the work on Pierre Bourdieu in relation to language and linguistics. We have seen the way language features on various levels of his work, both explicitly and implicitly. However, despite repeatedly coming back to and dwelling on issues of language, Bourdieu himself never undertook the type of detailed analyses that are now common practice in linguistic sciences. A second aim was therefore to offer practical exemplification of empirical studies and analyses of language in a range of contexts. Part I of the book gave some background to Bourdieu's social philosophy and its key underlying features. It also showed how his theory of practice can be developed with respect to issues of language and linguistics. We noted that the study of language and linguistics is a *field* which has yet to take on board a Bourdieusian perspective in any sustained manner. It is common to see Bourdieu referenced en passant, for example with respect to *linguistic capital* or the *linguistic market*. However, with one or two notable exceptions (for example, Hasan's critique discussed in the previous chapter, or the study of Albright and Lukes 2008 on literacy education), a truly Bourdieusian engagement to language is yet to emerge. A third major aim of this book was therefore to encourage such an engagement.

I have referred to the way that the philosophy of language became the philosophy of man during the twentieth century. This phenomenon and the explosion of the mass global communication systems mean that language pervades almost everything we do. Yet, in a post postmodern and pluri-disciplinary age, the sciences of language have themselves fragmented into multiple perspectives and practices. In some sense, there now seems to be less consensus over what language is and how it functions than there is about culture: a concept which itself is multidimensional in both its theory and practice. It is noticeable that, faced with a situation where language can be connected with almost any other socio-cultural feature, Bourdieu actually offers quite a limited range of conceptual tools for understanding its functions in social systems: it is almost theoretically ascetic. Yet, in terms of contemporary language and linguistic study, it appears to be based on a philosophy and epistemology which in many ways run counter to the predominant paradigms.

Part II of the book offered an account of the application of this conceptual toolbox to a range of language contexts. The exploration began with the mechanics of language itself in order to show how a Bourdieusian perspective might account for variation within a particular linguistic corpus. The principal point here was that it is never enough to simply analyse phonological, syntactic and semantic variations purely in terms of individual differences themselves. Such variation is deeply affected both by personal background – educational, professional and social *habitus* – and the specific *field* sites of operation. The *linguistic market* was shown to be something that operates across *fields* but actualized in particular contexts as they arise. *Linguistic capital* is similarly brought to bear on such contexts and finally shapes the sort of strategies that might be employed there, as individuals act with respect to their positioning with the structure of the *social space.*

Chapters 5, 6 and 7 explored aspects of and relations to language with respect to the State. Bourdieu's *linguistic market* presupposes a linguistic currency with specific exchange rates. For this to be so, there must be a base value, defined as *legitimate language,* which sets the standards against which all other language is measured. Of course, in the modern State, it would be unusual to find overt forms of imposition and censure, for example, in the way that indigenous languages were suppressed by colonialists in the past who subsequently imposed their own national language in their place. Despite an apparent greater tolerance towards regional variation, most modern nation states do, however, have an objectively recognized language which is expressed in terms of standard forms. That *legitimate language* is embedded in official and formal policies of the state. As chapter 5 of Part II shows, this legitimacy is refracted in ways which can be understood in terms of the ideology of particular language groups, minority groups and, indeed, the official language policy statements of the State itself. Bourdieu's main book on language – *Language and Symbolic Power* (1991c) – includes an entire section on *symbolic power* and the political *field.* Political delegation and representation are related to the theme of *legitimate language* as each case involves sanctioning others 'to speak on our behalf'. Of course, both are fraught with difficulties, as they inherently imply the expression of one set of *interests* being subordinated to another's. Language is always representational: the questions then are on whose behalf? in whose *interest*?

Where this representation is institutionalized ('I *am* the group' since I speak on their behalf), the effects are likely to be all the more pernicious and pervasive. The various chapters in Part II showed how these *interests* are expressed and represented in various linguistic contexts – through language. One of the main conduits for legitimate language to function is education, and Chapter 8 demonstrated how the language of the classroom can also be understood in similar terms: as the relations between centrally prescribed curricula, the training and background of teachers and the *habitus* of the students involved.

In response to these practical applications, Part III of the book set out to raise questions of methodology and, by implications, philosophy, as a way of framing a more systematic approach for a Bourdieusian study of language and linguistics. His critique of Chomskyan linguistics was noted, which, with its various offshoots, is possibly the most extensive linguistic paradigm in the world today. However, it would be wrong to regard this simply as a stand-off between Bourdieu and transformational grammarians, the former an 'externalist', the latter preoccupied with language as an innate characteristic of the human brain. Bourdieu is equally critical of essentialist views of language. So, for example, he is also at odds with Comte's and Saussure's understanding of language as some sort of 'common treasure' to which we all have access. He is equally critical of any view of language which sees it as possessing an inherent communicative function by its very nature. The latter would encompass a range of philosophical positions which regard language as somehow inherently communicative, as if existing in some utilitarian realm. These would include Locke's 'transmission of meaning', Grice's 'co-operative principle', Austin's 'illocutionary force' and Habermas' 'communicative action'. In each case, language is seen as having this innate property which establishes grounds for common consensus over sense and meaning, indeed, provides the conditions for this possibility. For these writers, cooperation and communication between men and women is possible, therefore, through language and because of language's very nature. This cannot be for Bourdieu.

Language, for him, is a socio-cognitive construction and, although the primary cognitive act of babies may indeed take place in some value-free realm where an individual interacts with their environment, the latter will increasingly be articulated in language and through language, and thus pre-constructed forms of thinking and thought – which are themselves value-laden by the fact that they come saturated with *interests* already existing within the *social space*. We have noted the centrality of *structure* for Bourdieu at both a subjective and objective level; structures (social and phenomenological) are indeed themselves cognitive, but also socio-cultural and therefore differential in terms of their positional provenance from within that space. For a writer such as Hasan, Bourdieu is simply substituting an externalist reading of language for an internalist one: a substitution with dangerous consequences in terms of the power to act. One result of Bourdieu's formalism, for her, is that language can never be seen as anything other than an expression of the social class structure of society and, consequently, that the dominated within society are active in their own domination by attempting to assimilate the language of the dominant – which they never can. As a result, there is no possibility of change. This again raises the political and practical consequences of Bourdieu's position and a further paradox: that a social philosophy that is all about change is accused of not being able to account for the possibility of change. Such a critique complements charges of determinism which have hung over Bourdieu's work for some decades, and despite the fact that the whole project is based on notions of flux and affinities rather than direct causality. This confusion has consequences for what we are to make of Bourdieu's approach in terms of policy and practical outcomes. To take the example of education, Hasan, in apparent contrast to Bourdieu, argues for pedagogic planning that is sensitive to variations in *habitus* in the belief that the social fatalism that seems to haunt Bourdieu's work might be neutralized. This proposal is related to the issue of 'entering teachers' consciousness' raised in Chapter 9. The possible result of such measures, she argues, could lead to a situation where *Pedagogic Action* itself might become less authoritative and the source of *symbolic violence*, and more the context for a kind of a kind of 'action literacy'. Here, *habitus* is used in this situation as a focus for assessing the 'discursive abilities' of individual learners as part of the processes of their language and learning. Greater equality and inclusiveness in education become a real possibility. Of course, this sort of compensatory technique has become well known in educational settings in recent decades. In fact, as part of the 'new' sociology of education of the 1970s and 1980s, it was common to advocate a change in attitude and approach to non-dominant cultures – as a possible source of resistance or celebration. However, finally, the logic of Bourdieu's theoretical position must surely be that such strategies are ultimately going to have little effect, especially as an emancipated form of pedagogy, because, inherently, they are still constituted by a logic of practice which runs counter to the differential logic on which the entire education system is based – one which, for (misrecognized) economic purposes, promotes a certain cultural prevalence over another one. But there are alternatives.

Change requires more than a different nomenclature or pedagogy. It requires an entire transformation in thinking, including the relationship between researchers and practitioners. It is often said – even by Bourdieu – that in order to get someone to think like you, you first need to get them to talk like you. The language that is used to discuss and describe language is therefore crucial. Bourdieu provides a language about language which invites the readers to 'think in these terms'. However, this 'new' way of seeing things – what Bourdieu called a *metanoia* – is more than the replacement of one set of concepts with another. I have suggested that they need to be seen less as descriptive metaphors and more as highly changed 'epistemological matrices' with their own innate, theoretical dynamic. Ultimately, the task might be to convince language and linguistic researchers to adopt Bourdieusian terms in place of their usual ones and, in so doing, to encourage them to 'think relationally' about both their object of study and their own relationship to it. This point relates to the emancipatory potential in Bourdieu's view of language. As his concepts offer the possibility of objectifying social processes, this move creates a certain distance from the latter. In a research *field* saturated with *interests*, it is not only the language about language adopted that is of critical importance. However, in order to avoid a Bourdieusian perspective – with all its concepts – becoming just another fraction of the academic (in this case linguistic) *field*, the conditions of the *field* themselves also have to change. That change will only come about as part of a process which includes a reflexive dimension to research, one that is both individual and collective. This principle lies at the basis of Bourdieu's Participant Objectivation as discussed in the previous chapter. Here, Bourdieu's concepts provide a form of 'language of association' for those working in this way. Indeed, his philosophy of language can then be seen as representing both an epistemology and a political ontology. It can also be regarded as offering a theory of practice against an intellectual status quo, which otherwise, Bourdieu argues, risks being submerged in a science of its own *field* rather than constructing a true 'science of science'.

This latter point raises questions about the whole raison d'être of Bourdieu's work, both on language and in its wider applications. Here in the early twenty-first century, language indeed dominates our society. The postmodernism condition has yet to play itself out. As part of this period, it is sometimes as if we are all caught in an endless ricochet of signifiers that come into being and evaporate before we hardly register their significance. In a world where impressions are frequently more important than substance, it is as if we are surrounded by signifiers with little, or nothing, to signify, as if the dynamic of social processes is more important than their substantive ends. The radical nature of Bourdieu's approach to language, including his wider views of social processes, needs to be seen as part of a resistance to these trends. Those working in this way act as kinds of 'praxeological agents' on its behalf. Finally, therefore, any consideration of Bourdieu on language and linguistics will always go beyond questions of method and science, to reach the heart of our world and the meaning we make of it.

Bibliography

The following is a list of the references used in this book. There are two aspects to the listing of Bourdieu's references which are to note.

First, Bourdieu always insisted that his work be read in terms of its 'socio-genesis', that is, in the light of both the theoretical and current events at the time that they were produced. Wherever possible, and to aid the reader, I have listed the English version first. However, in order to preserve the temporal dimension to his work, this is followed by details of the original French publication. It is to note that there are sometimes considerable differences between the two dates.

Second, Bourdieu collaborated with a number of individuals, and in different ways: for example, as joint co-author, or within a team. In this bibliography, I have elected to list both single-authored and collaborative publications together according to date, again in order to preserve and highlight the chronology of publications.

Ager, D. (1999) *Identity, Insecurity and Image: France and language.* Clevedon: Multilingual Matters.

Albright, J, and Lukes, A. (eds). (2008) *Pierre Bourdieu and Literacy Education.* Abingdon: Routledge.

Alexander, R. (2001) *Culture and Pedagogy: International Comparisons in Primary Education.* Oxford: Blackwell Press.

Alexander, R. (2004) *Towards Dialogic Teaching: Rethinking Classroom Talk.* Cambridge: Dialogos, University of Cambridge.

Althusser, L. (1994) Selected texts. In T. Eagleton (ed.). *Ideology* (pp. 87–111). New York: Longman.

Ammon, U. (1998) *Ist Deutsch noch internationale Wissenschaftssprache? Englisch auch für die Lehre an den deutschsprachigen Hochschulen.* Berlin: Mouton de Gruyter.

Ammon, U. (ed.). (2000) *The Dominance of English as the Language of Science: Effects on other languages and language communities.* Berlin: Mouton de Gruyter.

Anderson, J. (1983) *The Architecture of Cognition.* Cambridge, MA: Harvard University Press.

Anderson, J. (1985) *Cognitive Psychology and its Implications* 2nd edn. New York: Freeman.

Ashby, W. J. (1982) The drift of French Syntax, *Lingua*, 57, 26–46.

Atienza, E., Battaner, P., Bel, A., Borrás, L., Díaz, L., Hernández, C., et al. (1997) Una tipología de interferencias catalán-castellano a partir de las producciones escritas de los estudiantes universitarios. In F. J. Cantero, A. Mendoza and C. Romea Castro (eds). *Didáctica de la lengua y la literatura para una sociedad plurilingüe del siglo XXI* (pp. 577–582). Barcelona: Universitat de Barcelona.

Atienza, E., Battaner, P., Bel, A., Borrás, L., Díaz, L., Hernández, C., et al. (1998) Interferencia catalán-castellano en estudiantes universitarios bilingües. In P. Orero (ed.). *Actes del III Congrés Internacional sobre Traducció (Universitat Autònoma de Barcelona, March 1996)* (pp. 607–626). Barcelona: Universitat Autònoma de Barcelona.

Badia i Margarit, A. (1969) *La llengua dels barcelonins.* Barcelona: Edicions 62.

Badia i Margarit, A. (1975) *Llengua i cultura als Països Catalans.* Barcelona: Edicions 62.

Badia i Margarit, A. (1980) Peculiariadades del uso del castellano en las tierras de lengua catalana. In R. Velilla Barquero (ed.). *Actas del I Simposio para Profesores de Lengua y Literatura Españolas* (pp. 11–31). Madrid: Castalias.

Ball, R. V. (1983) Noun, pronoun and discourse structure in French, *Modern Languages,* 4, 229–239.

Barnes, D., Britton, J. and Torbe, M. (1969) *Language, the Learner and the School.* London: Penguin Press.

Barnes, D. (1976) *From Communication to Curriculum.* London: Penguin Books.

Barry, B. (2000) *Culture and Equality: An egalitarian critique of multiculturalism.* Cambridge MA: Harvard University Press.

Bastardas i Boada, A. (1986) *Llengua i immigració: La segona generació immigrant a la Catalunya no-metropolitana.* Barcelona: Edicions de la Magrana.

Billig, M. (1995) *Banal Nationalism.* London: Sage.

Blackledge, A. (2005) *Discourse and Power in a Multilingual World.* Amsterdam: John Benjamins.

Blackledge, A. and Creese, A. (2010) *Multilingualism. A Critical Perspective.* London, Continuum.

Blanc, M. and Biggs, P (1971) L'enquête socio-linguistique sur le français parlé à Orléans, *Le Français dans le Monde,* 85, 16–25.

Blas Arroyo, J. L. (2004) El español actual en las comunidades del ámbito lingüístico catalán. In R. Cano (ed.). *Historia de la lengua española* (pp. 1065–1086). Barcelona: Ariel.

Blommaert, J. (1996) Language and nationalism: Comparing Flanders and Tanzania, *Nations and Nationalism,* 2, 235–256.

Blommaert, J. (1999) The debate is open. In J. Blommaert (ed.). *Language Ideological Debates* (pp. 1–38). Berlin: Mouton de Gruyter.

Blommaert, J. (2001) Reflections from overseas guests. Linguistic ethnography in the UK. A BAAL/CUP seminar. University of Leicester 28–29 March 2001. http://www.lancs.ac.uk/fss/organisations/lingethn/leicesteroverseasreflections.rtf.

Blommaert, J. (2005) Situating language rights: English and Swahili in Tanzania revisited, *Journal of Sociolinguistics,* 9, 390–417.

Boix Fuster, E. (1993) *Triar no és trair: Identitat i llengua en els joves de Barcelona.* Barcelona: Edicions 62.

Boix, E., Payrató, L. and Vila, X. (1997) Espagnol-catalan. In H. Goebl, P. H. Nelde, Z. Stary and W. Wölck (eds). *Linguistique de contact: Manuel international des recherches contemporaines* (Vol. 2, pp. 1296–1302) Berlin: De Gruyter.

Borooah, V. K. (2005) Caste, inequality, and poverty in India, *Review of Development Economics,* 9/3, 399–414.

Borooah, V. K., Dubey, A. and Iyer, S. (2007) The effectiveness of jobs reservation: Caste, religion and economic status in India, *Development and Change,* 38/3, 423–445.

Bourdieu, P. (1958) *Sociologie de l'Algérie.* (New Revised and Corrected edn, 1961). Paris: Que Sais-je.

Bourdieu, P. (1961) Révolution dans la révolution, *Esprit, Janvier,* 27–40.

Bourdieu, P. (1962a) *The Algerians* (trans. A. C. M. Ross). Boston: Beacon Press.

Bourdieu, P. (1962b) Célibat et condition paysanne, *Etudes rurales,* 5–6, 32–136.

Bourdieu, P. (1962c) De la guerre révolutionnaire à la révolution. In F. Perroux (ed.). *L'Algérie de demain.* Paris: PUF.

Bourdieu, P. (with Darbel, A., Rivet, J. P. and Seibel, C) (1963) *Travail et travailleurs en Algérie.* Paris- The Hague: Mouton.

Bourdieu, P. (with Sayad, A) (1964a) *Le Déracinement, la crise de l'agriculture tradionelle en Algérie.* Paris: Les Editions de Minuit.

Bourdieu, P. (with Passeron, J-C) (1964b) *Les Étudiants et leurs études.* Paris-The Hague, Mouton, Cahiers du Centre de Sociologie Européenne.

Bourdieu, P. (1968) Structuralism and theory of sociological knowledge, *Social Research,* 35, 4, 681–706.

Bourdieu, P. (1971/1966) Intellectual field and creative project. In M. F. D. Young (ed.). *Knowledge and Control: New Directions for the Sociology of Education.* London: Collier Macmillan.

—Champ intellectual et project créateur, *Les Temps Modernes,* nov., 246, 865–906.

Bourdieu, P. (1972a) Les stratégies matromoniales dans le système de reproduction, *Annales,* 4–5, 1105–1127.

Bourdieu, P. (with Boltanski, L.) (1975) Le fétichisme de la langue, *Actes de la Recherche en Sciences Sociales,* 4, 2–32.

Bourdieu, P. (with Passeron, J-C) (1977a/1970) *Reproduction in Education, Society and Culture* (trans. R. Nice). London: Sage.

—(1970) *La Reproduction. Eléments por une théorie du système d' enseignement.* Paris: Editions de Minuit.

Bourdieu, P. (1977b/1972) *Outline of a Theory of Practice* (trans. R. Nice). Cambridge: Cambridge University Press.

—(1972) *Esquisse d'une théorie de la pratique. Précédé de trois études d'ethnologie kabyle.* Geneva: Droz.

Bourdieu, P. (1977c) The economics of linguistic exchanges (trans. R. Nice), *Social Science Information,* XVI, 6, 645–668.

Bourdieu, P. (Passeron, J-C) (1979a/1964) *The Inheritors, French Students and their Relation to Culture* (trans. R. Nice). Chicago: The University of Chicago Press.

—*Les héritiers, les étudiants et la Culture.* Paris: Les Editions de Minuit.

Bourdieu, P. (1982a) *Ce que parler veut dire. L'économie des échanges linguistiques.* Paris: Fayard.

Bourdieu, P. (1982b) *Leçon sur une leçon.* Paris: Les Editions de Minuit.

Bourdieu, P. (with Saint-Martin, M) (1982c) La Sainte Famille: L'épiscopat français dans le champ du pouvoir, *Actes de la Recherche en Sciences Sociales,* 44/45, 2–53.

Bourdieu, P. (1984/1979) *Distinction* (trans. R. Nice). Oxford: Polity.

—*La Distinction. Critique sociale du jugement.* Paris: Editions de Minuit.

Bourdieu, P. (with Salgas, J-C) (1985) Le rapport du Collège de France. Pierre Bourdieu s'explique, *La Quinzaine Littéraire,* 445, 8–10.

Bourdieu, P. (with Honneth, A., Kocyba, H and Schwibs, B) (1986) The struggle for symbolic order. An interview with Pierre Bourdieu, *Theory, Culture and Society,* 3, 3, 35–51.

Bourdieu, P. (1988/1984) *Homo Academicus* (trans. P. Collier). Oxford: Polity.

—*Homo academicus.* Paris: Les Editions de Minuit.

Bourdieu, P. (1989a) Reproduction interdite. La dimension symbolique de la domination économique, *Etudes Rurales,* 113–114, 15–36.

Bourdieu, P. (1989b) Social space and symbolic power, *Sociological Theory,* 7, 14–25.

Bourdieu, P. (with Wacquant, L) (1989c) Towards a reflexive sociology: A workshop with Pierre Bourdieu, *Sociological Theory,* 7, 1, 26–63.

Bourdieu, P. (with Boltanski, L., Castel, R. and Chamboredon, J. C) (1990a/1965) *Photography. A Middle-brow Art* (trans. S. Whiteside). Oxford: Polity.

—*Un Art moyen, essai sur les usages sociaux de la photographie.* Paris: Les Editions de Minuit.

Bourdieu, P. (with Darbel, A. and Schnapper, D) (1990b/1966) *The Love of Art. European Art Museums and their Public* (trans. C. Beattie and N. Merriman). Oxford: Polity Press.

—*L'Amour de l'art, les musées d'art et leur public.* Paris: Les Editions de Minuit.

Bourdieu, P. (1990c/1980) *The Logic of Practice.* (trans. R. Nice). Oxford: Polity.

—*Le sens pratique.* Paris: Les Editions de Minuit.

Bourdieu, P. (1990d/1987) *In Other Words: Essays Towards a Reflexive Sociology* (trans. M. Adamson). Oxford: Polity.

—*Choses dites.* Paris: Les Editions de Minuit.

Bourdieu, P. (with Chamboredon, J-C. and Passeron, J-C) (1991a/1968) *The Craft of Sociology* (trans. R. Nice). New York: Walter de Gruyter.

—*Le Métier de sociologue.* Paris: Mouton-Bordas.

Bourdieu, P. (1991b/1988) *The Political Ontology of Martin Heidegger* (trans. P. Collier). Oxford: Polity Press.

—*L'ontologie politique de Martin Heidegger.* Paris: Les Editions de Minuit.

Bourdieu, P. (1991c) *Language and Symbolic Power* (trans. G. Raymond and M. Adamson). Oxford: Polity Press.

Bourdieu, P. (1991d) Genesis and structure of the religious field. In J. B. Burnside, C. Calhoun and L. Florence (eds). *Comparative Social Research,* 13, 1–44.

—Genèse et structure du champ religieux, *Revue français de sociologie,* 12, 2, 295–334.

Bourdieu, P. (1991e) Political representation: Elements for a theory of the political field. In P. Bourdieu (1991c) *Language and Symbolic Power* (pp. 171–202). Oxford: Polity Press.

Bourdieu, P. (1991f) Delegation and political fetishism. In P. Bourdieu (1991c) *Language and Symbolic Power* (pp. 203–219). Oxford: Polity Press.

Bourdieu, P. (1991g) Introduction à la socioanalyse, *Actes de la Recherché en Sciences Sociales,* 90, 3–5.

Bourdieu, P. (1992a/1989) Principles for reflecting on the curriculum, *The Curriculum Journal,* 1, 3, 307–314.

—*Principes pour une réflexion sur les contenus d'enseignment.*

Bourdieu, P. (with Wacquant, L) (1992b) *An Invitation to Reflexive Sociology* (trans. L. Wacquant). Oxford: Polity Press.

—*Réponses. Pour une anthropologie réflexive.* Paris: Seuil.

Bourdieu, P. (1993a/1980) *Sociology in Question* (trans. R. Nice). London: Sage.

—*Questions de sociologie.* Paris: Les Editions de Minuit.

Bourdieu, P. (with Passeron, J-C and De Saint Martin, M) (1994/1965) *Academic Discourse.* Oxford: Polity.

—*Rapport Pédagogique et Communication.* The Hague: Mouton.

Bourdieu, P. (with Grenfell, M) (1995) *Entretiens.* CLE Papers 37: University of Southampton.

Bourdieu, P. (1996a/1989) *The State Nobility. Elite Schools in the Field of Power* (trans. L. C. Clough). Oxford: Polity Press.

—*La noblesse d'état. Grandes écoles et esprit de corps.* Paris: Les Editions de Minuit.

Bourdieu, P. (1996b/1992) *The Rules of Art* (trans. S. Emanuel). Oxford: Polity Press.

—*Les règles de l'art. Genèse et structure du champ littéraire.* Paris: Seuil.

Bourdieu, P. (1998a/1994) *Practical Reason.* Oxford: Polity Press.

—*Raisons pratiques. Sur la théorie de l'action.* Paris: Seuil.

Bourdieu, P. (1998b) *Acts of Resistance. Against the New Myths of our Time* (trans. R. Nice). Oxford: Polity Press.

—*Contre-feux.* Paris: Raisons d'Agir.

Bourdieu, P. (1998c/1996) *On Television and Journalism.* London: Pluto Press.

—*Sur la télévision, suivi de L'Emprise du journalisme.* Paris: Raisons d'agir.

Bourdieu, P. (1998d) The laughter of bishops. In P. Bourdieu, (1998a/1994) *Practical Reason.* Oxford: Polity Press, pp. 112–123.

—Le rire des évêques. In P. Bourdieu *Raisons pratiques. Sur la théorie de l'action* (pp. 202–213). Paris: Seuil.

Bourdieu, P. (1998e) On the economy of the Church. In P. Bourdieu, (1998a/1994) *Practical Reason* (pp. 124–126). Oxford: Polity Press.

—Annex: Propos sur l'économie de l'Église. In P. Bourdieu *Raisons pratiques. Sur la théorie de l'action* (pp. 215–217). Paris: Seuil.

Bourdieu, P. (1999a/1993) *The Weight of the World. Social Suffering in Contemporary Society* (trans. P. Parkhurst Ferguson, S. Emanuel, J. Johnson, S. T. Waryn). Oxford: Polity Press.

—*La Misère du monde.* Paris: Seuil.

Bourdieu, P. (1999b/1963) Statistics and Sociology, (trans. by Derek Robbins, Social Politics, Paper 10, March 1999, London: University of East London, first published as (1963) as Statistiques et Sociologie in Travail et Travailleurs en Algérie, Paris: Mouton.

Bourdieu, P. (2000a/1997) *Pascalian Meditations* (trans. R. Nice). Oxford: Polity Press.

—*Méditations pascaliennes.* Paris: Seuil.

Bourdieu, P. (2000b) *Les Structures sociales de l'économie.* Paris: Seuil.

—(2005) *The Social Structures of the Economy.* Cambridge: Polity Press.

Bourdieu, P. (with Wacquant, L) (2000c) La nouvelle vulgate planétaire, *Le Monde Diplomatique*, mai, 6–7.

Bourdieu, P. (2000d) Making the economic habitus. Algerian workers revisited (trans. R. Nice and L. Wacquant), *Ethnography*, 1, 1, 17–41.

Bourdieu, P. (2001a/1998) *Masculine Domination*. Oxford: Polity Press.
—*La Domination masculine*. Paris: Seuil.
Bourdieu, P. (2001b) *Contre-feux 2. Pour un mouvement social européen*. Paris: Raisons d'Agir.
Bourdieu, P. (2001c) *Science de la science et réflexivité*. Paris: Raisons d'Agir.
—(2004) *Science of Science and Reflexivity*. Cambridge: Polity Press.
Bourdieu, P. (2002) *Le bal des célibataires. Crise de la société en Béarn*. Paris: Seuil.
Bourdieu, P. (2003a) *Images d'Algérie*. Paris: Actes Sud.
Bourdieu, P. (2003b) Participation objectivation, *The Journal of the RoyalAnthropological Institute*, 9, 2, 281–94.
Bourdieu, P. (2006) The Forms of Capital. In H. Lauder, P. Brown, J-A. Dillabough and A. H. Halsey (eds). *Education, Globalisation and Social Change* (pp. 241–258). Oxford: Oxford University Press.
Bourdieu, P. (2007/2004) *Sketch for a Self-Analysis*. Oxford: Polity Press.
—*Esquisse pour une auto-analyse*. Paris: Raisons d'Agir.
Bourdieu, P. (eds). (Discepolo and F. Poupeau) (2008a) *Interventions* (2002) *Interventions (1961–2001)*. Marseilles: Agone.
Bourdieu, P. (2008b/2002) *The Bachelor's Ball*. Polity: Oxford.
—*Le bal des célibataires. Crise de la société en Béarn*. Paris: Seuil.
Bourdieu, P. (with Boltanski, L) (2008c/1976) *La Production de l'Idéologie Dominante*. Paris: Raisons d'Agir.
—*La production de l'idéologie dominante*, *Actes de la recherche en sciences sociales*, 2–3, 3–73.
Britton, J. (1970) *Language and Learning: The Importance of Speech in Children's Developmen*. London: Penguin.
Brutt-Griffler, J. (2002) Class, ethnicity and language rights: An analysis of British colonial policy in Lesotho and Sri Lanka and some implications for language policy, *Journal of Language, Identity and Education*, 1, 207–234.
Canagarajah, S. (2005) Dilemmas in planning English/vernacular relations in post-colonial communities, *Journal of Sociolinguistics*, 9, 418–447.
Carens, J. (2000) *Culture, Citizenship and Community: A contextual exploration of justice as evenhandedness*. Oxford: Oxford University Press.
Casanovas Catalá, M. (1996) Consecuencias de la interferencia lingüística en la morfosintaxis del español hablado en Lleida, *Verba*, 23, 405–415.
Casanovas Catalá, M. (1997) ¿Qué sucede cuando uno no es monolingüe? Algunas consecuencias de la interferencia léxica en el aprendizaje del léxico, *Lenguaje y Textos*, 10, 335–339.
Chomsky, N (1965) *Aspects of the Theory of Syntax*. Cambridge, MA: MIT.
Coulmas, F. (1998) Language rights: Interests of states, language groups and the individual, *Language Sciences*, 20, 63–72.
Crawford, J. (2008) *Advocating for English Learners*. Clevedon: Multilingual Matters.
Creese, A. (2008) Linguistic Ethnography. In K. A. King and N. H. Hornberger (eds). *Encyclopedia of Language and Education* (2nd edn, Vol. 10). *Research Methods in Language and Education* (pp. 229–241). Springer Science+Business Media LLC.
De Beaugrande, R. (1998) Society, education, linguistics, and language: Inclusion and exclusion in theory and practice, *Linguistics and Education*, 9, (2), 99–158.

de Certeau, M., Julia, D. and Revel, J. (1975) *Une Politique de la Langue. La Révolution Française et les Patois.* Paris: Editions Gallimard.

Department For Education and Science. (1992) *Circular 9/92: Initial Teacher Training (Secondary Phase).* London: HMSO.

DfES. (1998) *National Literacy Strategy: A Framework for Teaching.* London: DFES.

DfES. (1999) *English, National Curriculum Guidance.* London: DFES.

Department of Children, Schools and Families (DCSF). (2007a) *The Primary Strategy.* London: DCSF.

DCSF. (2007b) *Improving writing with a Focus on guided writing, Leading Improvement using the Primary Framework.* London: DCSF.

DCSF. (2007c) *Guided Writing for Year 5.* https://nationalstrategies.standards.dcsf. gov.uk/node/85981.

DCSF. (2009) *Deprivation and Education: Evidence on pupils in England, foundation Stage to Key Stage 4.* London: DCSF.

de Varennes, F. (1996) *Language, Minorities and Human Rights.* The Hague: Kluwer Law International.

DiGiacomo, S. M. (1999) Language ideological debates in an Olympic city: Barcelona 1992–1996. In J. Blommaert (ed.). *Language ideological debates* (pp. 105–142). Berlin: Mouton de Gruyter.

Di Maggio, P. (1979) Review essay on Pierre Bourdieu, *American Journal of Sociology,* 84, 1460–1474.

Dorian, N. (1998) Western language ideologies and small-language prospects. In L. Grenoble and L. Whaley (eds). *Endangered Languages: Language loss and community response* (pp. 3–21). Cambridge: Cambridge University Press.

Doyle, H. (1996) Referents of Catalan and Spanish for bilingual youths in Barcelona. In A. Roca and J. B. Jensen (eds). *Spanish in contact: Issues in bilingualism* (pp. 29–43). Somerville: Cascadilla Press.

Dreyfus, H. and Rabinow, P. (1993) 'Can there be a science of existential structure and social meaning?', In C. Calhoun, E. LiPuma and M. Postone *Bourdieu: Critical Perspectives* (pp. 35–44). Oxford: Polity Press.

Dua, H. (1994) *Hegemony of English.* Mysore: Yashoda Publications.

Duszak, A. (ed.) *Us and others: Social identities across languages, discourses and cultures* (pp. 159–185). Amsterdam: John Benjamins.

Edwards, C. (1994) *Pedagogical knowledge in a mathematics classroom – A stimulated recall exercise.* Unpublished Mimeograph: University of Southampton.

Edwards, D. and Mercer, N. (1987) *Common Knowledge: The development of understanding in the classroom.* London: Routledge.

Edwards, A. D. and Westgate, D. P. G. (1987) *Investigating Classroom Talk.* Lewes: Falmer Press.

Edwards, J. (1985) *Language, Society and Identity.* Oxford: Basil Blackwell.

Edwards, J. (1994) *Multilingualism.* London: Routledge.

Erickson, F. (1990) Qualitative Methods. In R. L. Linn and F. Erickson (eds). *Research in Teaching and Learning* (Vol. 2) (pp. 4–19). New York: MacMillan Publishing Company.

Erickson, F. (1996) Ethnographic microanalysis. In S. L. McKay and N. H. Hornberger (eds). *Sociolinguistics and Language Teaching* (pp. 283–306). New York: Cambridge University Press.

Fisher, A (2007) *Guided Reading: A lesson*. Unpublished transcription: University College St Mark and St John.

Fishman, J. (1968a) Sociolinguistics and the language problems of the developing countries. In J. Fishman, C. Ferguson, and J. Das Gupta (eds). *Language Problems of Developing Nations* (pp. 3–16). New York: John Wiley and Sons.

Fishman, J. (1968b) Some contrasts between linguistically homogeneous and linguistic heterogeneous polities. In J. Fishman, C. Ferguson, and J. Das Gupta (eds). *Language Problems of Developing Nations* (pp. 53–68). New York: John Wiley and Sons.

Fishman, J. (1968c) Language problems and types of political and sociocultural integration: A conceptual postscript. In J. Fishman, C. Ferguson, and J. Das Gupta (eds). *Language Problems of Developing Nations* (pp. 491–498). New York: John Wiley and Sons.

Fishman, J. (1989a) Language and ethnicity. In J. Fishman (ed.). *Language and Ethnicity in Minority Sociolinguistic Perspective* (pp. 23–65). Clevedon: Multilingual Matters (original, 1977).

Fishman, J. (1989b) Language and nationalism: Two integrative essays. Part 1. The nature of nationalism. In J. Fishman (ed.). *Language and Ethnicity in Minority Sociolinguistic Perspective* (pp. 97–175). Clevedon: Multilingual Matters (original, 1972).

Fishman, J. A. (1991) Three success stories (more or less) Modern Hebrew, French in Quebec and Catalan in Spain. In J. A. Fishman (ed.). *Reversing language shift: Theoretical and empirical foundations of assistance to threatened languages* (pp. 287–336). Clevedon: Multilingual Matters Ltd.

Flanders, N. A. (1965) *Interactional Analysis in the Classroom: A Manual for Observers*. Ann Arbor: University of Michigan, School of Education.

Fox, M. J. (1975) *Language and Development: A Retrospective Survey of Ford Foundation Language Projects 1952–1974*. New York: The Ford. Foundation.

Freeland, J. and Patrick, D. (2004) *Language Rights and Language 'Survival': A sociolinguistic exploration*. Manchester: St Jerome Publishing.

García Mouton, P. (1994) *Lenguas y dialectos de España*. Madrid: Arcolibros.

García, O. (2007) Foreword. In S. Makoni and A. Pennycook (eds). *Disinventing and Reconstituting Languages* (pp. xi–xv). Clevedon: Multilingual Matters.

Gard'ner, J. M. (2004) Heritage protection and social inclusion: A case study from the Bangladeshi community of East London, *International Journal of Heritage Studies*, 10/1, 75–92.

Gardner, K. (1995) *Global migrants, local lives: Travel and transformation in rural Bangladesh*. Oxford: Clarendon Press.

Gee, J. P. (1996) *Social Linguistics and Literacies: Ideology in Discourses*. London: Taylor and Francis.

Gellner, E. (1983) *Nations and nationalism: New perspectives on the past*. Oxford: Basil Blackwell.

Genesee, F. and Bourhis, R. Y. (1982) 'The social psychological significance of code switching in cross-cultural communication', *Journal of Language and Social Psychology*, 1, 1–27.

Giddens, A. (1984) *The Constitution of Society*. Berkeley: University of California Press.

Giles, H, and Powesland, P. F. (1975) *Speech Style and Social Evaluation.* London: Academic Press.

Goffman, E. (1959) *The Presentation of Self in Everyday Life.* Garden City: Doubleday.

Grau, R. (1992) Le statut juridique des droits linguistiques en France. In H. Giordan (ed.). *Les Minorités en Europe* (pp. 93–112). Paris: Editions Kimé.

Grenfell, M. (1998) Language and the Classroom, Chapter 5 in M. Grenfell and D. James (eds). (1998) *Bourdieu and Education: Acts of Practical Theory* (pp. 72–88). Falmer Press: London.

Grenfell, M. (1999) Language: Construction of an Object of Research. In M. Grenfell and M. Kelly (eds). *Pierre Bourdieu: Language, Culture and Education* (pp. 27–40). Bern: Peter Lang.

Grenfell, M. (2000) Learning and Teaching Strategies, Chapter 1 in S. Green (ed.) (2000) *New Perspectives on Teaching and Learning Modern Foreign Languages* (pp. 102–136). Clevedon: Multilingual Matters.

Grenfell, M. (2004a) *Pierre Bourdieu: Agent Provocateur.* London: Continuum.

Grenfell, M. (2004b) Bourdieu in the Classroom, Chapter 3 in J. Olsen (ed.). (2004) *Culture and Learning: Access and Opportunity in the Classroom* (pp. 49–72). IAP Publishers.

Grenfell, M. (2006) Bourdieu in the field: From the Béarn to Algeria – a timely response, *French Cultural Studies*, 17, 2, 223–240.

Grenfell, M. (2008) *Pierre Bourdieu: Key Concepts*, Stockfield: Acumen Publishing Limited.

Grenfell, M. and Hardy, C. (2003) Field Manoeuvres: Bourdieu and Young British Artists, *Space and Culture*, 6, 19–34.

Grenfell, M. and Hardy, C. (2006) When Two fields Collide, *International Journal for Arts in Society*, 1, 78–85.

Grenfell, M. and Hardy, C. (2007) *Art Rules: Pierre Bourdieu and the Visual Arts.* Oxford: Berg.

Grenfell, M. and James, D. (1998) *Bourdieu and Education: Acts of Practical Theory.* London: Falmer Press.

Grenfell, M. and James, D. (2004) Change in the field – changing the field: Bourdieu and the methodological practice of educational research, *British Journal of Sociology of Education*, 25, 4, 507–523.

Grenoble, L. and Whaley, L. (eds). *Endangered Languages: Language loss and community response.* Cambridge: Cambridge University Press.

Grillo, R. (1989) *Dominant Languages: Language and hierarchy in Britain and France.* Cambridge: Cambridge University Press.

Guarzino, L. E. (1997) The emergence of a transnational social formation and the mirage of return migration among Dominican transmigrants, *Identities*, 4, 2, 281–322.

Guenier, N., Genouvrier, E. and Khomsi, A. (1983) Le français devant la norme. In R, Bédard and J. Maurais (eds). *La Norme Linguistique.* Paris: Le Robert.

Gumperz, J. (1982) *Discourse Strategies.* Cambridge: Cambridge University Press.

Gumperz. J. J. (1999) On interactional sociolinguistic method. In S. Sarangi and C. Roberts (eds). *Talk, Work and Institutional Order* (pp. 453–471). Berlin: Mouton de Gruyter.

Habermas, J. (1984) *Theory of Communicative Action.* Boston: Beacon Press.

Hardy, C. (2007) 'Museums', Chapter 4 in Grenfell and Hardy (2007), *Art Rules: Pierre Bourdieu and the Visual Arts* (p. 283). Oxford: Berg.

Hardy, C. (2009) Bourdieu *and the Art of Education, A socio-theoretical Investigation of Education, Change and Art.* Unpublished PhD thesis, Southampton: University of Southampton.

Harker, R. (1984) On reproduction, habitus and education, *British Journal of Sociology of Education*, 5, 117–127.

Harker, R. (1990) Bourdieu: Education and reproduction. In R. Harker, C. Mahar, and C. Wilkes (eds). *An Introduction to the Work of Pierre Bourdieu: The practice of theory* (pp. 86–108). London: Macmillan.

Harker, R. and May, S. (1993) Code and habitus: Comparing the accounts of Bernstein and Bourdieu, *British Journal of Sociology of Education*, 14, 169–178.

Hart, B. and Risley, T. R. (1996) *Meaningful Differences in Everyday Experience of Young American Children*. London: Brookes Publishing.

Hasan, R. (1996) Literacy, everyday talk and society. In R. Hasan and G. Williams (eds). *Literacy in Society* (pp. 377–417). London: Longman.

Hasan, R. (1999) The disempowerment game: Bourdieu and language in literacy, *Linguistics and Education*, 10, 1, 25–87.

Heath, S. B. (1983) *Ways with words: Language, life, and work in communities and Classrooms.* Cambridge: Cambridge University Press.

Heller, M. (1995) Language choice, social institutions and symbolic domination, *Language in Society*, 24, 373–405.

Heller, M. (1999) *Linguistic Minorities and Modernity: A Sociolinguistic Ethnography.* New York: Longman.

Heller, M. (2007) Bilingualism as ideology and practice. In M. Heller (ed.) *Bilingualism: A social approach* (pp. 1–24). Basingstoke: Palgrave.

Heller, M. (2008) Doing Ethnography. In Li Wei and M. Moyer (eds). *The Blackwell Guide to Research Methods in Bilingualism and Multilingualism* (pp. 249–262). Oxford: Blackwell.

Héran, F. (1993) L'unification linguistique de la France, *Population et Sociétés*, 285, 1–4.

Hernández García, C. (1995) Algunas reflexiones sobre el español en las zonas bilingües: Propuesta de variables sociolingüísticas para la obtención de los infomantes del corpus de la variedad de español de Barcelona y su area metropolitana, *Anuari de Filologia*, 18, (F6), 87–105.

Hernández García, C. (1998) Anàlisi comparativa del nivell d'interferència lingüística català-castellà d'un grup d'universitaris de Barcelona (UPF). In *Actes de la Cinquena Trobada de Sociolingüistes Catalans: Barcelona, 24 i 25 d'abril de 1997.* Barcelona: Generalitat de Catalunya, Departament de Cultura.

Hicks, D. (1995) Discourse, learning, and teaching. In M. W. Apple (ed.) *Review of Research in Education* (pp. 49–95). Washington, DC: AERA.

Holborow, M. (1999) *The Politics of English: A Marxist view of language.* London: Sage.

Hornberger, N. (2007) Multilingual language policies and the continua of biliteracy: An ecological approach. In Garcia, O and Baker, C. (eds). *Bilingual Education. An Introductory Reader* (pp. 177–194). Clevedon: Multilingual Matters.

Huntingdon, S. (2005) *Who Are We? America's great debate.* New York: Free Press.

Hymes, D. (1968) The ethnography of speaking. In J. Fishman (ed.). *Readings in the Sociology of Language* (pp. 99–138). The Hague: Moulton.

Hymes, D. (1972) On communicative competence. In J. B. Pride and J. Holmes (eds). *Sociolinguistics* (pp. 49–76). Harmondsworth: Penguin.

Hymes, D. (1974) *Foundations in Sociolinguistics: An Ethnographic Approach.* Philadelphia: University of Pennsylvania Press.

Hymes, D. (1980) *Language in Education: Ethnolinguistic Essays.* Washington, DC: Center for Applied Linguistics.

Johnson, D. (1993) The making of the French nation. In M. Teich and R. Porter (eds). *The National Question in Europe in Historical Context* (pp. 35–62). Cambridge: Cambridge University Press.

Kijima, Y. (2006) Caste and tribe inequality: Evidence from India, 1983–1999, *Economic Development and Cultural Change,* 54, 369–404.

Kloss, H. (1968) Notes concerning a language-nation typology. In J. Fishman, C. Ferguson and J. Das Gupta (eds). *Language Problems of Developing Nations* (pp. 69–86). New York: John Wiley & Sons.

Kremnitz, G. (1995) Dimensionen und Dynamik kollektiver Identitäten (Biespiele aus dem okzitanischen und katalanischen Sprachgebiet), *Sociolingüística,* 9, 67–87.

Kymlicka, W. (1995) *Multicultural Citizenship: A liberal theory of minority rights.* Oxford: Clarendon Press.

Labov, W. (1972) *Sociolinguistic Patterns.* Philadelphia: University of Pennsylvania Press.

Labov, W. (1977) *Language in the Inner City.* Oxford: Blackwell.

Labov, W. (with Bourdieu, P) (1983) Le changement linguistique – entretien avec William Labov, *Actes de la Recherche en Sciences Sociales,* 46, 67–71.

Lankshear, C., Gee J. P., Knobel, M. and Searle, C. (1997) *Changing Literacies.* Buckingham: Open University Press.

LeRoux, B and Rouanet, H. (2004) *Geometric Data Analysis.* Dordrecht and London: Kluwer Academic Publishers.

Levitt, P. (2002) The ties that change: Relations to the ancestral home over the life cycle. In P. Levitt and M. C. waters (eds). *The Changing Face of Home* (pp. 123–144). New York, Russell Sage Foundation.

López del Castillo, L. (1984) *Llengua standard i nivells de llenguatge* 2nd edn. Barcelona: Laia.

Loubet del Bayle, J-L. (1969) *Les Non-Conformistes des Années 30.* Paris: Seuil.

Luke, A., McHoul, A. and Mey, J. (1990) On the limits of language planning: Class, state and power. In R. Baldauf and A. Luke (eds). *Language Planning and Education in Australia and the South Pacific* (pp. 25–44). Clevedon: Multilingual Matters.

Mahler, S. (2001) Transnational relationships: The struggle to communicate across borders, *Identities,* 7, 583–619.

Maira, S. (2002) *Desis in the House: Indian American Youth Culture in New York City.* Philadelphia: Temple University Press.

Makoni, S. and Pennycook, A. (2007) Disinventing and reconstituting languages in S. Makoni and A. Pennycook (eds). *Disinventing and Reconstituting Languages* (pp. 1–41). Clevedon: Multilingual Matters.

Mar-Molinero, C. (2006) The European linguistic legacy in a global era: Linguistic imperialism, Spanish and the *Instituto Cervantes*. In C. Mar-Molinero and P. Stevenson (eds). *Language Ideologies, Policies and Practices: Language and the Future of Europe* (pp. 76–90). London: Palgrave.

Marsá, F. (1986) Sobre concurrencia lingüística en Cataluña. In M. Alvar (ed.). *El castellano actual en las comunidades bilingües de España* (pp. 93–104). Salamanca: Junta de Castilla y León.

Maryns, K. and Blommaert, J. (2006) Conducting dissonance: Codeswitching and differential access to contexts in the Belgian asylum process. In C. Mar-Molinero and P. Stevenson (eds). *Language Ideologies, Policies and Practices: Language and the Future of Europe* (pp. 177–190). Basingstoke: Palgrave Macmillan.

Maurais, J. and Morris, M. (2003) *Languages in a Globalising World*. Cambridge: Cambridge University Press.

May, S. (2000) Accommodating and resisting minority language policy: The case of Wales. *International Journal of Bilingual Education and Bilingualism*, 3, 101–128.

May, S. (2001) *Language and Minority Rights: Ethnicity, Nationalism, and the Politics of Language*. London: Longman.

May, S. (2002) Developing greater ethnolinguistic democracy in Europe: Minority language policies, nation-states, and the question of tolerability, *Sociolinguistica*, 16, 1–13.

May, S. (2003) Misconceiving minority language rights: Implications for liberal political theory. In W. Kymlicka and A. Patten (eds). *Language Rights and Political Theory* (pp. 123–152). Oxford: Oxford University Press.

May, S. (2004) Rethinking linguistic human rights: Answering questions of identity, essentialism and mobility. In D. Patrick and J. Freeland (eds). *Language rights and language 'Survival': A sociolinguistic exploration* (pp. 35–53). Manchester: St Jerome Publishing.

May, S. (2005) Language rights: Moving the debate forward, *Journal of Sociolinguistics* 9/3, 319–347.

May, S. (2008) *Language and Minority Rights: Ethnicity, nationalism and the politics of language*. New York: Routledge.

McCarty, T. (ed.) (2010) *Ethnography in Language Policy*. New York: Routledge.

McGroarty, M. (2002) Evolving influences on education language policies. In J. Tollefson (ed.). *Language Policies in Education: Critical issues* (pp. 17–36). Mahwah, NJ: Lawrence Erlbaum Associates.

McGroarty, M. (2006) Neoliberal collusion or strategic simultaneity? On multiple rationales for language-in-education policies, *Language Policy*, 5, 3–13.

Mercer, N. (ed.) (1981) *Language in school and community*. London: Edward Arnold.

Mercer, N. and Edwards, A. D. (1981) Ground Rules for mutual understanding: A social psychological approach to classroom knowledge, Chapter 2 in N. Mercer (1981) *Language in School and Community*. London: Edward Arnold.

Mercer, N. (1995) *The Guided Construction of Knowledge: Talk amongst Teachers and Learners*. Clevedon, Avon: Multilingual Matters.

Mercer, N. and Edwards, D. (1981) Ground Rules for Mutual Understanding, Chapter 2 in N. Mercer N (1981) *Language in School and Community*. London: Edward Arnold.

Mey, J. (1985) *Whose Language? A Study in Linguistic Pragmatics.* Amsterdam: John Benjamins.

Mühlhäusler, P. (1996) *Linguistic Ecology: Language change and linguistic imperialism in the Pacific region.* London: Routledge.

Mullineaux, A. and Blanc, M. (1982) 'The problem of classifying the population sample in the sociolinguistic survey of Orleans in terms of socio-economic, social and educational categories', *Review of Applied Linguistics*, 55, 3–37.

Nelde, P., Strubell, M. and Williams, G. (1996) *Euromosaic: The production and reproduction of the minority language groups in the European Union.* Luxembourg: Office for Official Publications of the European Communities.

Norton, B. (2000) *Identity and Language Learning: Gender, ethnicity and educational change.* London: Longman.

OFSTED. (2008) *Mathematics: Understanding the Score.* London: OFSTED.

Olssen, J. (2004) *Culture and Learning: Access and Opportunity in the Classroom.* Connecticut: IAP.

Ó Riagáin, P. (1997) *Language Policy and Social Reproduction: Ireland 1893–1993.* Oxford: Clarendon Press.

Parekh, B. (2000) *Rethinking Multiculturalism: Cultural diversity and political theory.* London: Macmillan.

Patrick, D. (2005) Language rights in Indigenous communities: The case of the Inuit of Arctic Québec, *Journal of Sociolinguistics*, 9, 369–389.

Pavlenko, A. and Blackledge, A. (2004) New Theoretical Approaches to the Study of Negotiation of Identities in Multilingual Contexts. In A. Pavlenko and A. Blackledge (eds). *Negotiation of Identities in Multilingual Contexts*, (pp. 1–33). Clevedon: Multilingual Matters.

Payrató, L. (1985) *La interferència lingüística: Comentaris i exemples català-castellà.* Barcelona: Curial/Abadia de Montserrat.

Pennycook, A. (1994) *The Cultural Politics of English as an International Language.* London: Longman.

Pennycook, A. (1998a) The right to language: Towards a situated ethics of language possibilities, *Language Sciences*, 20, 73–87.

Pennycook, A. (1998b) *English and the Discourses of Colonialism.* London: Routledge.

Pennycook, A. (2000) English, politics, ideology: From colonial celebration to postcolonial performativity. In T. Ricento (ed.). *Ideology, Politics and Language Policies: Focus on English* (pp. 107–120). Amsterdam; John Benjamins.

—Peuple et Culture (1945) *Un Peuple: Une Culture.* Paris: PEC.

Phillipson, R. (1992). *Linguistic Imperialism.* Oxford: Oxford University Press.

Phillipson, R. (1998) Globalizing English: Are linguistic human rights an alternative to linguistic imperialism? *Language Sciences*, 20, 101–112.

Phillipson, R. (2003) *English-Only Europe. Challenging language policy.* London: Routledge.

Pinto, L. (1998) *Pierre Bourdieu et la théorie du monde social.* Paris: Albin Michel.

Popper, K. R. (1968) *The Logic of Scientific Discovery.* London: Hutchinson.

Pujolar, J. (2007) Bilingualism and the nation-state in the post-national era. In M. Heller (ed.) *Bilingualism: A Social Approach.* Basingstoke: Palgrave.

QCA. (1999) *National Curriculum.* London: HMSO.

Quiniou-Tempereau, R. (1988) *The Breton Language in Primary Education in Brittany, France.* Leeuwarden: Fryske Akodemy.

Rampton, B. (1995) *Crossing: Language and ethnicity among adolescents.* London: Longman.

Rampton, B. (2007) Neo-Hymesian linguistic ethnography in the United Kingdom, *Journal of Sociolinguistics,* 11/5, 584–607. Web version: http://www3.interscience. wiley.com/cgi-bin/fulltext/117980211 pp. 1–15.

Rampton, B., Roberts, C., Leung, C. and Harris, R. (2002) Methodology in the analysis of classroom discourse, *Applied Linguistics, 23,* (3) 373–392.

Rampton, B., Tusting, K., Maybin, J., Barwell, R., Creese, A. and Lytra, V. (2004) UK linguistic ethnography: A discussion paper. www.ling-ethnog.org.uk.

Ricento, T. (ed.) (2006) *An Introduction to Language Policy.* New York: Blackwell.

Rorty, R. (1979) *Philosophy and the Mirror of Nature.* Princeton: Princeton University Press.

Rouvière, D. (n.d.) *LinguisticBehaviour according to the Social Context: The Nominal Phrase in Spoken French.* Unpublished Mimeograph, Birkbeck College: University of London.

Rubin, J. and Jernudd, B. (eds). (1971) *Can Language be Planned? Sociolinguistic theory and practice for developing nations.* Hawaii: University of Hawaii Press.

Sankoff, D. and Laberge, S. (1978) The linguistic market and the statistical variability. In D. Sankoff (ed.). *Linguistic Variation – Models and Methods.* New York: Academic Press.

Schiffman, H. (1996) *Linguistic Culture and Language Policy.* London: Routledge.

Schlesinger, A. (1992) *The Disuniting of America: Reflections on a multicultural society.* New York: W. W. Norton and Co.

Schmid, C. (2001) *The Politics of Language: Conflict, identity, and cultural pluralism in comparative perspective.* Oxford: Oxford University Press.

Schön, D. (1983) *The Reflective Practitioner: How Professionals think about Action.* New York: Basic Books.

Sinner, C. (2002) The construction of identity and group boundaries in Catalan Spanish. In A. C. Sinner (2004) *El castellano de Cataluña.* Tübingen: Niemeyer.

Sinner, C. and Wesch, A. (2008) El castellano en las tierras de lengua catalana: Estado de la cuestión. In C. Sinner and A. Wesch (eds). *El castellano en las tierras de habla catalana* (pp. 11–55). Madrid/Frankfurt: Iberoamericana/Vervuert.

Stevenson, P. (2006) 'National' languages in transnational contexts: Language, migration and citizenship in Europe. In C. Mar-Molinero, P. Stevenson and C. Mar-Molinero (eds). *Language Ideologies, Policies and Practices: Language and the Future of Europe* (pp. 147–161). London: Palgrave.

Street, B. (1984) *Literacy in Theory and Practice.* Cambridge: CUP.

Stubbe, M., Lane, C., Hilder, J., Vine, E., Vine, B., Marra, M., Holmes, J. and Weatherall, A. (2003) Multiple discourse analyses of a workplace interaction, *Discourse Studies,* 5, (3), 351–388.

Stubbs, M. (1976) *Language, Schools and Classrooms.* London: Methuen.

Tajfel, H. (1982) The Social Psychology of Minorities. In C. Husband (ed.). *Race in Britain: Continuity and Change.* London: Hutchinson, U. L.

Teachers Development Agency. (2006) *Professional Standards for Teachers.* London: TDA.

Thompson, J. (1991) Editor's Introduction. In P. Bourdieu (ed.). *Language and SymbolicPower* (pp. 1–31). Cambridge: Polity Press.

Tough, J. (1977) *The Development of Meaning.* London: George Allen and Unwin.

Tusting, K. and Maybin, J. (2007) Linguistic ethnography and interdisciplinarity: Opening the discussion, *Journal of Sociolinguistics,* 11/5, 575–583.

Vann, R. E. (1995) Constructing Catalanism: Motion verbs, demonstratives, and locatives in the Spanish of Barcelona, *Catalan Review,* 9, (2), 253–274.

Vann, R. E. (1996) *Pragmatic and cultural aspects of an emergent language variety: The construction of Catalan Spanish deictic expressions.* Unpublished Doctoral dissertation (University Microfilms No. 9633318), The University of Texas at Austin, Austin.

Vann, R. E. (1998a) Aspects of Spanish deictic expressions in Barcelona: A quantitative examination, *Language Variation and Change,* 10, 263–288.

Vann, R. E. (1998b) Pragmatic transfer from less developed to more developed systems: Spanish deictic terms in Barcelona. In A. Schwegler, B. Tranel and M. Uribe-Etxebarría (eds). *Romance linguistics: Theoretical perspectives* (pp. 307–317). Amsterdam: John Benjamins.

Vann, R. E. (1999a) An empirical perspective on practice: Operationalizing Bourdieu's notions of linguistic habitus. In M. Grenfell and M. Kelly (eds). *Pierre Bourdieu: Language, culture and education. Theory into practice* (pp. 73–83). Bern & London: Peter Lang.

Vann, R. E. (1999b) Language exposure in Catalonia: An example of indoctrinating linguistic ideology, *WORD,* 50.2, 191–209.

Vann, R. E. (1999c) Reversal of linguistic fortune: Dimensions of language conflict in autonomous Catalonia, *Language and Communication,* 19.4, 317–327.

Vann, R. E. (2000a) An empirical perspective on practice: Operationalizing Bourdieu's notions of linguistic habitus. In D. Robbins (ed.). *Masters of contemporary social thought: Pierre Bourdieu* (pp. 170–178). London: Sage.

Vann, R. E. (2000b) Constructing reality in bicultural communication: Catalan ways of speaking Spanish, *Intercultural Communication Studies,* X:1, 113–124.

Vann, R. E. (2001) El castellà catalanitzat a Barcelona: Perspectives lingüístiques i cultural, *Catalan Review,* 15, (1), 117–131.

Vann, R. E. (2002) Linguistic ideology in Spain's ivory tower: (Not) Analyzing Catalan Spanish, *Multilingua,* 21, (2/3), 227–246.

Vann, R. E. (2003) The construction of Catalanist identities: Group history and individual practice. In A. Lorenzo Suárez, C. Cabeza Pereiro and X. P. Rodriguez-Yanez (eds). *Comunidades e individuos bilingües* (pp. 166–174). Vigo, Spain: Servicio de Publicacións da Universidade de Vigo.

Vann, R. E. (2004) Language ideology in public practice: Civic movements in Catalonia. In A. M. Lorenzo Suárez, F. Ramallo and X. P. Rodríguez-Yáñez (eds). *Socialización bilingüe e adquisición lingüística bilingüe: Actas do Segundo Simposio Internacional sobre o Bilingüismo* (pp. 1741–1751). Vigo: Servizo de Publicacións da Universidade de Vigo.

Vann, R. E. (2006) Frustrations of the documentary linguist: The state of the art in digital language archiving and the archive that wasn't [Electronic Version]. *Proceedings of the 2006 E-MELD Workshop on Digital Language Documentation (Tools and Standards: The State of the Art), 20–22 June 2006, Michigan State University, East Lansing, MI.* Retrieved 3 January 2007. Available from http://emeld.org/workshop/2006/proceedings.html.

Vann, R. E. (2007) Doing Catalan Spanish: Pragmatic resources and discourse strategies in ways of speaking Spanish in Barcelona. In J. Holmquist, A. Lorenzino and L. Sayahi (eds). *Selected Proceedings of the Third Workshop on Spanish Sociolinguistics* (pp. 183–192). Somerville, MA: Cascadilla Proceedings Project (print and web edns; web edn available at www.lingref.com, document #1539).

Vann, R. E. (2009a) *Materials for the sociolinguistic description and corpus-based study of Spanish in Barcelona: Toward a documentation of colloquial Spanish in naturally occurring groups.* Lewiston: Mellen.

Vann, R. E. (2009b) On the importance of spontaneous speech innovations in language contact situations. In K. Braunmüller and J. House (eds). *Convergence and divergence in language contact situations* (pp. 153–182). Amsterdam: John Benjamins.

Vertovec, S. (2009) *Transnationalism.* London, Routledge.

Vološinov, V. (1973) *Marxism and the Philosophy of Language.* Cambridge: Harvard University Press (original, 1929).

Vygotsky, L. (1962) *Thought and Language.* Cambridge: MIT Press.

Vygotsky, L. (1978) *Mind in Society: The Development of Higher Psychological Processes.* London: Harvard University Press.

Weber, E. (1976) *Peasants into Frenchmen: The modernization of rural France 1870–1914.* Stanford, CA.: Stanford University Press.

Weinstein, B. (1983) *The Civic Tongue: Political consequences of language choices.* New York: Longman.

Weinstein, B. (1990) *Language Policy and Political Development.* Norwood, NJ.: Ablex.

Wenger, E. (1999) Communities of Practice: Learning as a social system, *The Systems Thinker*, 9, 5.

Wenger, K. J. and Ernst-Slavit, G. (1999) Learning to Teach in a Linguistic Market, *Journal of Classroom Interaction*, 34, 2, 45–57.

Wesch, A. (1997) El español hablado de Barcelona y el influjo del catalán. Esbozo de un programa de investigación, *Verba*, 24, 287–312.

Wesch, A. (2002) La investigación sobre variedades del español hablado en contacto con el catalán (particularmente en Cataluña y Baleares): Estado de la cuestión y perspectivas para el futuro. In M. T. Echenique Elizondo and J. Sánchez Méndez (eds). *Actas del V Congreso Internacional de Historia de la Lengua Española* (Vol. 2, pp. 1857–1872). Madrid: Gredos.

Whorf, B. L. (1940): 'Science and Linguistics', *Technology Review* 42, (6), 229–231 and 247–248.

Woolard, K. (1985) Language variation and cultural hegemony: Toward an integration of sociolinguistic and social theory, *American Ethnologist*, 12, (4), 738–748.

Woolard, K. (1989) *Double talk: Bilingualism and the politics of ethnicity in Catalonia.* Stanford, CA: Stanford University Press.

Woolard, K. (1998) Introduction: Language ideology as a field of inquiry. In B. Schieffelin, K. Woolard and P. Kroskrity (eds). *Language Ideologies: Practice and theory* (pp. 3–47). New York: Oxford University Press.

Woolard, K. and Schieffelin, B. (1994) Language ideology, *Annual Review of Anthropology*, 23, 55–82.

Wright, S. (2000) *Community and Communication: The role of language in nation state building and European integration.* Clevedon: Multilingual Matters.

Young, M. (ed.) *Knowledge and Control: New Directions for the Sociology of Education.*
    London: Collier Macmillan.
Zamora Vicente, A. (1989) *Dialectología española* 2nd edn. Madrid: Gredos.
Zuengler, J. and Mori, J. (2002) Microanalyses of classroom discourse: A critical
    consideration of method, *Applied Linguistics,* 23, (3), 283–288.

Contributors

Michael Grenfell is Chair of Education at Trinity College, University of Dublin, Ireland. He previously worked for 20 years in UK universities. His research interests include: second language learning and teaching; teacher education; and the philosophy of education, in particular with respect to research methodology. He has published extensively on language in education. He has also taken a special interest in the work of Pierre Bourdieu with whom he had a long association over a number of years. He was three times visiting scholar at the *École des hautes études* in Paris. He is a frequent journal article writer and conference attendee. He is also the author of 11 books including; *Pierre Bourdieu: Agent Provocateur* (Continuum, 2004); *Bourdieu, Education and Training* (Continuum, 2007); *Art Rules* (with C. Hardy, Berg, 2007); and *Pierre Bourdieu: Key Concepts* (Acumen, 2008).

Adrian Blackledge is Professor of Bilingualism in the School of Education, University of Birmingham. His research interests include the politics of multilingualism, linguistic ethnography, education of linguistic minority students, negotiation of identities in multilingual contexts and language testing, citizenship, and immigration. His publications include *Multilingualism, A Critical Perspective* (with Angela Creese, Continuum 2010), *Discourse and Power in a Multilingual World* (John Benjamins 2005), *Negotiation of Identities in Multilingual Contexts* (with Aneta Pavlenko Multilingual Matters 2004), *Multilingualism, Second Language Learning and Gender* (Mouton de Gruyter 2001 co-edited with Aneta Pavlenko, Ingrid Piller and Marya Teutsch-Dwyer) and *Literacy, Power, and Social Justice* (Trentham Books 2001).

Cheryl Hardy is an independent researcher and tutor at the University of Winchester, England, where she was also Director of Professional and Postgraduate Development. She also works for the Children and Young People Service at Milton Keynes, with particular responsibility for literacy. Her research interests include social inclusion, literacy, visual literacy and teachers' professional development. She has undertaken a substantial number of projects using a methodological approach based on Bourdieu's theory of practice. She has published a co-authored book, *Art Rules* (with M. Grenfell, Berg, 2007), and contributed chapters to other books, including *Pierre Bourdieu: Key Concepts* (Acumen, 2008) and *Language Across the Curriculum* (Routledge, 2002). Other current projects includes publications on photography and further work on women artists, language and classroom ethnography.

Stephen May is Professor of Education in the School of Critical Studies in Education, Faculty of Education, University of Auckland, New Zealand. He has published 8 books and over 70 articles and chapters in the areas of language diversity, language rights and the wider politics of ethnicity, bilingualism and multiculturalism, and has drawn regularly on the work of Bourdieu in so doing. His book *Language and Minority Rights* (Longman 2001, Routledge 2008) was shortlisted for the BAAL 2002 Book Prize and recognized as an American Library Association Choice Outstanding Academic Title in 2008. Stephen is also a Founding Editor of the interdisciplinary journal *Ethnicities* (Sage), and Associate Editor of the journal *Language Policy* (Springer).

Dr. Robert E. Vann is Professor in the Department of Spanish at Western Michigan University in Kalamazoo, Michigan, where he teaches courses in Spanish language, culture and linguistics. He received his B.A. in Spanish and his M.A. in Spanish linguistics at The University of Illinois at Urbana-Champaign; he received his Ph.D. in Iberoromance linguistics and philology at The University of Texas at Austin. Research interests have generally focused on Spanish language, culture and society in Catalonia, and include (1) documentation and digital preservation of spoken language data, (2) social, cultural and linguistic effects of language contact and bilingualism, (3) variation in ways of speaking, and (4) ways of constructing linguistic identities and ideologies. Recent publications include: (2009a). *Materials for the sociolinguistic description and corpus-based study of Spanish in Barcelona: Toward a documentation of colloquial Spanish in naturally occurring groups.* Lewiston, NY: Mellen; (2009b). 'On the importance of spontaneous speech innovations in language contact situations.' In K. Braunmüller & J. House (eds.), *Convergence and Divergence in Language Contact Situations* (pp. 153–81). Amsterdam: John Benjamins.

Index

Lightning Source UK Ltd.
Milton Keynes UK
02 March 2011

168502UK00001B/30/P